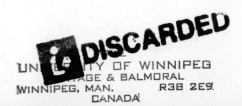

COMMON SENSE FOR HARD TIMES

COMMON SENSE
FOR HARD TIMES

The Power of the Powerless to Cope with Everyday life
and Transform Society in The Nineteen Seventies

JEREMY BRECHER & TIM COSTELLO

TWO CONTINENTS
INSTITUTE FOR POLICY STUDIES

Library of Congress Catalog Card Number: 76-7270
FIRST PRINTING

Two Continents Publishing Group, Ltd.
30 East 42nd St.
New York, NY 10017

Institute for Policy Studies

Printed in the United States of America
Design direction: Tony Lane
Book design: Richard Seireeni
Redesign: Jim True

Library of Congress Cataloging in Publication Data

Brecher, Jeremy.
  Common sense for hard times.

  Bibliography: p.
  Includes index.
  1. Labor and laboring classes--United States--1970-
2. Labor and laboring classes--United States--Political
activity. I. Costello, Tim, joint author. II. Title.
HD8072.B724   301.44'42'0973   76-7270
ISBN 0-8467-0149-9
ISBN 0-8467-0175-8 pbk.

This book is for Gillian and Helen, Fanya, Moira and Jill, and Dorothy Lee

CONTENTS

"Those Who Take the Meat from the Table"

Teach contentment.
Those for whom the taxes are destined
Demand sacrifice.
Those who eat their fill speak to the hungry
Of wonderful times to come.
Those who lead the country into the abyss
Call ruling too difficult
For ordinary men.

—Bertolt Brecht, *Selected Poems*

ACKNOWLEDGMENTS

Whatever is of merit in this book is due largely to the hundreds of people from whom we have learned in discussions, arguments and interviews over the past few years. We wish we could list them individually. Our thanks go to all, particularly to those with whom we have worked on jobs and projects.

As we traveled around the country, many people put us up and helped us get started in unfamiliar communities. We would especially like to thank Ingred and Joe Eyer, Steve Sapolsky, Jesse and Marty Glaberman, Fredy and Lorraine Perlman, Alice and Staughton Lynd, Tony Barsotti, Reggie Daniels, Patricia and Michael Athay, Joe Paulaka, and the denizens of Mohawk Avenue in Chicago.

We would like to thank Jill Cutler, Alan Rinzler and Edward Brecher for painstaking editorial assistance as well as substantive suggestions.

Many people read and commented on all or parts of the manuscript. Their criticisms and suggestions have been extremely helpful; they are in no way responsible for opinions or errors in this book. We would like to thank Tony Barsotti, Millard Berry, Mary Corcoran, Helen Costello, Sean Costello, Reggie Daniels, Joe Eyer, Marty Glaberman, Dorothy Lee, Ronald Lee, Liz Long, Staughton Lynd, Fredy Perlman, Peter Rachleff, Marc Raskin, Steven Rosenthal, Steve Sapolsky, Katherine Stone, Ingrid Waldron, Caroline Ware and Heather Weiss. We are grateful to Jim True, who took us in hand through the trials of redesign and production. We would like to thank the Institute for Policy Studies, who stood by us in hard times. Martin Gold, Liberation News Service, and the AFL-CIO kindly supplied us with graphics. Our lawyer, Catherine G. Roraback, and our agent, Mary Yost, helped keep us going.

Finally, we would like to thank all our friends who put up with us during the writing of this book.

Squeezed between inflation and unemployment, most people are finding their conditions of life growing worse and worse. Retail prices have continued to rise while unemployment has reached the highest level since the Great Depression. This chart gives one indication of the deterioration: the decline in spendable weekly earnings of nonsupervisory workers on private payrolls, measured in constant (1967) dollars. Most people don't need statistics, however, to know that life is getting harder.

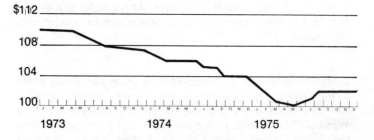

Source: *News,* U.S. Department of Labor. Bureau of Labor Statistics. January 21, 1976

INTRODUCTION

"Hard times" — they're something difficult to pin down, even when you can feel them all around you. It's not just high prices, or the difficulty of finding a job or trouble getting fuel, housing and food, the things you need to live. Hard times really mean an end to everything wrapped up in the phrase "living well."

Faced with deteriorating conditions, threatened by the destruction of their established way of life, millions of people over the past two years have begun questioning aspects of their society they have long taken for granted and turning to actions they have never before considered. As a contribution to this process, this book will examine the problems of daily life as they are experienced; uncover their roots in the way our society is organized; report on the ways people are already getting together to cope with them; and show how these actions can be made the starting point for a challenge to the power of those who control the life of our society.

Until recently, such a challenge seemed unnecessary — indeed undesirable — to most Americans. For since the Great Depression some forty years ago, most people have lived better each year than they did the year before and expected such improvement to continue into the future.

But now that expectation has been undermined. For many people, the standard of living began to decline in the mid-60's. During 1974 and early 1975, real take-home pay for a typical worker decreased 9.5% as a result of inflation[1] — a loss which has yet to be made up. Meanwhile, unemployment reached the highest levels since the Great Depression — and remained there through nearly a year of reputed "business upswing." What once seemed like a good income is now hardly enough to get by on. Many people do not eat as well, have been forced to give up hopes and plans, or find it necessary to take on extra work.

*Footnotes have been provided for readers seeking sources for quotations, suggestions for further reading and discussion of various technical issues, starting on page 231.

Does the future promise an end to such conditions? The chances seem slim. The country might well experience a rapid but temporary "business revival" — accompanied by a resurgence of inflation. Alternatively, revival may falter and unemployment rise still higher. Neither development would alter the underlying deterioration of living conditions for most people. For while business indices may fluctuate and politicians may promise that "prosperity is just around the corner," in reality we are in the midst of a world-wide economic crisis with no end in sight. Most people recognize this; as pollster Peter D. Hart stated at the end of 1975, "The public does not expect any substantial improvement in economic conditions in the foreseeable future. The public believes that the current respite from the severe difficulties of a year ago is nothing more than the calm before the storm."

The particular forms taken by hard times today may be different from those of the past, inflation and shortages may have joined unemployment, but the basic reality for most people — living less well — is the same. And when their way of life is threatened, people have little choice but to try to do something about it. As a union official warned, working people are

> "scared as hell. Unless we get straightened out, we are in for a hell of a lot of trouble. I'm not talking about strikes. I'm talking about real social upheaval. We'll see riots in supermarkets, gasoline stations and other places.[2]

Such actions have already begun. The past two years have seen the largest protest in American history — the nationwide consumer boycott of meat. They saw the truckers' blockades, the first coordinated national tie-up of traffic ever. They saw the largest strike wave since 1946. They saw an unprecedented industry-wide wildcat strike by coal miners against employers, union, and government. They saw a series of occupations of factories and other workplaces, practically unknown in the U.S. since the 1930's.

Many people are trying to figure out just what kinds of action can be effective. At a gas station in Lincoln, Nebraska, we overheard two men talking. The older one, about fifty, said:

> The thing that gets me is that what you have to pay for food, gas, rent, you name it, keeps going up, but if you're a worker, your wages don't go up. It doesn't matter whether you work construction or in a factory or drive a truck or anything else, it's all the same.

The younger one, about twenty-five, replied, "I think we should strike." The other answered:

> I think what we should do is turn Robin Hood, go out and take the stuff from the rich and give it to the poor people. After all, they're stealing from us, especially the ones up in Washington.

Once again, as in John Steinbeck's description of the Great Depression of the 1930s:

> In the eyes of the people there is a failure. . . . In the souls of the people the grapes of wrath are filling and growing heavy, growing heavy for the vintage.[3]

That wrath results from the fact that those who own and manage this society are proving themselves unwilling and unable to provide a decent life for the majority. They can no longer be looked to for solutions to the problems most people have to cope with day by day. Whatever action they take, they will take in their own interest. People have become the victims of a system which functions to meet the needs of the rich and powerful. The choice for the majority is to either accept a continuing deterioration of their way of life or break the power of those who now control society.

A basic argument runs through every chapter of this book. The life of our society is based on the cooperative labor of the great majority who do the work; it is controlled by the small minority of owners, managers, businessmen, politicians and bureaucrats for whom they work. For most people, every aspect of daily life is shaped by the power of the dominant minority. What you experience at work, what you have available to meet your needs at home, the very environment in which you live—all depend upon the often chaotic interaction of decisions made by the rich and powerful.

When things go smoothly, when the ways to achieve a good life seem evident, most people see this control by others as something to accept, not something to challenge. But when, as now, people's needs go unmet, when the future looks bleak, when the power of that minority promises nothing but misery, insecurity and endless labor, then it is time to put an end to the system of minority control.

The means to do so are at hand. Our society is created by what working people do in their daily life. Corporations would crumble, governments collapse and armies disintegrate if those whose activity made them up simply refused to continue the behavior that maintains them. If the majority took control of their own activity, they would have the power to shape this activity as they choose, and thereby shape society. This reality gives ordinary people, who often appear so powerless, a great potential power. What is necessary to end minority rule is for the majority to *use that power*.

Even in normal times, people join together in a variety of ways—strikes, informal resistance on the job, consumer boycotts, community protests—to challenge particular aspects of minority power. In the past two years, under the pressure of deteriorating conditions of life, millions of people have adopted such techniques of action. For those who do not own or run this society, the key to making a good life under today's conditions is to turn these actions into a concerted challenge to every aspect of minority control.

Each of us evolves a strategy for living in the world. It is pieced together from what we learned as children, what we have observed others doing, what we have learned from our own experience and the ideas we have of what might work in the future. Such strategies can be quite conscious plans and decisions or they can be largely a matter of unconscious habit, just repeating what an individual—or his social group—has "always done." Strategies that are well adapted to real social conditions work—people find their activity meaningful and useful in getting what they need and want. But when realities change, the old strategies may stop working; accepted practices no longer "make sense" or achieve their objectives. We believe this is exactly what is happening today.

The basic strategy most people have adopted over the past quarter of a century has been an acceptance of the existing organization of society and an attempt to make their way within it as individuals. There have been exceptions: many people have joined together to defend their interests on a small scale or to protest particular policies. But the basic strategy for making a good life has been to get more education, find a higher-paying job and move into a better neighborhood *as individuals*. Because of an expanding economy, relative social stability and luck in forestalling a variety of potential social disasters, such a strategy by and large has worked.

It is natural to cling to strategies that have worked in the past, but dangerous to do so when reality has changed so that the strategy no longer fits. We believe that the strategy of individual advancement within the existing organization of society can now only lead to individual and social disaster.

When old strategies break down, it is natural to look for new ones. One possibility, to which some people are turning today, is a kind of fatalism, often justified in spiritual or religious terms, that abandons any effort to act in the world. As one young man told us: "If I can't change my scene, I have to change my head." Such fatalism was also a common reaction to the beginning of the Great Depression, and this attitude weakened every effort to end the horrible and unnecessary suffering of that period. Another method is to work through the established political institutions to select representatives who will make necessary changes. Such approaches have been notoriously unsuccessful of late, both because the political apparatus itself overwhelmingly favors those with wealth and power, and because the main centers of power in our society lie beyond the control of elected politicians. A third possibility is to try to solve the problems of one race or nation at the expense of others, often by force. This approach reached its logical conclusion in the military aggression and mass exterminations by the Nazis. A fourth possibility is to organize all society under a giant government bureaucracy, whose managers make all decisions and direct the labor of everyone. The tyrannical outcome of such an approach is indicated by the state socialism of the countries in the Eastern bloc.

We can learn from history that these approaches do not work, but we cannot learn what will work. To solve our problems we shall have to create something new, a type of social organization that presently does not exist. Only by acting in new ways, analyzing the results and trying again can we develop the means to create such a society. Such a process is risky—but far less risky than continuing to follow strategies which we know are doomed.

Fortunately, the elements of an alternative strategy are already being forged in the activity and thought of millions of people. The actions and discussions recounted throughout this book indicate that many of the ideas and tactics necessary to challenge minority power are already widespread. These familiar approaches, applied on a massive scale for more far-reaching objectives, would provide the majority of working people with an irresistible social power. With such power, they could wrest control of society from the owners, managers, bureaucrats and politicians, and organize their activities to meet their own needs.

Such a task may seem impossible. But the development of society has already laid the basis for it. Our entire life is now based on the interdependence of millions of people all over the world, each living on products the others produce; this interdependence creates a network of social cooperation which, if people took control of it, would allow them to shape their mutual activity.

Most people already use cooperative strategies on a small scale at certain points in the course of their daily lives. As the great majority of society and the creators of its life, they possess a power potentially greater than any other social force. Faced with deteriorating conditions and disastrous alternatives, that majority can choose to expand the scope of its cooperation to the point of taking complete control of its social activity. Only such a strategy can promise survival, security and a daily life not sacrificed to the needs of the few.

Such action is often viewed as impossible because of the supposedly fixed characteristics of the working people who make up the majority of our society. There are a number of stereotypes by which workers are commonly portrayed. Sometimes they are presented as a "silent majority," one-dimensional puppets dedicated to preserving the status quo, whatever it may be. Alternatively, they are seen as dissatisfied and alienated, perhaps potential followers of left-wing or right-wing politicians. They may be portrayed as intolerant Archie Bunkers and ignorant "Joe Six-Packs" or as sinister "authoritarian personalities." Occasionally they are viewed as ripe for revolution, if only given the "right" leadership. [4]

We believe all such stereotypes contain more insult than insight. All bear the mark of some other group—most often politicians, managers or intellectuals—looking down their noses, threatened and uneasy, at the majority of society. In this book, we view people not as fixed objects to be classified and labelled, but as human beings engaged in making their own lives. From this perspective, it is possible to make sense of most people's actions as reasonable responses to the situations they face, given the information and resources available to them. Throughout American history, as the conditions faced by the majority have changed, so have their responses. At those times when collective action has seemed necessary and promising, millions of people have in fact turned to it as a means of solving their problems. Mass strikes and other actions by working people, often acting outside of any official union or political channels, have been a repeated feature of American life, but one which has been largely omitted from history books. Likewise today, collective action by working people is often massive, but frequently passes with little notice.

The sheer fact that people's experiences take place entirely within the existing society often makes the idea of any fundamental change in that society seem a mere fantasy. A lower level manager at an auto plant in Detroit told us: "Someone will always have to come out on top. It's human nature, and animal nature too. It's always been that way and it always will be."

We believe that such assumptions are false. Society can be transformed because of the following facts about human nature—facts borne out, we believe, by the whole of human history:

Human beings can change. They are far less guided than other animals by fixed, inborn instincts which direct their action. For that reason, human history has been a history of change. At any given time people's existing patterns may seem so fixed as to be immutable. Yet over and over again, people have in fact been able to transform their patterns of thinking and living when it has become clear that their old strategies no longer work. They have been able to do so with amazing speed when necessary.

Human beings can cooperate. Even more than other mammals, they are social beings, interdependent and equipped with complex means to communicate with each other, to make joint plans and to modulate each other's behavior. This by no means implies that people always cooperate. Nor is this capacity always used for good—cooperation may be arbitrarily limited to a narrow group or used for the most destructive of purposes. But the ability to cooperate is there and people can use it, if they so choose, to serve their individual needs far more effectively than they ever could alone.

Human beings can think. For individuals and groups, action is not just a reflex; it is guided by people's ideas about the world in which they live. These ideas do not arise in a realm cut off from the world of action and experience; on the contrary, there is a constant back-and-forth exchange between the realm of ideas and the world in which people face and cope with the problems of daily life. The ideas on which people act are their tools for functioning in that world; they are guided by past experience and by possibilities for future action of individuals and groups. To understand how people think and act, it is necessary to examine the contexts out of which their thought and action come. And to decide how to act, it is necessary to examine the realities in which you find yourself and to evaluate your ideas in terms of them.

We believe human beings can realistically hope to create good lives for themselves as long as they retain the capacity to change, to cooperate, to think and to create new social solutions to the problems they face.

Introduction

In this book, we have tried to combine insights and information from a number of different sources. Much of the book is based on a trip we took around the country in the summer of 1973, visiting the pleasure spots—Philadelphia, Pittsburgh, Cleveland, Detroit, Gary, Seattle, Portland, Los Angeles and smaller towns in between. Many of our insights have come from the Teamsters with whom Tim works, and with whom many of our ideas were discussed. We have drawn on Jeremy's research in labor history to try to understand the historical roots of what is going on today. We have tried to bring to bear whatever we could find that others have written on the subjects we were pursuing.

The problems people face today are global in origin; all humanity will have to cooperate in their solution. While the context of this book is limited to the United States, the action it calls for will have to cross all boundaries of nationality and place in order to be effective. Indeed, those boundaries and the forces that preserve them are among the greatest obstacles to creating a secure basis for a good life.

We hope readers will not take this book as any kind of last word, but rather as a starting point from which they can take what is useful to them, criticize what seems wrong and add what they know from their own experience. We wrote it, not to prove any argument or theory, but because we want to participate with others who share the same problems in a common effort to avert impending catastrophe and make a good life for ourselves. Above all, we have tried to develop a method for analyzing the social world and the roots of its problems—a method that others can apply for themselves.

Throughout this book, our starting point for thinking about society is not what happens in the president's Oval Office or the board rooms of some powerful corporation, but the basic life situation of ordinary people. We focus on daily life for two reasons. First, as we have emphasized, our whole society is based on the daily activity of working people—taking control of that activity is the key to transforming society. Second, daily life is what most people are most concerned with, and rightly so. Living well day by day, not some abstract principle or future glory, should be the objective of social life. What happens every day is the actual substance of human life; if it is unpleasant, stunting, impoverished or unfree, any political, religious or philosophical justification is hollow.

Almost everyone has experienced times that have been good, when they have felt happy and fulfilled. Almost everyone can remember activities that have been enjoyable and creative expressions of themselves. Of course, what people want and need changes over time and differs for different individuals. But a good life depends on having the freedom to do what you want and having the resources with which to do it. If they had the choice, most people would no doubt choose a way of life which makes such experiences possible.

The relative prosperity of the past quarter of a century raised hopes that our society might be entering an era of "post-scarcity" in which such a good life would be available to all. But that prospect now seems highly unlikely. For most people, the few years they are given here on earth must be dedicated primarily to making a living at work they would rarely do by choice, under the command of employers who use their labor for their own purposes. Even that employment is rarely secure; the threat of being out of work lurks constantly and from time to time is realized. After a lifetime of such labor, people are sent into retirement with a few years of pensioned-off old age left before they die. With the advent of hard times, even the relatively high standard of living which has been enjoyed since the Great Depression and has helped compensate for the other meannesses of life is being replaced by a life of scraping to get by. At the same time, the natural and social environment is descending into a mire of pollution and decay, destroying the overall quality of life. Finally, the future promises a continuation of the chronic international warfare that has marked recent decades, taking the lives of many who fight and accompanied always by the threat of mass destruction through nuclear, chemical and biological war.

Nearly two hundred years ago, on the eve of the American Revolution, Thomas Paine wrote in his famous pamphlet *Common Sense* that "a long habit of not thinking a thing *wrong,* gives it a superficial appearance of being *right.*"[5] Paine asserted that the domination of the North American colonies by Britain, accepted for over a century as inevitable and even desirable, was in fact a form of slavery which promised nothing but impoverishment and oppression for those subjected to it. His argument for a complete end to British power in America rapidly swept a country in economic and political crisis; the discussion and action it provoked helped lay the groundwork for the revolution that was to come. We believe that today the time has come for a complete end to the power of owners, managers, politicians and bureaucrats over the lives of the majority who now must work for them. This power may superficially appear to be legitimate simply because it has so long been accepted, but today it guarantees impoverishment and oppression for the majority of our society. The opportunity to declare its independence from that power—indeed the chance to abolish it—lies in the hands of that majority.

AFL-CIO News

I

WORKING

"We have made this daily experience—the power of employers
over the labors of others—the starting point for this
book because it is the key to understanding our society and its present
crisis. It is through their control of other people's labor
—so easily taken for granted—that employers can shape every
aspect of life, on and off the job alike. Only by abolishing
that power can people get control of their lives,
either at work or away from it."

1. THE TIME OF YOUR LIFE

We were sitting in a kitchen in Chicago drinking coffee, while Sam Howard was making sandwiches to take to work. Sam worked swing shift in the morgue at a Chicago newspaper, and it was nearly three o'clock. What Sam said to us could have been said by tens of millions of other people that day:

> It's terrible having your whole day revolve around work. No matter what you're doing, you always have to keep an eye on that clock. It's not that I would worry about showing up late for the company—I wouldn't mind getting fired that much anyway. But it would just mean more work for the other guys.

Whatever else it is, for most people work is unfreedom. It means giving up the time of your life to an employer to use for his purposes. Work consumes more time than anything else most people do during their waking hours. Contrary to a widespread myth, full-time workers work just about as long on the average today as they did forty or fifty years ago—nearly fifty hours a week on the job or commuting to and from it.[1]

We have made this daily experience—the power of employers over the labor of others—the starting point for this book because it is the key to understanding our society and its present crisis. It is through their control of other people's labor—so easily taken for granted—that employers can shape every aspect of life, on and off the job alike. Only by abolishing that power can people get control of their lives, either at work or away from it.

Having to spend the time of your life working for someone else often seems as inescapable as death itself. The reason is obvious— for all but a privileged few work is the main source of income. In a society where almost everything you need has to be paid for, the amount of money you have goes a long way toward determining the quality of life. No doubt "money doesn't buy happiness," but the lack of it can bring misery. As Bertolt Brecht put it:

> Ah, how very sorely they're mistaken,
> They who think that money doesn't count.
> Fruitfulness turns into famine
> When the kindly stream gives out.
> Each one starts to yell and grabs it where he can.
> Even were it not so hard to live
> He who doesn't hunger yet is fearful. . . .
> Good plus money, too, is what it takes
> To keep man virtuous without a slip.[2]

Most people in our society have barely enough to support themselves for a few weeks or months into the future—many are even in debt. The most recent U.S. government study available, made in 1962, found that 44 percent of American households had less than $5000 in assets, and 60 percent had less than $10,000.[3] The wages that most people receive from their employers, even when enough to provide relative comfort, consign them to what a forty-five-year-old Teamster in Boston called a "week-to-week, paycheck-to-paycheck life." In the week-to-week world of most people, loss of a job can be a catastrophe, especially in times of high unemployment. Finding and keeping a job becomes an absolute necessity. As an old chant of the Wobblies—members of the militant Industrial Workers of the World in the early years of this century—put it: "We go to work to get the dough to buy the goods to get the strength to go to work to get the dough. . . ." Such conditions make insecurity a way of life.

Why does the need for goods and services—and the money with which to buy them—lead to having to sell the time of your life to someone else? The answer is evident. People cannot produce the things they need out of thin air with their bare hands. To produce requires natural resources and the tools, equipment and machinery that people have made in the past, not to mention something to live on while you are producing. But most people possess none of these things; they have barely enough to support themselves for a few weeks or months. The sophisticated machines, large factories, fleets of ships, trains and trucks, the vast tracts of oil fields, farmlands and coal mines, are owned by a small minority. These are the means by which the great bulk of society's needs are met. And since the only thing most people have to exchange for the things they need is the time of their lives, they have to go to work for those who own these means of production if they are to live.

Most People Possess Little Wealth

The most recent government figures on the distribution of wealth show that in 1962, 60 percent of consumer units possessed less than $10,000 wealth—including their cars, homes and savings. Our society is rich, but most people have little share in its wealth. Most families have no way to live for more than a few weeks or months without working.

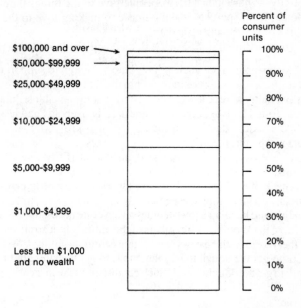

Source: *Social Indicators, 1973*. U.S. Department of Commerce, Washington, D.C., 1973.

The news media have recently been full of reports that workers, especially young workers, are dissatisfied with their work. College professors have announced the astonishing finding that a large proportion of jobs are boring, unfulfilling and detested. But it doesn't take a sociological survey to find out how people feel about work—just try asking the next five people you meet.

What makes so many people resent the work they have to do? It is not just an irrational railing against the fact that, no matter what kind of society they live in, people have to produce the things they need. Most people understand that the products they consume do not spring ready-to-use from the earth; they know that you have to change what nature offers to meet your needs.

Nor does this resentment of work stem from a desire to be as passive as possible, to lie around and do nothing at all. Many of the people we talked with had passionate interests of their own which they would have pursued if they had not had to work. Indeed, many of life's greatest pleasures and satisfactions come from people's own activity—witness the energy people give to the things they do by choice, from sports to making music to making love to the finest works of craftsmanship and art.

There are often some aspects of their activity at work that people enjoy. For many, work provides an important part of their social contact with others. The work itself may at times be interesting, challenging or pleasurable. And even if it is not, the job may provide a framework of activity around which life can be organized. Since they are born, raised and live as adults in a society where most people are expected to spend the heart of their days working, work is the normal way to be active in the world. A thirty-eight-year-old truck driver explained:

> I like the layoff time. Life is more than work. When I was younger I used to work all the time, all year 'round with just a short vacation—I'm talking fifty, sixty or more hours a week. Hey, no more. My wife works, I get by and take a lot of time during the summer. But I still work more than I have to, I suppose, because it gets me out of the house in the winter. Every year I get laid off, you know, I can't wait for the layoff. But after a while, a couple of months, I want to get back. It's not the job; Christ! That's monotonous, doing the same thing every day—I don't care for it—but it gets me out.

But if most people enjoy activity, most jobs are anything but an expression of their interest in an activity they would pursue for its own sake. On the contrary, going to work usually means giving up the possibility of determining your own activity, and relinquishing this control to the employer who has hired you. At times, such work can provide some measure of satisfaction but it is, above all, time when you are not free to pursue your own activities and desires. Such work is all too meaningful—it means giving up the time of your life. The real reason people resent work is that it is first and foremost the realm of unfreedom.

In theory, of course, people are free to choose their work. But most jobs are hardly what people would do, given the choice. Few people plan to grow up to install gas tanks in Chevrolets or to work as file clerks in insurance offices. Even those who get specialized education or training usually have to choose their occupation on the basis of where the jobs are available—otherwise, they have little chance of finding a job that uses their training. What job you're in depends more than anything on what job openings you find—often as much a matter of accident as anything else.

As resentment about work has grown more visible in the past few years, managers, academics and a variety of would-be reformers have proposed various schemes for "job enrichment" to make work more fulfilling and expressive of personal needs.[4] But such plans, however well-meaning, do little more than gild the bars of the prison to which people are consigned for the best part of their days. They may alleviate some of the worst abuses, but they cannot touch the basic source of resentment about work in our society—the fact that it is forced servitude.

Even the more specific grievances about work result directly from this condition of subordination. The fact that you have to spend your time under the control of someone else means that you spend it under conditions that at best are not what you would freely choose, at worst downright destructive to the mind and body. Irene Pastrio, a young woman who worked in a clothing factory in Pittsburgh, Pennsylvania, told us:

> The air is so bad that when you blow your nose it's full of lint and blood. People's arms are green from working on newly dyed uniforms.

Howard Kalado, a young man who had worked in the U.S. Steel mills, in Gary, Indiana, spoke of equally bad conditions:

> I already lost about half my hearing working there in one year. And all the time I was breathing hot filings and dust from the heated steel—that doesn't do you any good, either.

Howard had escaped the mills and gone to college, but he lost his savings and went into debt trying to start a community newspaper. When we met him, he had just gone back to work in the mills. He put his feelings succinctly: "Yesterday was the worst day of my life."

It is not only your time that an employer extracts. You have to give up control of your every movement, turn over your muscles, nerves and mind to someone else to use as he or she sees fit. A waitress in Boston told us:

> Waitressing is totally demanding, physically and mentally. Take Brigham's, for example, working at a counter. Even if no one is there, you're supposed to be busy all the time. Even if there's nothing to do the manager will yell at you if you don't look busy. . . . Then you have to remember the orders. At Brigham's, for example, I handled eleven at a time, carrying them all in my head. One restaurant here has a menu literally half the size of the table—it's a sort of joke—and the waitress may have to master a hundred or more different possible orders. If you're like me and your mind turns to jelly under pressure, it can be a real nightmare. . . .
>
> Since the job is supposed to be totally mindless, you feel really stupid when they yell at you for making mistakes, although the work is mentally very demanding in fact. It's as if the whole thing was designed just to humiliate you.

Such humiliation is possible because of workers' subordination. Employers are in a position to treat them like children. Irene Pastrio, the clothing factory worker, told us:

> The man who hired me said, ''You don't want to work here, you're too intelligent.'' He talked as if the other women who worked there were mules. . . . It is literally true that they would instruct me in how to hold my little finger while running the sewing machine.

A worker from another sweatshop in Portland, Oregon, told us that you actually had to raise your hand to go to the bathroom.

Along with the authority of the supervisor goes the attempt to squeeze more labor out of workers. A student at the University of Massachusetts described a job at an ice cream chain:

> What really gets to you on a job like that is having the supervisor always breathing down your neck, keeping you turning out the orders as fast as you can bear it. It's like being on piece rate, where you have to turn out so many pieces in an hour.

The pressure to work fast for the employer's benefit can greatly reduce whatever intrinsic satisfactions a job might have. This was

17

brought out when we went on a late-night call-in radio show in Detroit, most of whose callers were just coming off the night shift from the auto plants. One of them expressed a sentiment voiced by many who called:

> How can you have "pride in your work" when the company doesn't care? They just want to make production. When I first started I tried to do the job right, but after a few months I decided what's the point, they don't care.

We talked to one worker who loved his job. Steven Harper was about twenty-five, and his great passion was for skilled craft work. He made guitars as a hobby, and would have liked to make violins for a living. He loved working with tools, so he considered himself very lucky to get a job as an apprentice toolmaker at a tool and die shop in Warren, Michigan, a suburb of Detroit. The company made machines for the auto industry, such as one which would take a rough casting at one end and produce a finished carburetor at the other. Such a machine might be fifteen feet by thirty feet, and require tolerances of 2/1000 of an inch. Because tool and die makers are highly skilled workers and nobody else can do the job, their relation to the employer and the work is quite unusual. Steven told us:

> I've never heard a foreman tell anybody to work harder. . . . It doesn't matter how many times you have to do it as long as you get it right. The guys work at a nice easy pace. The foremen don't really discipline the workers at all—they're more like master workmen. They've been working there for thirty years and know how to do everything. They are under pressure themselves to speed the work, but they never hassle the workers.

Steven Harper found his job as an apprentice toolmaker overwhelmingly better than his previous jobs in auto assembly lines and forge departments, but he still wanted to get away from it eventually if he could. For one thing, he wanted to pursue the activity that interested him most, making musical instruments. For another, as he told us: "I just don't like having to get up and go to work every day, just to meet someone else's schedule."

It all adds up to the fact that the various complaints about work are rooted in having to give up the time of your life to the control of someone else. It's a bit like selling yourself into slavery, only it's done a little at a time. Of course, unlike a slave, you can always quit.

But then you will just have to go to work for another employer. So, in effect, a worker is a slave to employers as a group—you get to pick your master. Conditions may be better or worse, but as long as people live in a society where those who do the work are a group distinct from those who control it, this basic situation will remain the same. As someone once put it: "You either own it or you work for it."

Of course, many people look for avenues of escape. Some start small businesses so they can be their own bosses. A young truck driver in Pittsburgh told us he didn't like truck driving, didn't like having a boss: "I'd like to have my own business and have some 290-pound guys who like to work for me. I'd sit on my ass, travel and do what I wanted while they did the work."

But 400,000 small firms go out of business annually, 100,000 of them in their first year, carrying with them the broken hopes and lost savings of their owners.[5] And even those few who manage to survive in business often find competitive conditions so bad that they would be better off as workers. "I had a gas station for a while," a factory worker in Pittsburgh explained, "but the gas business wasn't so good, and I didn't like the long hours."

Others try to escape by going back to school, but the motto "For a good job, get a good education" rings more hollow every year. While the cost of college soars wildly, jobs for the college-educated grow increasingly scarce—an estimated four-fifths of all new jobs in the 1970s will not require a college degree.[6] We found many people with at least some college education working as unskilled and semiskilled workers in factories all over the country. Andrew Korenko, for example, a crane operator at Republic Steel in Cleveland, had graduated from college in liberal arts, but was unable to find any work except in the mills. Even when college graduates do find work that requires their degree, the job is often characterized by the same lack of creativity, subordination to authority and pressure to produce as other labor.

Many people, especially younger people, work for a few months, save up some money and then quit for as long as they can survive—reviving the work pattern of migratory workers half a century ago. In this way they are able to avoid working for a while, but sooner or later they find themselves forced to look for another job.

Drugs and booze form another avenue of escape. An auto worker in Detroit told us: "You ought to write a whole chapter about dope." Another auto worker explained: "Some people say how can you work stoned? But I figure, how can you do it not stoned?'' And Andrew Korenko at Republic Steel said: "People start looking around to see who has any grass after about 7:30 p.m.—that's when the bosses go home. A few older guys smoke dope, and some of them bring a jug.'' A young worker in Portland, Oregon, pointed to the rows of frame houses surrounding his own and said: "The kids here know what work is like; that's why they spend their time instead just hanging out and doing downs.''

Many people try to escape from a job that seems intolerable by looking for another job somewhere else. Yet for most people, this and all other seeming paths of escape lead right back to selling the time of their lives to an employer. They will continue to do so as long as most people don't themselves possess the means to produce what they need to live.

Many people, recognizing that they cannot escape this position, try to pay as little attention as possible to the realm of work. They figure, why think about work—you might just as well think about sleep. You have to do it, and there's nothing you can do to change it. They try to blot out work as much as possible and consider their real lives to be what they do away from work. One is making a living; the other living. Such a separation between work and nonwork worlds may not have been possible in the days when people worked on farms and in home workshops, but today when you finish your labor time you leave the workplace and your employer's direct authority behind. You enter a region which, compared with work, is a world of freedom, or at least of some choice. By slipping into a private world, you can create for yourself the illusion that you are free. As an old-time Wobbly militant put it: "There is a time-clock mentality, that when you punch out from the job all your involvement with the rest of society is over.'' At home, separated both from the workplace and those with whom you work, it is possible to forget the reality of work like a bad dream and think of yourself as a "citizen,'' equal with all others, free to establish your own life style, rather than as a worker who takes orders from a boss or the movements of a machine all day. Such a fantasy does little more to eradicate the miseries of work than the dreams of a prisoner that he is free. It leaves the realities of powerlessness intact in all realms of life.

No doubt people will always have to engage in some activities to meet their needs. But there is no reason that they should always have to do so for the benefit and under the control of employers separate from themselves. As the next chapter will show, the way production is organized in our society is something relatively new. If workers could gain control of their labor, they could transform the realm of work from an expression of servitude to an expression of their own needs and purposes—a chosen activity radically unlike the forced labor people must suffer through today. By taking control of their work, they could also take control of the society it creates.

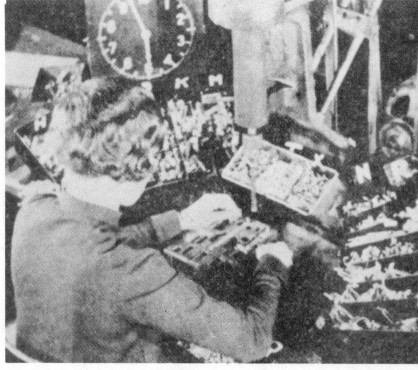

2. HOW DID WE EVER END UP HERE

THE WELL-BOTTOMED POTS

The daily experience of being controlled by others conflicts with the belief that people in our society are free and equal individuals. That belief is rooted in a past that was far different from today.

At the founding of the United States two hundred years ago, employees in the modern sense were a rarity. About two-thirds of Americans were farmers, working farms they owned themselves. A large proportion of the rest were independent artisans, who, like the farmers, owned their own tools and materials and sold their products themselves, mostly to people in their town or backwoods area. Occasionally neighbors might join together when the labor of many hands was required to build a house, barn or ship, but generally the early American families worked for themselves on their own property, dividing up the tasks by age and sex. They often had to work hard for scanty return, but they decided themselves how and when they would work, and whatever they produced they owned themselves.

People made most of the products they needed at home. Edward Wakefield, an economist, described the situation in 1833:

> Free Americans, who cultivate the soil, follow many other occupations. Some portion of the furniture and tools which they use is commonly made by themselves. They frequently build their own houses, and carry to market, at whatever distance, the produce of their own industry. They are spinners and weavers; they make soap and candles, as well as, in many cases, shoes and clothes for their own use. In America cultivation of land is often the secondary pursuit of a blacksmith, a miller, or a shop-keeper. [1]

Such people had little need for economic involvement with others because they were largely self-sufficient.

Since most people could work for themselves, there was little reason for them to work for others. Indeed, the economist Wakefield complained:

> Where land is cheap and all men are free, where everyone who so pleases can easily obtain a piece of land for himself, not only is labour very dear, as respects the labourer's share of the product, but the difficulty is to obtain combined labor at any price.[2]

These conditions seemed natural and right to most early Americans. Individual proprietorship—the private ownership of the means of production—was felt to mean that all were free, all were equal and all were independent. The slogan "let every pot sit on its own bottom" seemed both practical and self-evidently just, for the simple reason that every pot had a bottom to sit on—every farmer could have land, every artisan his own shop. Although there were great variations in wealth, most people did not have to work for someone else—at least permanently—and rarely could anyone exercise power over others through a monopoly of the means of livelihood. The conception of economic individualism that reflected these conditions has marked American society down to the present and is the basis of the belief that it is a land of freedom and equality.

In reality, of course, there were always exceptions to this pattern. The most glaring was slavery. Europeans had early bought slaves in Africa to work the mines and sugar plantations of the West Indies and South America; later, when the North American colonies were formed, traders imported slaves into all of them. The northern colonies and the mountain regions of the South tried slavery to meet the shortage of "combined labor," but it did not prove profitable and virtually died out. In the lowlands of the South, natural conditions proved excellent for crops like rice, tobacco, sugar and later cotton—crops for which a plantation system with slave labor was well suited. The result was the importation of large numbers of African slaves into these areas. By the first census of 1790, nearly one-fifth of all Americans, and two-fifths of those in the South, were African slaves.[3] Other exceptions to the rule of self-employment occurred in the major cities (where less than 4 percent of the population lived in 1820), which provided considerable employment for porters, carmen, longshoremen, seamen, house servants, seamstresses, and other wage laborers.[4] Many people first came to America as indentured servants, sentenced by courts in Europe or agreeing to work for employers in America in exchange for their boat fare. Even in rural areas, a mason, carpenter or other artisan might hire himself out to work for others. In the years to come, the control of labor by employers was to move from the margins of society to become its central structure.

"UNNATURAL RELATIONS"[5]

The market for which early artisans produced was small, since people made most of the things they needed themselves, and it was local, since transportation was expensive and most communities had their own craftsmen. But toward the beginning of the nineteenth century cities began to grow, larger areas to the south and west were settled, and canals and railroads reduced transportation costs to a tenth or even a twentieth of former rates. This caused markets for manufactured goods to grow as well, and master workmen began to employ journeyman assistants to help them increase their production.

At first the journeyman worked side by side with the master and received only moderately less income and respect; he could expect to become a master himself within a few years. As the market continued to expand, merchants—who, unlike the master workmen, bought and sold but did not produce goods—began dealing over large areas and buying products wherever they were cheapest. This put all their suppliers into competition, no matter where they were. The whole process was clearly, if not enthusiastically, portrayed by a Massachusetts labor paper in 1847:

> The rich are growing richer and the poor, poorer, and Mammon is usurping sovereignty in all places. In proportion as railroads and canals are constructed, these mammoth establishments in tanning, shoemaking, saddlery, blacksmithing, and every department of work and skill, send their productions and fabrics to distant parts of the country, and reduce smaller capitalists . . . constantly killing out their rivals and monopolizing the business to themselves.[6]

Master workmen responded to the new conditions by hiring more journeymen, subdividing, lengthening and intensifying their labor and cutting their wages. Merchants with capital and access to markets began to sponsor large-scale production themselves. A group of Philadelphia shoemakers protested in 1835:

> If we take a retrospective view of our trade we will find that
> . . . the trade has been gradually sinking, at least so far as the
> interests of the journeymen are concerned. The cunning men
> from the East have come to our city, and having capital
> themselves or joining with those who had, have embarked in
> our business and realized large fortunes by reducing our
> wages. . . .[7]

Thus evolved the forerunners of the modern industrial employer and the modern employee. Many workers understood, resented and opposed their increasing subjugation to employers, which directly contradicted the principles of freedom and economic independence of the early economy. In 1854, for example, a group of highly skilled piano makers declared that working for a daily wage—in contrast to working for themselves and selling their own product—was equivalent to slavery. They hoped that

> the day is far distant when they[wage earners] will so far forget
> what is due to manhood as to glory in a system forced on them
> by their necessity and in opposition to their feelings of
> independence and self-respect. May the piano trade long be
> spared such exhibitions of the degrading power of the day
> [wage] system.[8]

Similarly, the *Awl,* published in Lynn, Massachusetts, by an association of shoemakers, compared their situation to slavery:

> We are slaves in the strictest sense of the word. For do we not
> have to toil from the rising of the sun to the going down of the
> same for our masters—aye, masters, and for our daily bread?[9]

These changes made the older ideology of economic individualism largely obsolete. The workplace of the individual artisan was no longer efficient enough to compete economically; only an enterprise which could hire many workers and buy and sell on a large scale would thrive. Many individuals, no longer able to own the means of production necessary to make a living, had to go to work for someone else and ceased to be self-sufficient and economically independent. As enterprises grew, more and more people came to work for the same employer, thus becoming members of a work group and of a working class, with common problems, common interests and a common antagonism to their employers.

Almost as soon as there were workers, there were strikes over particular grievances. In many trades, such as shoemaking and printing, trade unions developed to set wages and other conditions of labor. The reasons for such combinations were made clear in a statement of the National Typographical Society in 1850:

> To remedy the many disastrous grievances arising from this disparity of power [between employer and employed] combination for mutual agreement in determining rates of wages and for concert of action in maintaining them, has been resorted to in many trades and principally in our own. Its success has abundantly demonstrated its utility. Indeed, while the present wage system continues in operation, as an immediate protection from pressing calamities, it is clearly the only effective means which labor can adopt. So far as it extends it destroys competition in the labor market, unites the working people and produces a sort of equilibrium in the power of the conflicting classes.[10]

As many workers came to see their problems as common to other workers, whatever their trade, working class movements developed, demanding reforms to improve workers' position in society—free public schools, an end to imprisonment for debt and, above all, a shorter working day. Yet early American workers by no means accepted the idea that they might permanently remain in what seemed to them the unnatural position of employees, and much of their organized effort was directed toward alternatives to the emerging system of capitalism. They participated in attempts to create producers' cooperatives, rural utopian communities and movements to keep public lands available for settlement as an escape from permanent status as workers. While none of these strategies proved to be a viable alternative to the new system—known to friends and foes alike as capitalism—they indicate that in its early stages workers were looking for such alternatives.[11] As the printers' union continued in its argument for working class organization:

> [We] regard such an organization not only as an agent of immediate relief, but also as an essential to the ultimate destruction of those unnatural relations at present subsisting between the interests of the employing and the employed classes. . . .
>
> A combination merely to fix and sustain a scale of prices is of minor importance compared with that combination which looks to an ultimate redemption of labor . . . when labor determines to sell itself no longer to speculators, but to become its own employer, to own and enjoy itself and the fruit thereof, the necessity for scales of prices will have passed away and

labor will be forever rescued from the control of the
capitalist.[12]

THE "INDUSTRIAL REVOLUTION"

Labor for others might have remained an island surrounded by a sea
of individual proprietorship, had the methods of production themselves not been revolutionized by the development of machinery. A
series of inventions, starting with the power loom, the spinning
machine and the steam engine, made it possible to do by machine the
work that had previously been done by skilled human labor.
Machine production required a larger initial outlay of money than
an artisan had spent on his tools and materials, and to be efficient it
required many more people working together. Thus it accelerated
the tendency toward the concentration of many workers in one
enterprise. Large-scale machine production was cheaper than the
old craft production, so that one group of artisans after another was
driven out of business and into the factory by its competition.

The first substantial use of machinery was in the cotton mills
established in such towns as Lowell and Fall River, Massachusetts,
early in the nineteenth century. Machine production made cloth far
cheaper to produce:

> In 1815, when cotton cloth was still woven chiefly by hand
> . . . the price of ordinary cloth for sheeting was forty cents a
> yard. In 1822 it had fallen to twenty-two cents, and in 1829 to
> four and one-half cents.[13]

The reason for this reduction was increased productivity—the larger
amount produced by each worker in a given time. Where a hand-
wheel spinner spun about 4 skeins of yarn a day, a mill spinner in
1815 could tend spindles producing 180 skeins. By 1860, factory
production had completely eliminated home production of cotton
fabrics.[14]

Throughout the course of the nineteenth century, machinery
replaced hundreds of jobs in scores of industries that were once
performed by hand, and even created new industries to perform
functions unthought of before. New inventions were introduced
almost daily. Milling machines, sewing machines, water
turbines—the list could go on and on. Thousands of factories sprang
up, employing an ever greater proportion of the population. This
"industrial revolution" transformed the pattern of laborers working for employers from the exception to the rule in American society.

The spread of machinery under the control of owners seeking profits strengthened the tendency toward polarization between a class of employers with large personal fortunes and a class of employees who worked for them. This was evident to contemporaries. A doctor in the textile mill town of Lowell, Massachusetts, wrote in 1841 that the introduction of machinery meant that

> those who labor are not only required to toil longer than before, but, compared with their employers, are as a class sinking day by day to a still deeper degradation. [15]

A newspaper published by a group of workers in the same town stated:

> That the factory system contains in itself the elements of slavery, we think no sound reasoning can deny, and every day continues to add power to its incorporate sovereignty, while the sovereignty of the working people decreases in the same degree. [16]

And a cotton factory manager in Fall River, Massachusetts, declared in 1855:

> I regard my work-people just as I regard my machinery. So long as they can do my work for what I choose to pay them, I keep them, getting out of them all I can. . . . When my machines get old and useless, I reject them and get new, and these people are part of my machinery. [17]

Many of the basic trends established in the "industrial revolution" continue to this day. First trains, then cars and trucks, next airplanes, jets and pipelines and now rockets, have speeded up, extended or cheapened transportation. Telegraph, telephone, radio, movies and television have speeded and widened direct, mass communication. Steam, electricity, oil and atomic power have increased the amount and flexibility of energy sources. Output per worker has advanced by leaps and bounds as new machinery and processes—increasingly created by deliberate scientific research—have become the basis for virtually all production (rationalized for maximum productive efficiency) and now are becoming increasingly automated and computerized. Companies have grown into corporations and then multinational conglomerates. And an ever-growing part of the American people has become employees.

29

THE CONTROL OF PRODUCTION

Instead of working for themselves, people had to go to work for those who owned the means of production. But in the early days of capitalism, it was usually the workers, not the owners, who directed the work itself. This was because only the workers had the knowledge and skills required to produce. While some owners might be skilled workers themselves, they were more likely to be merchants—businessmen who might know about buying, selling and making money, but not about production. As Frederick Winslow Taylor, the inventor of time-and-motion studies, wrote in 1905 in his *Principles of Scientific Management:*

> In the best of the ordinary types of management, the managers recognize the fact that the 500 or 1000 workmen, included in the twenty or thirty trades, who are under them, possess this mass of traditional knowledge, a large part of which is not in the possession of the management. The management, of course, includes foremen and superintendents, who themselves have been in most cases first-class workers at their trades. And yet these foremen and superintendents know, better than anyone else, that their own knowledge and personal skill falls far short of the combined knowledge and dexterity of all the workmen under them.[18]

Only through a long and sometimes bloody struggle did employers establish their present domination of the workplace. To do so, they had to break the power of the skilled workers and gain control of the skills needed to produce. In some cases, such as the textile industry, the power of the earlier skilled workers was destroyed at the same time that factories and machine production developed; in others, workers' power was broken only long after mechanization occurred. Many aspects of this struggle are unknown, even to historians, yet it shaped the whole structure of modern work. Fortunately, a thorough study by Katherine Stone[19] has uncovered that history for the steel industry, revealing much about how employers came to have so much power over work. Other industries, and even many white-collar occupations, have gone through much the same transformation.

The steel industry of the late nineteenth century was already divided into workers and employers. But curiously enough, the employers had little control over the actual work of making steel. Production was run by teams of highly skilled workers who hired their own helpers and organized their own labor, using equipment and raw materials supplied by the employer. There were no supervisors hired by the owners to organize production and direct the workers. Only the skilled steelworkers knew the complex and tricky process of producing steel, learned through years of experience. They were organized into a union, the Amalgamated Association of Iron, Steel and Tin Workers. A company historian testily described the power over production formalized in the union contract at the Homestead mill in 1889:

> Every department and sub-department had its workmen's "committee," with a "chairman" and full corps of officers. . . . During the ensuing three years hardly a day passed that a "committee" did not come forward with some demand or grievance. If a man with a desirable job died or left the works, his position could not be filled without the consent and approval of an Amalgamated committee. . . . The method of apportioning the work, of regulating the turns, of altering the machinery, in short, every detail of working the great plant, was subject to the interference of some busybody representing the Amalgamated Association. Some of this meddling was specified under the agreement that had been signed by the Carnegies, but much of it was not; it was only in line with the general policy of the union. . . . The heats of a turn were designated, as were the weights of the various charges constituting a heat. The product per worker was limited; the proportion of scrap that might be used in running a furnace was fixed; the quality of pig-iron was stated; the puddlers' use of brick and fire clay was forbidden, with exceptions; the labor of assistants was defined; the teaching of other workmen was prohibited, nor might one man lend his tools to another except as provided for.[20]

John Fitch, in the classic Pittsburgh Survey, confirmed the power the skilled steelworkers had over production:

> A prominent official of the Carnegie Steel Company told me that before the strike of 1892, when the union was firmly entrenched in Homestead, the men ran the mill and the foreman had little authority. There were innumerable vexations. Incompetent men had to be retained in the employ of the company, and changes for the improvement of the mill could not be made without the consent of the mill committees. I had opportunity to talk with a considerable number of men employed at Homestead before 1892, among them several prominent leaders of the strike. From these conversations I

31

gathered little that would contradict the statement of the
official, and much that would corroborate it.[21]

The employers wanted to increase output and introduce new
machinery, and they saw the workers' control of production as a
block to this. As Henry Clay Frick, chairman of the Carnegie Steel
Company, wrote to Andrew Carnegie in 1892: "The mills have
never been able to turn out the product they should owing to being
held back by the Amalgamated men."[22]

The company decided to wrest control of production from the
workers. It ordered three hundred guards, closed the works, laid off
all the workers and announced that it would henceforth operate
nonunion. There ensued a bloody conflict in which dozens of men
were killed in battles between the Homestead workers and Pinkerton
detectives, strike breakers and state militiamen. After four months,
the workers were finally defeated and forced to return to work on the
company's terms.[23] With the employer in control, the skilled
workers could no longer determine who was hired, who promoted,
how the work was divided, what machines were introduced, how
much was produced in each heat and its quality, the materials to be
used or the teaching of skills. The direction of production had been
taken over by the employer. The steel companies, and most other
employers as well, were eventually able to impose this new pattern
throughout industry.

Only a few occupations today resemble the earlier pattern of
highly skilled workers directing their own work. The toolmakers
with whom Steven Harper worked (see page 18) were still all-around
craftsmen, much like those of the nineteenth century. Their remark-
able working conditions reflected their unusually powerful position.
But in the great majority of work situations, as in the case of the steel
industry, the power to organize production has long since been
secured by the employers, whether through violent struggles like the
Homestead strike or through less dramatic means. The lack of
control over the work situation that most workers experience is the
result.

THE TRANSFORMATION OF THE BOSS

Originally, most businesses were directly owned and managed by
single individuals or partners. Many small businesses continue on
this basis today, although primarily in the less profitable fields like
retail trade and services. Because of their competitive situation, low
profit rates and invulnerability to unionization, these small com-

panies generally pay low wages. They provide a great deal of the employment for women and the working poor; indeed, a large proportion of them survive only by paying substandard wages.

Throughout the history of capitalism, however, the tendency has been to concentrate more and more workers into larger and larger companies. We have seen how this process began with the growth of markets and was augmented by the development of technology. It was further accelerated by the combination of businesses into larger and larger units to try to increase profits and counter the effects of heightened competition.[24] In the late nineteenth and early twentieth centuries, thousands of small companies were reorganized into a few hundred huge ones, dominating the major industries of the nation. At the same time, companies began taking over the functions of their suppliers and merchants. The U.S. Steel Corporation, for example, owned and managed mines, ships, railroads, blast furnaces, rolling mills, other plants and its own marketing operation—every step from the raw materials in the earth to the final sale.

An individual capitalist or even two or three partners could hardly supervise an enterprise of such size and complexity. Over many decades, therefore, a new management structure has developed, through which decisions are made and activities supervised in almost all large-scale modern businesses. At the top are a half-dozen or fewer high-level officials—generally the president, the chairman of the board, and a few vice-presidents and members of the executive committee. They make the basic decisions about company objectives and the allocation of funds, but have little to do with the day-to-day functioning of the enterprise. Under them are officials responsible for divisions of the company or particular departments such as finance, marketing, production, purchasing. Below them are large numbers of middle-level managers responsible for supervising day-to-day operations in plants, offices and stores. At the lowest level of the management hierarchy are foremen and supervisors who command the workers who actually do the work. To service this vast bureaucracy, there developed a large group of clerical and other white-collar workers. In their day-to-day experiences at work, most workers in large companies—white- and blue-collar alike—are supervised not by a capitalist, but by a low-level manager who is both a boss and an employee himself.

When businesses were owned and managed by identifiable individuals, it was easy to pinpoint a class of capitalists and employers. But the development of a complex hierarchy of managers, who often own no share of the company at all, makes it seem somewhat unclear just who workers really are working for.

Along with the growth of business size and management hierarchy, there developed a legal form—the corporation—which further obscured the social division of power and wealth. In legal terms, a corporation is an artificial person which can make contracts, assume debts, own other companies and conduct economic business as if it were a human being. As this form of organization came to dominate

Who Owns the Corporations

It is well known that most production in our society is controlled by the powerful private corporations. It is not so well understood that four-fifths of the privately-held corporate stock is owned by a tiny minority of barely one million families. The great majority of workers in effect work to produce profits that belong primarily to this small group.

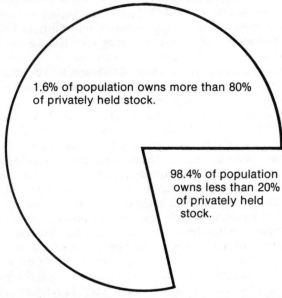

1.6% of population owns more than 80% of privately held stock.

98.4% of population owns less than 20% of privately held stock.

Source for statistics: Robert Lampman, *The Share of Top Wealth-holders in National Wealth, 1922–1956.* Princeton University Press, Princeton, N.J., 1962. Graph drawn by Mark Wilson.

more and more of the economy, it became ever harder to identify single individuals for whom others worked; the "artificial person" of the corporation came to be experienced as the employer, for whom the immediate boss was just another employee. The existence of a "capitalist class" dominating the economy became less and less evident. By World War I, corporations turned out more than 80 percent of the goods manufactured in America.[25]

Corporations, instead of being the property of a single owner or a few partners, issued stock which could be bought by anyone with the money. It is often difficult, therefore, to find out just who really owns a corporation. Though it may appear that ownership has been democratized, with thousands of individuals receiving the profits, a great deal of careful research has proved otherwise.[26] The most thorough available study of the subject, conducted by Professor Robert Lampman of the University of Wisconsin and published by the National Bureau of Economic Research, found that a tiny group of 1.6 percent of the American people—fewer than two million individuals—owned more than 80 percent of privately held stock.[27] Many other studies have essentially confirmed Lampman's results.

The ownership of big business by individual capitalists has thus been transformed into the collective ownership of the entire corporate economy by a small, wealthy minority. Not only is the ownership of each corporation spread among many members of this group, but most of its members own stock in a number of different companies. The bulk of the profits produced by all the employees of all corporations belongs to this group as a whole.

INTERDEPENDENCE AND SERVITUDE

Looking back in 1900, the United States Census described the sharp contrast between the production system of early America and that which followed it:

> Until about 1850, the bulk of general manufacturing done in the United States was carried on in the shop and the household, by the labor of the family or individual proprietors, with apprentice assistants, as contrasted with the present system of factory labor, compensated by wages, and assisted by power.[28]

This change in production was the core of a revolution in the whole organization of society.[29] At one time, each family unit was largely self-sufficient, producing most of the goods it needed itself. The new system was based on a completely different division of labor. Each product was produced by the cooperation of a number of different workers, who made little else. Each individual did only one part of a vast social labor. In return, he received a share—though by no means necessarily an equal one—of what the whole labor of society produced. He necessarily depended on the labor of thousands of other workers who produced the things he needed, just as thousands

35

of others depended on the things he helped produce. This interdependence became a basic characteristic of modern society.

Such a division of labor was essential if society was to make use of the new, large-scale technology introduced by the industrial revolution. Most machine processes required the cooperation of a number of workers. At the same time, each ensemble of workers and machines could produce goods sufficient for thousands or even millions. There was no way independent individuals alone could have utilized such techniques.

Unfortunately, this cooperation did not generally take the form of individuals getting together to produce for each other's needs. Most people simply did not possess the wealth to obtain the factories and machines needed for industrial production. Instead, the entire development of large-scale economic production and cooperation took place under the control of those with the wealth to buy means of production and hire workers. The interdependence of workers was not reflected in any direct communication or planning among them. Cooperation in production appeared only in that many workers were hired by the same employer. The reality of workers producing for each other was manifested only in the fact that all workers bought from various companies products that had been made by other workers.

The new capitalist system grew by leaps and bounds, drawing more and more workers into its net. Between 1850 and 1910, the number of wage earners increased sevenfold.[30] Wage labor became the standard pattern not only in manufacturing, but in mining, lumbering, transportation and construction. Office and sales work became largely a realm of employees, usually paid in the salary rather than the wage form. Even in farming, wage labor became prominent.

The progress of the economy toward greater integration and productivity was at the same time a progressive elimination of economic independence. Most people had little choice but to go to work for someone else. The methods of production that might have made it possible for people to cooperate directly in producing what they needed were used instead to subordinate the majority to the power of a few.

This pattern, in one form or another, exists not only in America, but in all the countries of the modern world. All "capitalist" countries resemble the United States closely in this regard; in "communist" countries, title to the means of production is lodged in the state, but workers continue to work for large-scale enterprises controlled by a minority of managers and politicians from the ruling party. In both cases, the time of their lives remains dominated by others.

Whether some day working people can achieve "the ultimate destruction of those unnatural relations" between workers and employers, whether the time will come "when labor determines to sell itself no longer to speculators, but to become its own employer, to own and enjoy itself and the fruit thereof . . . forever rescued from the control of the capitalist," depends on the actions they choose to take. As we shall see in the next chapter, however, employers do not hesitate to use their power over the workplace to prevent workers from cooperating in their own interests even for much lesser goals.

3. THE STRUCTURE OF WORK

THE EMPLOYER'S STRATEGY SHAPES
THE EXPERIENCE OF WORK

It seems natural: you don't have any money, so you have to go to work. At work, the workplace and the equipment in it belong to those who own the enterprise. So does what the workers produce. The owners or their representatives are the bosses. They decide who to hire and who to fire. They determine the purpose of the work and dictate its technique. They divide up the tasks and assign them to various workers, telling each one what to do, when and how to do it. You expect to carry out their orders, using your own ingenuity to a greater or lesser extent depending on the particular job.

Yet as we have seen, there is nothing natural about this situation at all. It resulted from a historical process through which one social class developed power over another. The entire structure of modern work—the conditions under which people spend much of their life—results from that process.

Early American farmers and artisans had considerable control over the hours and pace of their work, and set their own balance between their need for various products of labor and their desire for free time. Their work pattern was far different from the steady concentration on the same task with few breaks, eight hours or more a day, day after day, week after week, that characterizes modern labor. The early shoe worker of Lynn, Massachusetts, for example, was farmer and fisherman as well as artisan:

> He felt that he could work in the fields or in the shop as he chose, and when disinclined for either he could lock up his "ten-footer" (the small shoe shop beside his home) and go fishing. When it was too cold for work indoors or out, he sat in his kitchen reading.[1]

When an apprentice left his work at night,

> he might be expected back in the morning, but there were no
> special grounds for the expectation. He might drop in the next
> morning or the next week.[2]

The right to use your own time in your own way, even at work, was so well-established that when, in 1854, New York lithograph companies issued rules against having visitors while at work, the printers made it an issue in a strike on the ground that it was "conflicting with the liberties of American working-men."[3] A woman who spent time long ago among cotton mill workers in southern Appalachia told us that in the early years of this century they absented themselves to go fishing whenever they felt like it. Employers apparently accepted their right to do so. When the boss would inquire where they had been, their laconic and self-satisfied reply was "goin' fishin'."[4]

When employers took control of the work process, such worker independence presented them with a terrible problem. All their wealth, all their complex machinery and all their apparent power could produce nothing unless they could make the workers work. As an early nineteenth-century British economist wrote of the rise of factory production:

> The main difficulty . . . lay . . . above all in training human
> beings to renounce their desultory habits of work and to
> identify themselves with the unvarying regularity of the
> complex automaton.[5]

This difficulty has never been fully overcome. As we shall see in the next chapter, workers can find a multitude of ways to use their time at work for themselves rather than their employers. They develop secret techniques to conceal such actions from their employer. Even more threatening, they can combine in strikes and related actions that can considerably weaken the employer's power.

To counter these forms of worker resistance and establish an authoritarian "work discipline," employers evolved a number of institutions and policies characteristic of modern workplaces. In some cases, employers understood clearly the effects of these structures and introduced them deliberately. In other cases they may simply have tried a variety of structures and retained those which—from the employer's point of view—seemed to work. Later generations of managers may have continued them without even knowing why they were adopted. But whatever their origin, they constitute a collection of strategies which make workers work and discourage them from combining against the employer.

These job structures determine much about the quality of people's lives at work. A careful look at the reasons for them indicates that in the main the miseries of work do not result from the unchangeable nature of work itself; nor are they simply due to "unenlightened management," subject to cure by the introduction of "job enrichment" and similar "enlightened" managerial policies which could "humanize" work without changing the actual power of the employer. The present structure of work is the result of policies which are, in most cases, already "enlightened" from the point of view of the employer—a point of view whose objective is to get as much work as possible out of workers, under conditions where the lion's share of the benefit does not go to the workers. The structure of work could be far different, but only if its control is taken away from those who now possess it.

The modern workplace brings groups of workers together and gives them a common interest in conflict with the employer. A major goal of employers, therefore, has been to structure the workplace in ways that divide workers up, promote loyalty to the company, and prevent them from getting together. To develop a strategy to fight for their own interests on the job, workers need to understand and counter the strategies that are being used against them.

Every job and every workplace has its own characteristics, changing over time. A few basic structures, however, can be recognized in most of them.

"SUBJECT TO BE DISCHARGED"

From the early days of masters and journeymen down to the present, the most obvious way for employers to establish power over workers was direct economic coercion—to fire those who would not obey. In 1842, when employers were extending their control over many industries, a New York labor paper complained:

> The capitalists have taken to bossing all the mechanical trades, while the practical mechanic [worker] has become a journeyman, subject to be discharged at every pretended "miff" of his purse-proud employer.[6]

No doubt tens of millions of workers have been fired for one or another "miff" in the generations since.

Actually, firing is used surprisingly infrequently as a means of disciplining workers; demotion and suspension are far more common, along with harassment designed to make workers quit. But firing remains the employer's reserve threat. As an auto worker in Lordstown, Ohio, reported:

> The whole plant runs on fear. The top guy in that plant is scared of somebody in Detroit. And the guy below him is scared of him and, man, it comes right down to the foremen, and the foremen are scared to death. And when they're scared to death they really put the heat on the people, and the people are scared to death 'cause they're afraid to lose their jobs. And they know if they don't do the work they will lose their jobs. . . .[7]

Much the same could be said of any factory, office or other workplace. The employer's power to cut off a worker's economic sustenance remains the stick in the closet backing up all management authority. The vulnerability of workers to such intimidation lies in economic dependence—the fact that you have to have a job in order to live.

As a New York truck driver said: "Clubs are still trumps."

THE MANAGEMENT CADRE

One of the near-universal features of contemporary workplaces is the division of the personnel into a minority of managers and a majority of other workers. The managers organize the work and direct the workers. This situation may seem quite natural, since the managers possess most of the skills and knowledge needed to run the enterprise. In fact, managerial authority over work developed not because workers were *unable* to direct their work themselves, but rather to prevent them from doing so.

In early industry, as we saw in the last chapter, production and knowledge about production were often controlled by skilled workers. Employers took control of production in order to break that power. But if workers were no longer to direct their own work, employers had to find an alternative means to control it. To organize the work and command the workers, a new cadre of managers was established. In 1919, the president of a training school for foremen described the ideal of this cadre: "From the foreman to the president right straight through, you have got one body of mind workers, and they do but two things: they organize knowledge and then they use the knowledge as organized."[8]

In reality, power and authority were as important as knowledge to the managerial role. A steel company official compared the new organization of authority in industry to that of the "army, with the necessary distinction between the commissioned officers and the ranks''; such a comparison was frequent and appropriate.[9]

Unfortunately, the superior souls chosen for management were not born with the knowledge of how to direct production. If they really wanted to run the work, there had to be what Frederick Taylor described as

> the deliberate gathering in on the part of those on management's side of all the great mass of traditional knowledge, which in the past has been in the hands of the workman, and in the physical skill and knack of the workman, which he has acquired through years of experience.[10]

Most of the technical and scientific knowledge thus ''gathered in'' was transferred to special engineering, laboratory and planning departments. Typical was Taylor's advice that ''all possible brain work should be removed from the shop and centered in the planning or laying-out department.'' In many if not most workplaces, much of this knowledge is actually kept secret from those who do the work. A young man from Oregon related his experience of this:

> I wanted to learn how to make musical instruments, so I applied for a job at a factory where they made high-quality flutes. When a job came open they called me and I took it. I was a skilled worker, one of about forty people who worked there. Of course, it was like any factory: they wanted to break me in on one job and keep me there. They tried to make sure I didn't learn about the whole process. I was able to learn a lot anyway by keeping my eyes open. Finally, one guy who worked there, who had frustrated ambitions to become a foreman, caught me making sketches of the way certain keys were made. He turned me in to the boss, and it was made pretty clear to me that I'd better not get caught doing it again.

It is often impossible for workers to find out about schedules for future work, or even on what shift they will be the following week, let alone information on the production process or management's long-range planning. It would be hard to find more telling evidence that knowledge is centralized in the management cadre not primarily to increase the intelligence with which work is performed, but rather to reduce the power that workers can exercise over it.

As knowledge passed to special departments, authority over workers was given to foremen and other ''front-line supervisors.'' In the early days of American industry, foremen were characteristically lead workers in labor gangs. In the steel industry, for example, they had little authority over the skilled workers and did manual labor themselves. But when employers took control of the production process, they tried to create for foremen a new status separate from the rest of the labor force and with authority over it. An editorial in *Iron Age* in 1905 quotes approvingly a superintendent lecturing foremen:

> You men have no business to have your coats off when on duty in your shops unless you are warm. You have no business to take the tools out of a workman's hands to do his work. Your business is to secure results from other men's work. . . . A man cannot work with his hands and at the same time give intelligent supervision to a gang of men, and the foreman who does this is apt to lose control of his men while he is weakening the confidence of his employers in his ability as a general.[11]

Management developed special training programs for foremen in line with their new role. But this training usually has little to do with production itself—a fact evident to many workers, as we shall see. Supervisor training is largely concerned instead with managing workers. Such weighty topics are studied as "organizational structure and communication," "intergroup relations" and "organizational psychology." At times this training can approach the ludicrous. A front-line manager at a large computer company told us:

> At one training session we played a game where the instructor held a handkerchief. Two trainees stood on either side, each trying to "steal the bacon" without getting tagged by the other. I know it sounds rather humorous; the only thing is, the company always observes how you react, and every time we have one of these training sessions, you look around the next week and you notice that someone has disappeared from the organization.

Supervision by foremen remains characteristic of industries like steel which developed in the late nineteenth and early twentieth centuries. Most other jobs have some variant of this pattern. In many occupations of more recent origin, authority over workers is held by professionals or technicians. In hospitals, doctors and nurses often are the bosses for the various grades of workers below them. In factories with advanced technology, such as in the chemical industry, chemists and technicians often directly supervise the blue-collar work force. In many stores and other small businesses, the employees are supervised directly by the owner. In offices, it is common practice to give some workers management titles and make them responsible for supervising other workers as well as doing their own work. The reason for this pattern may well be that in offices, the speed of work is not so often set by the machine, and therefore only close supervision can make sure that workers actually work.

Front-line supervisors, whatever their titles, directly wield the power of employers over their workers. They exercise an authority which contradicts every ideal of equality and freedom. They are in a position to command and harass the workers under them, and often to demote, suspend and fire them as well. Subjection to their authority may well be the specific aspect of work that workers dislike most intensely. Yet the front-line supervisor is usually an employee himself, only partly separated from those he directs, making a small or moderate amount more than them. The attitude of many workers toward him is a mixture of hatred, pity and contempt, reflecting the ambiguity of his position. As Andrew Korenko put it:

> In a funny way, a lot of the workers have sympathy for the foremen, even though they hate them too. They're caught in the middle—the company on one side, the workers on the other. Some of them will help out. A few of the older ones were hired off the shop floor, but most of them now come out of college. They can't really boss—they don't know anything about production. They don't do much—the people that work there know how to do the work and do it. The foremen just have a disciplinary function.

And a track maintenance worker in Detroit told us:

> People give the foremen a real hard time. They don't talk to them. Our foreman's name is Alison. They all call him Alice, except me; I always call him "Prick."

As we shall see in Chapter 4, the sparring between foremen and workers is not all verbal. Foremen are not called "front-line managers" for nothing; they represent the employer in the daily battle to keep workers under control and to make them work.

TIED TO THE MACHINE

One of the most common criticisms of industrial society is that it turns human beings into mere appendages of machines, controlled by "the unvarying regularity of the complex automaton." It is an illusion, however, that machinery per se dictates such a pattern of work. Rather it is the way in which today's machines are designed and used. If workers controlled the design and use of the machinery, it would be possible to create far different schedules and rhythms. The subservience of many workers to ''their'' machines is a product of their subservience to their employers. It results from the deliberate effort of employers to use machines as a way to control those who work for them.

One of the first attempts to use machines to control how hard workers worked occurred in the nineteenth-century cotton mills. When the mills were first founded, there was little systematic attempt to use every second of the workers' time. A former textile mill worker, Harriet Robinson, remembered that in the early 1840s,

> the girls were obliged to tend no more looms and frames than they could easily take care of and they had plenty of time to sit and rest. I have known a girl to sit idle twenty or thirty minutes at a time.[12]

But employers soon discovered they could greatly increase their production simply by running the machines faster and having each worker run more of them. Between the 1830s and the 1870s, the number of looms and the number of picks per minute a worker had to tend doubled and perhaps tripled.[13] This so-called stretch-out put an end to the once-leisurely pace and greatly increased the amount of labor extracted. Such crude speed-up techniques are still everyday occurrences in all kinds of jobs. To complement these tactics, employers have had equipment redesigned to extract more work from fewer workers; indeed, engineering science has built this managerial objective into its basic principles. A steelworker told us:

> The old-timers agree that the work has gotten worse. It's speeded up by introducing new machinery, increasing the number of jobs per person and cutting crews. My crew was cut in half when we moved to the new plant. The provisions in the union contract give no protection. The company has a free hand in introducing new machinery, setting crew sizes and scheduling.

Nor is this simply a question of introducing more ''productive'' machines. Generally, the organization of the workplace as a whole is designed with the objective of making workers work well. The placement of desks in an office, the layout of a department store, the moving belt of an assembly line—all involve strategies devised by employers to make workers work.

The design of machinery and other aspects of the production process has also been an important means for employers to combat workers' power. Traditionally, the more skilled workers have been, the more power they have had over their work. Mechanization made it possible for employers to do without the highly-skilled industrial craftsmen, and therefore made it possible to break their power. As the British inventor/industrialist Nasmyth said more than a century ago:

> The characteristic feature of our modern mechanical improvements is the introduction of self-acting tool machinery. What every mechanical workman has now to do, and what every boy can do, is not to work himself but to superintend the beautiful labor of the machine. The whole class of workmen that depend exclusively on their skill, is now done away with.[14]

In the United States, a study in 1921 found that little skill was required in most industries either using or building machinery, such as steel, shoe, clothing, meat-packing, baking, canning, hardware and tobacco.[15]

This process was evident in the history of the American steel industry. The traditional skills of heating, roughing, catching and rolling, once performed only by very highly skilled workers wielding tools, were instead built into the machines. The crushing defeat of the skilled steelworkers at Homestead (see page 32) could never be recouped because employers were no longer dependent on their skills.

The process continues to this day. Employers introduce equipment which reduces skill levels wherever they believe it will pay to do so. Automation and computers are reducing the need for human skills in factory and office alike. The fact that today machinery is designed to keep the element of human skill to a minimum helps explain both the mindlessness of most work and the powerlessness of most workers.

JOB DIVISION

Any work process consists of a series of operations, performed simultaneously or in succession. When skilled craftsmen controlled production, they carefully regulated which workers could perform any given operation to be sure that their work was not broken down into components that required less skill. Once management established control of production, it set about redividing jobs. Its usual objective was to break down the production process into many separate jobs, each as simple as possible. This process—considered

47

by management the "rationalization" of work—had two virtues for managers: By making each operation as simple as possible, it allowed employers to hire workers with no skills and train them in a few weeks or even a few hours, thus making the employers independent of skilled labor; by reducing the job to one constantly repeated operation, it made it possible to speed up the jobs to an extreme degree.

This subdivision of jobs is often closely coordinated with the physical design of the production process and its machines. The automobile assembly line is an extreme example of combining production engineering and job subdivision to squeeze out every possible drop of labor. In his autobiography, Henry Ford, inventor of the auto assembly line, described its development:

> Along about April 1, 1913, we first tried the experiment of an assembly line. . . . We had previously assembled the fly-wheel magneto in the usual method. With one workman doing a complete job he could turn out from 30 to 40 pieces in a 9 hour day, or about 20 minutes to an assembly. What he did alone was then spread into 20 operations; that cut down the assembly time to 13 minutes, 10 seconds. Then we raised the height of the line 8 inches—that was in 1914—and cut the time to 7 minutes.
>
> That line established the efficiency of the method and we now use it everywhere. The assembly of the motor, formerly done by one man, is now divided into 48 operations—those men do the work that 3 times their number formerly did.[16]

Thus the assembly line, the great symbol of modern production, was above all a means to increase the amount each worker turned out by eliminating every second that he was not actually producing.

Subdivision of jobs greatly weakened workers' power; those performing such simple tasks could easily be replaced. The results are evident today. When we asked a young auto worker in Detroit about using walkouts as a tactic to improve the job, he replied it would be ineffective because the workers would simply be fired and replaced: "We're just trained monkeys."

The subdivision of jobs was often based on time-and-motion studies which established supposedly "scientific" judgments about the "one best way" to do each operation and how much time it should require. Frederick Taylor, the inventor of so-called "scientific management," developed techniques for analyzing people at work to break down each job into its component movements, and the time-study man with stop watch in hand became a stock figure in American industry.

The reduction of work to a single repeated function makes it far more boring and deadening than it need be. The monotony of repetitive jobs has often been portrayed by journalists and social scientists as the prime source of discontent about work. In reality, monotony is only one source among many, but it remains one of the most degrading results of the power employers wield over workers.

The extreme subdivision of jobs, in addition to its evident inhumanity, has at times proved less than effective for management's purposes. The extreme boredom it engenders often generates poor quality work, high turnover and general worker resistance. Many managements are therefore cautiously experimenting with various forms of "job enrichment" or "job enlargement," amidst considerable ballyhoo about "the Job Revolution." In a Manhattan bank, for instance, until recently checks were processed in production-line fashion, each worker performing a simple repetitive step of the process, such as copying out a single digit of the account number. Job enlargement consisted of giving each individual responsibility for processing the entire check, including handling any questions about the results that customers might raise. In Sweden, there are even attempts to break up auto production into subassembly operations, in which teams of workers have responsibility for one cluster of parts, deciding in what order to work, who will do what job and the rhythm of work.

Such job enlargement may ease some of the more brutal effects of "scientific management." A young woman who worked at Techtronics, a factory in Portland, Oregon, where job enrichment techniques were applied, told us:

> They have this job enrichment. You assemble a whole unit;
> each person does a number of different operations. Bad as it is,
> I know when I'm working it would be worse if I had to do just
> one operation.

But job enlargement can be simply a way to increase the difficulty and responsibility of jobs without increasing their pay. In 1973, for example, a book somewhat extravagantly titled *The Job Revolution*, by ex-*Fortune* editor Judson Gooding, hailed the new General Motors Vega plant at Lordstown, Ohio, as a prime example of a "forward-looking approach to improving auto assembly jobs"; his book had barely appeared when a highly publicized strike against speed-up made the Lordstown Vega plant a national symbol of intolerable work conditions.

Having three operations on a production line instead of one may look good in a company press release; but speed-up by any other name is just as bad. As long as control of the workplace remains in the hands of employers, the extent to which "job enlargement" is introduced, and the extent to which it genuinely benefits workers, will be determined less by how much it "humanizes" work than by how much it enlarges profits.

JOB HIERARCHIES

On most jobs, workers are stratified into a number of different job categories and pay grades. At first sight, these may appear to result directly from the nature of the various functions to be performed. But in reality, they are one more weapon in the employer's arsenal of control.

During the late nineteenth and early twentieth centuries, machine production and the subdivision of jobs tended to equalize the amount of skill needed to do various jobs. Where it might once have taken from four to seven years' apprenticeship to master a trade, the overwhelming majority of jobs were redesigned to be learned in a few weeks or months. A group of British iron masters who visited the United States around the turn of the century reported:

> The tendency in the American steel industry is to reduce by every possible means the number of highly-skilled men employed and more and more to establish the general wage on the basis of common unskilled labour. This is not a new thing, but it becomes every year more accentuated as a result of the use of automatic appliances which unskilled labor is usually competent to control.[17]

By World War I, such skill reduction had reached the point where the time required to train workers in the shipyard trades averaged only nineteen days.[18]

Of course, many workers classified as "unskilled" or "semi-skilled" actually possess a tremendous range of skills and knowledge that they have acquired on the job. There are usually knacks and tricks that may take a considerable time to learn; even more expertise is required to cope with the difficulties that arise when machines break down, bosses don't know what they are doing or other special conditions arise. This may be true for the simplest jobs, as well as those that are classified as more skilled. Many workers have had the experience of being skipped many skill grades to jobs that supposedly required long previous training, only to find that they are not much harder than the "unskilled" jobs they held before. Most "skilled" jobs require little formal training, unless it is demanded by apprenticeship or other regulations. A number of workers told us that, as a steelworker put it: "On every job, you learn what to do from the other workers, just watching them and then doing it yourself." Except for a few remaining highly skilled occupations, most jobs can be learned by most people in a relatively short period of time.

In a few places like the auto industry, the result of this equalization of skills has been a general equalization, with most jobs offering similar pay and status. But such equality presented problems for management. It gave individual workers little incentive to compete with each other for management's favor in order to "get ahead," and it strengthened the basis for workers' cooperation with each other against the employer, by making clear their common position and common interests.

Both problems were clearly recognized by employers. An industrial manager named Meyer Blumfield, for example, wrote in 1918·

> A good deal of literature has been published within the last dozen years in which scathing criticism is made of what has come to be known as "blind alley" or "dead-end" jobs. By these phrases is meant work of a character which leads to nothing in the way of further interest, opportunity, acquisition of skill, experience or anything else which makes an appeal to normal human intelligence and ambition.

He added revealingly: "The work itself is not under attack as much as the lack of incentive and appeal in the scheme of management."[19]

Frederick Taylor warned of other dire consequences of treating all workers equally:

> When employers herd their men together in classes, pay all of each class the same wages, and offer none of them inducements to work harder or do better than the average, the only remedy for the men comes in combination; and frequently the only possible answer to encroachments on the part of their employers is a strike.[20]

To counter these results of job equalization, the management of many companies deliberately divided their work force into different job grades and categories, linked by promotion hierarchies. While this was by no means required by the production process itself, and left the jobs as unsatisfying as ever, it offered workers some chance to "get ahead." As Bloomfield continued:

> A liberal system of promotions and transfers has therefore become one of the most familiar features of a modern person- nel plan, and some of the most interesting achievements of

management may be traced to the workings of such a system.[21]

Most large companies today have developed such complex systems of job grades and promotion hierarchies. While ostensibly benefiting the employees, they actually serve as a means to motivate workers to work in the present by dangling before them the carrot of future advancement. At its most effective, this technique can lead workers not only to perform as their employers desire, but to adopt the attitudes they think their employers would like them to hold. It can likewise turn workers against one another in a scramble for each other's jobs. Many of the conflicts on the job between different age, race, sex and other groups grow out of competition for the more favored ranges of the job hierarchy. Job stratification even has powerful effects off the job, determining much of the inequality of income and status that marks our society at large.

Such advancement hierarchies continue to be constructed today, sometimes under the banner of "job enrichment." For example, the telephone company has great difficulty keeping people at work on the low-paid and onerous job of operator. In Los Angeles in 1969, the turnover of operators reached 65 percent; many operators simply grew disgusted with the job after six to nine months and quit. Rather than change the job or raise the pay, the manager in charge started promoting a certain number of operators to better paid and more prestigious jobs as "service representatives," a position which had previously been filled from outside the company. He brags that during the first eight months of 1970, the number of operators lost decreased by nearly 40 percent, as workers kept their detested jobs in the hopes of rising to something better.

Many promotion systems have been modified, often under union pressure, to provide for advancement on the basis of seniority. Such a system, if administered fairly, would still tend to divide workers into conflicting interest groups, but at least it would protect them against being punished with bad job assignments. In fact, favoritism often plays as great a role as seniority in such systems, contract clauses notwithstanding. An assembler at a lightbulb factory in Cleveland told us:

> People working here are still taking home $130 a week after fifteen years, the same as I make after two. There really is no advancement. One opening came up for a good job; six people bid for it, but were turned down as "theoretically unqualified." The boss's nephew, right out of high school, got the job. The second guy ever to go from assembly to the tool and

die department was the son of the president of the union. People were outraged. People in general just don't advance.

A steelworker confirmed this:

> I tried to bid out of my job as crane operator but it's a dead-end job and it's a nervous job moving weights over people. They have a hard time getting people to stay on it so they won't let me go. It's a grade 9 which isn't too good. There really is no seniority. Other things being equal there is seniority, but the company decides if other things are equal. A lot of guys stay grade 9 for twenty years. Others go right up if they have connections. There is a lot of favoritism.

Under such conditions advancement by seniority is little more than a fraud.

The effects of job hierarchies were apparent to many workers when they were introduced. Nearly seventy years ago, the founders of the Industrial Workers of the World described with precision the new pattern of labor and its objective:

> Laborers are no longer classified by difference in trade skill, but the employer assigns them according to the machine to which they are attached. These divisions, far from representing differences in skill or interests among the laborers, are imposed by the employers that workers may be pitted against one another and spurred to greater exertion in the shop, and that all resistance to capitalist tyranny may be weakened by artificial distinctions.[22]

The management strategy of divide and rule can be just as apparent to workers today, as a teamster explained:

> They just try to keep us fighting among ourselves. They love that. Show a little favoritism here, give certain people the cream, it makes some people happy and some people mad. The ones that are happy aren't going to say anything and the ones that are mad usually get mad at the people who are getting the cream.

FORMS OF PAYMENT

The forms in which workers are paid are often used as techniques for dividing them and making them work. The most obvious of these is the distinction between wages and salaries. Employers measure the labor of some workers by the month or year and some by the hour to draw a line between those they want to feel like "part of the organization" and those they want to feel like merely "hired hands." This distinction, trivial to begin with, becomes increasingly meaningless in reality, as salaried employees lose their immunity to layoff and firing. But employers cultivate this division to keep those they have categorized as wage and salary workers apart.

This separation often goes to extremes. Many workplaces have separate parking lots, cafeterias and even bathrooms for "salaried" and "hourly" employees, reminiscent of the segregated facilities for blacks and whites that once prevailed in the South. The status distinctions are often emphasized further by different clothing; salaried workers, for instance, often wear suits and white shirts, while wage workers are required to wear blue or green work uniforms.

Employers often attempt to tie wages to output. In some workplaces, especially those which don't produce a physical commodity, this is not practical; the majority of jobs are simply paid by time. But many employers, especially in manufacturing, use payment plans as a carrot to motivate workers to increase output. The most obvious means of doing this is to pay workers in proportion to the amount they produce—the piece-rate system. The purpose of piece-rate payment was to encourage workers to drive themselves to produce more. But the result instead was often to provoke a constant battle over the rates for each job. When rates were set high, workers could often increase their output enough to make exceptionally high wages. Management generally responded by cutting the rates. This process proved to workers that trying to maximize individual output was not to their advantage at all; they often responded by getting together to set informal ceilings on the output for each job (for examples, see Chapter 4). In short, piece rates often produced the exact opposite of the effect management intended. Today, the piece-rate system prevails primarily in the garment and other industries marked by many small, highly competitive companies, where workers' cooperation is weak.

To overcome the problems with piece rates, management next turned to more sophisticated incentives. These gave workers a bonus for high output. *Iron Age,* for example, recommended a plan "to pay the more efficient workman only one-half of what he saves by speeding up." It described one case where

> for every extra $1 the man earned by his extra effort, the manufacturers would gain $7. Not a bad investment, this

premium system. It betters the workingman's condition materially, and, best of all, improves his frame of mind.[23]

As time went on, incentive plans became more and more complex, combining a maze of day rates and individual and group bonuses. Howard Kalado described a meeting where the general foremen explained a new wage-payment system:

> I looked at the paper they were handing out. I'm a college graduate, I studied math, and I couldn't make head or tail of it, but the workers just said, "Sure, sure." So I said, "This is fine, but will we make more money or less?" I guess they weren't used to questions, because the foremen didn't quite know what to say. Finally one of them said, "More, if you work hard."

Bonus systems can also be used to turn workers against each other. A manufacturer queried in 1928 explained eloquently why he had adopted output incentives:

> To break up the flat rate for the various classes of workers. This is the surest preventive of strikes and discontent. When all are paid one rate, it is the simplest and almost the inevitable thing for all to unite in support of a common demand. When each worker is paid according to his record there is not the same community of interest. The good worker who is adequately paid does not consider himself aggrieved so willingly nor will he so freely jeopardize his standing by joining with the so-called "Marginal Worker." There are not likely to be union strikes where there is no union of interest.[24]

In many cases, however, workers have been able to turn incentive systems to their own advantage as they did with piece rates. Forty-five years ago, a manufacturer warned that the group bonus "has a strong tendency to make the men organize, at least informally, in cliques and become somewhat dictatorial."[25] At times, workers have even fought to maintain or extend incentive systems. In the 1950s, the United Steelworkers union pressured the steel industry into introducing incentive pay for workers in coke ovens and blast furnaces, even though "most industrial engineers were of the opinion that workers could exert no positive influence over production in these units and any incentive installed would represent an outright gift."[26]

Some of the recent schemes for "job enrichment" are essentially new descriptions for group incentives and bonuses. But the main trend in management is away from such incentive plans. Management has considerably increased its ability to make workers work through the timing of the production process itself, backed by close supervision. The result has been a tendency away from output incentives and toward so-called "measured day work," in which workers are paid a flat hourly rate and required to expend a measured amount of labor. But incentive systems remain in a great many workplaces to this day.

RATIONAL FOR WHOM?

Any workplace is a collection of people, equipment and materials organized to produce some intended result. But in our society that organization takes the form of a minority with power controlling the great majority of workers. The key to understanding the workplace as it is experienced day by day is to recognize that it is shaped not only by the work to be done, but also by management's need to control those who do it. Insecurity of employment, the managerial structure, the selection and organization of equipment, the assignment of tasks, the hierarchy of jobs, the form in which workers are paid— these basic structures of work in our society, far from expressing any "technological necessity," are all used as means for the control of workers.

Many of these control techniques have been described by management theorists as aspects of the "rationalization" of work. They may well be rational from the point of view of those who are in control and want to stay there. Examined from other perspectives, however, they are totally irrational. When it comes to getting the work done easily and efficiently, for example, managerial control may be nothing but an interference. A track maintenance worker at a steel company in Detroit gave an illustration of this:

> Until recently, each maintenance crew had responsibility for the track in one section of the plant. But the company felt the crews were getting too together—in some cases the foremen were going out to buy beer for the guys at work, and workers were coming in and sleeping most of the shift. So they changed the system; now they send each crew out wherever they are needed all over the plant. The result is that the accident rate has been soaring from poorly maintained track. But I guess they got what they wanted.

Many workers can cite similar cases.

The present organization of the workplace is irrational in a still more profound sense. In it, many people cooperate on the various parts of a common task. But those who do the work cannot directly coordinate their efforts. Those in one work group cannot, for example, decide how to divide up the work among themselves, nor can they arrange a convenient scheduling of work with another department. Both the knowledge and the authority for such coordination are jealously guarded by management. Therefore workers, instead of cooperating through their own intelligence and social capacity, are supposed to do so only through obedience to the plans and orders of management. Thus, the entire structure of work in our society is based on denying and obstructing the majority of the population's ability to think, cooperate and create. That ability could only be realized if people controlled their work themselves.

Of course, the schemes that exist in the heads of managers and on the drawing boards of engineers do not always determine what happens in reality. The actual pace of work, even in a highly mechanized workplace, is often set by jockeying between workers and management. Production really depends on the problem-solving capacity of those on the spot.

However sophisticated the techniques of management control become, in the end they mostly boil down to the carrot and the stick. They comprise a system of rewards and punishments designed to condition workers' day-to-day behavior and their basic life ambitions. But therein lies the weakness. Unlike laboratory rats, workers can understand the objectives of those who try to manipulate them through rewards and punishments. And as we shall see in the next chapter, they can devise their own strategies to counter those of management. For, to paraphrase Bertolt Brecht:

> Your warplane is a powerful weapon, general,
> But it has one fault:
>   It needs a pilot.
> Your machine is a great producer, capitalist,
> But it has one fault:
>   It needs a worker.
> Your worker is a marvelous creature, boss,
> But he has one fault:
>   He has a brain.[27]

Cidne Hart/Liberation News Service

4. RESISTANCE ON THE JOB

WORKERS' STRATEGIES

When you go to work you give the employer the right to control your activity. Not only that, you are faced with an elaborate organization of authority and technology designed to maintain and perpetuate that control. Your activity and your cooperation with other workers is supposed to be entirely at management's direction.

Under such circumstances, workers might appear to be nothing but tools in the hands of their employers. Unfortunately for employers, however, workers are not just tools; even after they go to work they remain human beings, pursuing their own ends, their own satisfactions and their own freedom. Worse still, they retain their human ability to think and to relate to each other directly, even though they are only supposed to follow orders and relate through management.

There are a number of ways that workers attempt to deal with the power of their employers. We find it helpful to think of these as alternative strategies. This does not mean that workers always think out a conscious strategy. But even when these strategies are largely a matter of habit, they are still ways of acting to achieve a purpose in a context. Few individuals or groups use any one of these strategies exclusively; most workers resort to most of them at one time or another.

One basic strategy is to try actively to please the employer and follow his desires. The structure of the workplace, with its rewards and punishments, is designed to elicit such a response. In our experience, however, this attitude in its pure form is quite rare. Only a very small proportion of workers have any real expectation of "getting ahead" on the job beyond whatever advancement they can expect with seniority. Workers sometimes feel a psychological identification with their employer; a number of women employees at a factory in a rural area, for example, felt proud of what they had contributed to the growth of "their" company. As we shall see in Part III, identification with the employer has traditionally been much more common in white- than in blue-collar occupations. So far as we can judge, however, workers who want to please, impress and loyally serve their employers are quite exceptional in all but management jobs.

A more common strategy is to do whatever you have to do to stay out of trouble with the employer, without doing any more work than you have to. Take it easy but keep your nose clean. Such an attitude is often based on a belief that neither individual attempts to get ahead nor cooperation by workers against the employer have much to offer. This attitude is exemplified by old-timers who urge young troublemakers to learn to "live around" the sore spots in their relations with management.

These two strategies involve little direct conflict with the employer. Others, however, are based on defiance of management's power. Some of these, discussed in the next section, "Guerrilla Tactics," involve secret cooperation among workers for such tactics as output restriction and sabotage, based on their ability to conceal from management what they are really doing. Outright confrontation with management, such as walkouts, sitdowns and wildcat strikes, which make use of workers' power to halt production, are discussed under "Stopping the Works."

The choice of strategies may be embedded in individual and group values. A person who believes in always trying to prove himself better than others in what he does is actually choosing a strategy of getting ahead individually at the expense of others. Someone who, in contrast, believes in helping those who face the same problems he does, is in fact opting for a strategy of collective struggle. An important example of this is the strong feeling of many workers from blue-collar working-class backgrounds that "scabbing" by working when other workers are on strike, or even crossing a picket-line, is morally repugnant. A teamster from an old union background said: "Personally, I could never scab. I just couldn't bring myself to do it—I'd die first. I guess I was just raised that way." Such a feeling, whatever else it may be, is an expression in moral terms of a strategy based on workers' solidarity and mutual support.

To some extent the choice of strategies varies from individual to individual. These individual differences seemed most important to a foreman who—perhaps unknowingly echoing Frederick Taylor—told us:

> The workplace is like a bell curve. At one end are a few
> workers who will do anything for you, who will work hard no

matter what. They'll give the company their all, sometimes more than it really deserves. Then there are the majority of workers in the middle. They'll do what is really required but no more. Finally at the other end are the bad ones. They're the guys who will look for any excuse to get out of work and always try to find some way to goof off. The problem for your front-line supervisor is to keep them from influencing the rest. If they get to the ones in the middle and begin to pull them down, you're in bad trouble.

The selection of strategies may have even more to do with the history, experience and situation of the work group as a whole than with the individuals who make it up. A new group of workers just coming together for the first time have no relationships with each other except those which the employer imposes on them. They have little basis for cooperation. Over time, however, they talk, get to know each other and develop a complex web of interrelationships. Common interests become apparent. Within such a context, the possibility of cooperative strategies may open up. The success or failure of such ventures becomes part of the shared experience of the group. Since such strategies usually depend on considerable unity among the participants, the group exerts social pressure on its members not to break ranks. New workers are carefully indoctrinated in the values and practices of the group. Thus the strategies of the various individuals may be primarily influenced by the strategy of the group as a whole. In turn, each individual tries to fulfill his or her needs through the action of the group. Such a work group can become what a sociologist who took a job as a machinist once described as "a guerrilla band at war with management."

The choice of strategies is also influenced by many factors originating outside the workplace. Although these influences would be difficult to establish statistically, there are several we think are particularly important at present. First, there is a general decrease throughout our culture—especially among young people—of respect for authority. This makes many people less willing to simply accept whatever they are told to do, more willing to try strategies that challenge the employer's authority. Second, there is a parallel decline in the willing acceptance of a life spent doing onerous work for someone else. This often makes grievances on the job seem more irritating, and makes people less willing simply to "live around" them. Third, there is the evident onset of "hard times." This has several conflicting effects. On the one hand, it makes people much more cautious about taking any action that might result in losing their jobs. On the other hand, it creates a general sense of discontent and rejection of the status quo. The feeling that people need to act to improve their conditions often translates into increased militance on the job. Finally, many companies, pressed financially themselves, try to take advantage of workers' increased economic vulnerability by increasing workloads and "tightening up." This direct deterioration of conditions on the job undermines the strategy of "going along with the company" and encourages strategies of resistance. Most people we talked with agreed that over the past few years resistance on the job has been increasing.

GUERRILLA TACTICS

In recent years, Americans have become all too familiar with the tactics of guerrilla warfare by which a native population can resist a centralized and apparently vastly superior military and political force. When the authorities are watching, the guerrillas appear to be nothing but peasants going about their business. They seem to obey directions willingly, yet somehow what is ordered rarely seems to get done—the population, too numerous to watch every second, practices a silent noncooperation. Once the authorities turn their backs, the peasants change into a resistance army, harassing them when the opportunity arises. Yet when the official military attacks, the guerrillas avoid a confrontation and appear to simply fade away.

The workers on many jobs apply a strategy strikingly similar to that of guerrilla warfare. They try to avoid outright confrontation with management which might lead to firings and other reprisals. Yet they try to improve their own conditions as much as they can through secret cooperation. Their objectives may include controlling the pace of work, winning free time for their own use, making life on the job more interesting and pleasurable, altering unsafe and uncomfortable conditions, diminishing the authority of the boss, improving pay and benefits and even getting the job done in a more socially constructive way. Their actions constitute a conspiracy to improve the quality of life on the job.

Time for Yourself As we have seen, management has developed elaborate techniques for controlling the pace at which workers work. But workers have developed their own tactics to gain counter-control for themselves. This requires cooperation; if some workers go too fast, management can use them as a lever against the rest. When new workers first come on a job, there is often a contest between management and the other workers for their allegiance on this issue. A woman who phoned when we spoke on a late-night call-in show in Detroit told us:

My husband's been working in an auto plant here for five years. When he first started he was really, you know, gung ho—trying to do the job well and get it done fast. But the people that work there really got down on him, telling him to work slower and everything. His father worked there too and he asked him what he should do and his father told him to go along and slow up.

Did he? we asked.

Oh yes, he did slow up. Now they've got a new guy coming in and they're having to teach him the same way.

At a manufacturing plant in Gloucester, Massachusetts, an older worker told a newcomer to the job:

> The hours are long
> And the pay is small
> So take your time
> And screw them all.

Management first developed piece-rate and incentive pay to counter such "restriction of output." Under these payment systems, workers get paid more if they produce more. The hitch is that when workers are able to earn far above a normal wage on a particular job, management often reduces the payment per piece. The result is that, in the long run, a worker who works as hard as possible only increases the amount of work required to make a normal wage on that job. Workers under many such plans have found ways to fight this technique of speed-up. One way is by setting their own ceiling on how much production to turn out on each job. An assembler on an electrical production line in Cleveland explained:

We work on group incentive pay. We set the rate ourselves at eighty pieces. We can do the job in six hours. No one tries to speed up the job—they feel that they wouldn't really make any more money if they worked harder. The company more or less accepts the rate. But right now we have a new foreman who tries to make us work the full eight hours, even if we make the rate earlier. I tell him, the company pays me for my work; it doesn't buy my life. If I finish the amount of work defined in the contract, then I'm free. They've got an incentive system; well, John, what are you going to do, we're just not feeling very ambitious.

In some cases, workers may vary the pace of work instead of setting a fixed ceiling. Terry Cole, who had worked at Chrysler and Great Lakes Steel, reported:

> People in each department at Chrysler and Great Lakes decided informally each day whether they would make the production or incentive quotas. It's done by consensus: One guy will say, "I'm too tired to work hard today"; someone else will say, "Yeah, but I'd really like to finish up an hour early," and gradually they work it out.

A production mechanic in a truck-building plant described another way such actions get organized:

> In our part of the plant there were three work gangs, maybe sixty or seventy-five people in all. Our gang was the most together, although we had one guy in skilled trades who was a real suck-ass for the company. We had gotten together when the company had sent in a new foreman who tried to push everyone around. We just didn't get the work done while he was boss, and when the company discovered he wasn't getting out production, they took him out of there.
> One Friday on the night shift, we were talking in our gang and somebody—actually it was the suck-ass—said, why don't we do six trucks tonight instead of eight. We talked about it and everyone agreed it was a good idea. But it was hard to do it just in our section. So we went and talked to the individuals in the adjoining two sections that we thought would be sympathetic and told them what we wanted to do. They discussed it with each other and pretty soon we had sixty or seventy people cooperating on the slowdown. Each group used whatever techniques they had already worked out to slow things down. We even talked to a few people we knew in other parts of the plant and they started slowing things down too, though most of them weren't in such a key place to do it. Anyway, before the shift was half over supervision was out of the office and down on the floor, going crazy trying to figure out why production wasn't getting out. But the thing was so well concealed and coordinated that they never did figure out that there was any kind of deliberate slowdown under way.

Not surprisingly, management often tries to break up such cooperation by pitting workers against each other. A foreman at a large computer company described one way it's done:

> There are definitely work groups who deliberately slow down

the pace of work. For them, something is always going wrong with the equipment. When something goes wrong, they always blame it on something or someone else. Sometimes we have to take the entire work group and make them exchange places with another group that has been producing well, to show that it is the workers and not the equipment that's at fault. If they still don't get out production, then we know who's responsible.

Where the pace of work is set by the machines themselves, controlling it may require workers to make alterations in the machinery. A steelworker told us that in his mill there are slowdowns all the time. We asked him how do you slow down when you are dealing with a continuous process?

You can break down the mill by sending a bar through too fast. Or maybe the guys might ask the crane operator to drop a piece down too hard, which screws things up. Or he can pull a piece in such a way that the cable comes off the pulley. When the mill breaks down, it might be four or five hours before it's fixed. Whenever the electrician comes he always forgets his tools—people cooperate that way—so he has to go back to get them, even for the smallest job. The mill breaks down probably a couple of times a week. People do it to keep the company from stockpiling, as well as to get a break. No one would say anything to the company about it even though they might be afraid to participate themselves.

Does the company know? we asked. "Sure, but there's nothing they can do about it. There's thirty-five or forty people could have done it."

Techniques for altering equipment are widely known. A worker in Pittsburgh informed us: "In the machine shop sabotage is easy—just forget to put oil in the machine, or something like that." An auto worker told us: "Sabotage goes on all the time. You don't know who does it but the line's always stopping and you know it could be any one of thirty people."

Sometimes workers are able to win quite substantial blocks of time for themselves. A young man working at Great Lakes Steel in Detroit described to us an extreme case:

I work in track maintenance—the job used to be called a gandy dancer. When I came on the job, they told me the last time they went on strike was 1959. I thought, oh wow, this must be like a company shop. But when I saw what goes on, I came to the conclusion that they had been on strike for fourteen years.

The way we get the most free time is going to and from the jobs. We'll just go out to a shanty in a deserted part of the yard, do a couple of joints and hang out for an hour or two. If they challenge it, we just say we got held up by a train going to the job or there was a furnace we couldn't go by without a safety man. Nobody works too hard. I get in four hours of reading a night, myself.

I'm on the second shift. We used to do only emergency work. Then the company began sending us out to do routine maintenance as well. We used evasion tactics to stop it. We would shovel dirt, but only pick up a tiny bit in each shovelful—then, awhile later, someone else would shovel it back. We worked for hours, but lo and behold, nothing got done. When the foreman complained, we said, "What do you want, we've been working steady." Spike-hammer handles are supposed to be unbreakable. Well, when we go out on a job, we'll break three or four of them. Then we'll take turns using the one that's left while the other guys hang around and take it easy.

By contract we don't have to work if the safety man says a condition is unsafe. We have two safety men. One is an old union man; we can't do much about him. The other position we rotate among ourselves. The safety man doesn't have to do anything, so this gives everybody a chance to take it easy for a while.

The struggle over time sometimes has a comical dimension, as a foreman at a large computer corporation related:

Some of these guys you wouldn't believe. I came in one day at ten to eight and Joe was there jumping up and down like this. [He imitates someone on a pogo stick.] I said, "Joe, what's happening?" He said, "Oh, man, I got to go to the can so bad." I said, "So, why don't you go?" He said, "Are you crazy, do you think I'm going to go to the can on my time?" Sure enough, ten minutes later when work started he made a beeline for the bathroom and didn't show up till half-an-hour later.

Workers' Strategy for "Job Enrichment" In recent years there has been considerable public concern about "boring work" and a variety of proposals to make work more interesting through "job enrichment." However, workers find a number of ways of their own to make work less boring. Sally Maxwell, a young woman currently working as a printer in the office of an auto company in Detroit, was formerly employed in a factory and at a post office:

Wherever I work, I try to think of things to do to liven the place up. I try to do something different every day. One day I just Xeroxed off a sheet under the company letterhead with a few cracks about what was going on as an office newsletter. Another time the union steward came around with a question-naire asking what we thought the union should do for us. He was someone I intuitively distrusted, who spent most of his time talking with the supervisors. So I wrote down, "There should be fewer bosses and the union officials shouldn't spend so much time hanging around with them." I passed it around the office and everyone cracked up. Then we had a big discussion about whether I should hand it in. "Everybody knows it, but you're not supposed to say it," they told me. Finally we agreed that I should not expose myself so much until I had my ninety days in. But it sure got us all talking. People really get off on stuff like that.

At the post office, everybody took it easy. People would pull five trucks together and blow a joint. We used to goof a lot.

One time I was taking the mail up to a plant that was pouring huge clouds of pollution into the air. Just then a dude in a business suit got out of a Cadillac and said, "Give me the mail." I figured he had to be the general manager or some-thing, so I said, "I'm not going to give you this mail till you stop putting that stuff into the air." When I got back to the post office the superintendent was waiting for me because the dude had called him up. "What happened today?" he says. I'd forgotten it by then, you know, because I was stoned. Then I remembered: "Oh yeah, I wouldn't give this guy his mail until he stopped polluting." He goes through this rap about me having to deliver the mail anyway, but I told him I wouldn't do it so he just found someone else to do it.

At times, workers counter the repetitiveness of jobs by establish-ing job rotation. We talked with Jerry Sands, a black auto worker at a plant outside of Detroit, who told us how job rotation had gotten started on his job.

The brother who worked next to me wanted to get a drink of water; I was a few pieces ahead, so I walked around the table and began running my buddy's job. When he came back he just took my old place. That gave us the idea, and we began trading

> off regularly. Pretty soon a Chicano who worked further up the
> line suggested that we begin rotating regularly.

We asked about people who didn't want to rotate.

> There were a few guys with the easy jobs at the beginning and
> end of the line who didn't want to rotate. So we got some of our
> guys with more seniority to bump them around. There are a
> few old-timers who don't want to rotate, but we've got the
> foreman pretty much under our control, and he's easing them
> out.
>   On one line, they like to work fast for forty minutes, then
> take a rest for twenty. There was one older worker who
> couldn't take the pace; so we put him on an easy job and rotated
> around him.

The idea spread. The next line, also mostly young workers, began to
imitate the rotation idea. The company eventually broke up the
original group and dispersed it around the plant. But wherever its
members came together on a line, they started rotating with each
other there. Jerry explained the two advantages of rotating: "Because the jobs are quite different, rotation helped break up the
monotony. It also helped equalize the work, spreading the hard and
easy jobs around."

Another example of rotation came from Sam Howard, a clerical
worker in the morgue of a Chicago newspaper, who reported:

> There are eight of us who work in my department. It's mostly a
> nonunion company. In the morgue we've organized ourselves,
> so we don't really need a union. The work used to be organized
> by seniority—the two guys at the bottom did all the work, and
> the people at the top didn't do anything. Everyone was always
> on everybody else's back—the whole atmosphere was really
> tense. Finally one day one of the guys at the bottom just blew
> up. So we all just stopped working and talked about it for a
> couple of hours. We decided to divide up the work equally and
> do it together. Now we start by doing a bunch of miscellaneous
> preliminary jobs. Then we throw dice and the winners get first
> pick of the various filing jobs. The whole atmosphere is a lot
> better now—everyone gets along and the old sense of pressure
> is gone. The supervisor has his own job to do, so he just leaves
> us alone.

Similarly, a worker at a Veterans' Administration hospital, where
militants had won most of the union positions, told us:

People are very organized, but they don't pay much attention
to the union. There used to be individual job assignments.
Now people in each unit get together and divide up the work
themselves.

Academic authorities have at times pointed out that work sometimes offers less opportunity for self-expression than might be
considered desirable. However, workers sometimes find their own
ways to express their thoughts and feelings on the job, and to exercise
their own creativity. During the 1972 Presidential campaign, for
example, some younger workers in a recreational equipment factory
managed to achieve self-expression by pasting "Nixon Sucks"
stickers on six thousand bumper pool sets they had manufactured.
Another example was given us by a West Coast radio disc jockey:

The engineers make $7.50 an hour, but they're bored out of
their skulls. They'll do anything they can to get at the station, if
they can do it without getting caught.

The company has a tape machine which records everything
that goes out over the air. My engineer spent many tedious
hours recently connecting a microphone in such a way that I
could say stuff on the air that wouldn't get recorded.

They'll go to extraordinary lengths for a goof, just to break
up the boredom. One time they took a daytime TV show about
doctors and spliced into it footage from that night's horror
movie—the only one that ever grossed me out to the point that I
had to turn it off. As the serious-looking doctor on the
afternoon show announced, "We're going to have to operate," suddenly the screen was filled with pictures of people
eating rotting arms, drinking eyeballs and engaging in other
questionable medical procedures. The parent company sent in
people from L.A. to nail the culprits, but it was done so
skillfully that they were never able to find out who was
responsible.

Sometimes what workers do with time they win is constructive as
well as creative, as in the case of "government work." We asked a
business agent and several workers at one plant whether people ever
made things for themselves in their extra time. One of the workers
replied:

Oh, you mean government work? Yeah, we do that all the
time, though you can't do as much on the day shift when the
bosses are around. Guys will bring in their hunting equipment
to work on, or make something for their car. I didn't even

know what government work was when I came here, but I found out soon enough.

"See these metal name plates on my desk?" the business agent added with a smile. "They're government work."

In a certain sense, all these activities are attacks by workers on the authority of management. But we found, especially in the auto industry, that such attacks can take a more direct form. An auto worker told us:

> The spot-welding department over at the Chrysler Jefferson plant—they call it the jungle because there are so many wires hanging down that it looks like vines. They can shoot sparks something like thirty feet with those welders. Guys come home looking scarred and suntanned from them. Anyone comes through with a white shirt, they turn the welders on them. There was a kid—just a kid from engineering—walked through with a white shirt, you know, by the time he got to the other side he didn't have a shirt. They thought he was a foreman or something.

Jerry Sands said of his plant:

> When they created the new shift, they put on a lot of young foremen. Most of them pretty much let the workers do what they want; they know that's the only way they'll ever get production out. They're afraid of the workers anyway—several foremen have been taken down.

An Interest in Your Work   Employers often complain that their workers are not interested in what they produce. Because their product belongs to someone else, this is often quite true. However, workers at times reach out for at least some power over the product itself.

One such effort is known to management as "inventory shrinkage." It refers to the direct appropriation of the product by the immediate producers. We picked up a hitchhiker from Leadville, Colorado, who gave us an example of how interested workers can be in the quality of their product:

> The miners there have something they call highgrading. If they hit a vein of high-grade ore, they don't tell the boss about it; instead they take some home every night in their lunchbox.

70

Taxi drivers have developed the technique of "riding with the flag up"—that is, without using the taxi meter—for the same purpose. New York City taxi officials complained that this practice doubled in 1973.

> Usually the drivers are young and articulate, their offers come late at night and, for most trips around midtown Manhattan, the most frequently suggested "fee" is $2. Usually the approach is: "Do you mind if I make this one for myself?"[1]

At times, the interest in the product can be more altruistic. A young man was working in a company which processed books for libraries. Among its other services, it selected for libraries those of their present books they should discard. This employee discovered that the company was choosing the most valuable books for discarding and then selling them itself. He tipped off the libraries and had the pleasure of watching the librarians enter the warehouse and open up the boxes wherein the books subject to this sophisticated pilfering had been concealed.

Real concern about the product of their work is far more common among people who perform non-profit services for other human beings than among those who produce things for someone else's profit. A woman who worked at a home for mentally retarded kids told us:

> Our shift is really together. It's all younger people. A whole bunch of us came on together a few months ago. During the day shift they run the place like a factory—they relate to the kids as things, not as people. We've really changed things since we got here, and you can really see it in the kids. They are really changing—kids are learning who never learned before. But we freak out the people in the office. For example, we stopped wearing uniforms. We can justify that in terms of the kids, anyway; it's not good for them to deal constantly with identically-dressed ladies. Another thing—we started visiting other homes, just to get ideas about possible ways to do things better. The office really came down on us for that; they said we weren't "professionally qualified."

But even factory workers can have reason to take an interest in what they produce, especially if its purpose is clearly known. We talked with a young worker at a company that made walkie-talkies for police forces and the like. The Chicago Police Department had

71

ordered 500 walkie-talkies of a fancy new design. Knowing their destination, workers systematically sabotaged them: "The engineers never could figure out why more than half of them never worked. They finally decided to redesign the whole system." Another time they got an order from the Federal Bureau of Narcotics for a few hundred walkie-talkies. Some of the workers decided to make a contribution to the cause from their own stash. "I just hope they tried to use those walkie-talkies along with some of those marijuana-sniffing dogs—otherwise, what a waste!"

Many people view informal on-the-job action as little more than an expression of individual frustration, hostility or laziness. Several young steelworkers from Gary, Indiana, who were active in trying to reform the union agreed that "sabotage happens all the time. . . . Sure, everybody looks for a way to get out of work. I had a job once drilling holes in pipes. We'd just not bother putting holes in half of them." They felt such action was of little significance.

No doubt there are times when such actions are in fact merely the isolated acts of individuals. But more often they grow out of a whole social milieu which makes them possible. Even such an individual act of resistance as dropping a bolt in a production line would be risky if other workers did not at least tacitly tolerate it. At a minimum it requires that no one inform the company of what is being done. Other guerrilla tactics require considerable group discipline. For example, when workers on piece rates control output, they have to discuss and decide among themselves the proper production for each job. Then they have to make sure that a high proportion of workers abide by the decision. Those who do not are generally punished by social ostracism. When new people come on the job they have to be taught the rules that workers have established for regulating the work; they must be socialized into the practices of the group.

STOPPING THE WORKS

Guerrilla tactics are inevitably quite limited in what they can achieve. If they cause the employer more than modest damage, he can retaliate with a variety of disciplinary moves—from reassigning jobs to firing workers for "bad attitudes" or "poor work habits." Consequently, workers at times have to resort to stopping production completely—going on strike. Strikes, in contrast to guerrilla tactics, are direct confrontations, in which workers and the employer each try to hurt the other enough to force concessions.

Work stoppages can be simply extensions of the tactics we have already discussed. For example, when grievances arise, workers often use short work stoppages and walkouts to force the employer to settle with them. An auto worker told us he knew of twelve wild-cats in Detroit in the preceding year. Six were one-shift heat walkouts—people just walked out when the heat got too high. The others were over firings and speed-up, lasting anywhere from one shift to five days. A UAW committeewoman who had been working in auto plants for decades listed the same causes for wildcats and added:

> There are not nearly as many walkouts now as there were in the time right after World War II, but they have definitely been increasing over the past few years. The walkouts come from the rank and file; even the lowest levels of the union are not involved.

The V.A. hospital worker quoted above similarly told us that they pull a work stoppage in a unit whenever grievances aren't settled rapidly.

A social worker in Chicago described some other uses for direct confrontation:

> In the welfare department, people pull various work stoppages and sabotage the work. Of course, at times it is really doing management's job for them. If some bureaucrat, for instance, comes up with a new form that takes the welfare workers twice as long to fill out, the copies of the form are likely just to disappear in great quantities, until it is finally phased back out.
>
> Once they expanded the work of one section but continued with only two finance clerks, through whom every application had to pass. Eventually they had tens of thousands of applications backed up at the bottleneck. So all the workers in that section just stopped working one day and refused to continue until something was done. Next day they had additional clerks on the job. In some cities, the welfare workers would take the files for all their cases in excess of official guidelines and dump them en masse in the welfare headquarters.

Andrew Korenko told us:

> I operate a crane and I have to swing stuff over men's heads. The equipment is lousy. I stopped the mill four or five times

> when things weren't right. People refuse a lot of times to operate bad equipment.

Are you afraid of getting in trouble? we asked.

> No. They just send someone to fix it. The company knows the equipment is no good.

Of course, the company wasn't always so accepting:

> A couple of millwrights got in trouble six weeks ago because they refused to work in an unsafe place. They got suspended. It's the old story—it's in arbitration now.

We asked if other workers did anything about it:

> No, they didn't walk out or anything—they just collected money for them, and a lot of people went to the union meeting.

Such work stoppages are of course by no means something new. A retired iron worker and crane operator we met in a bar in Portland, Oregon, said:

> I've walked off jobs many times—you have to respect yourself. Like in Idaho we were working a few years ago on the side of a mountain. It was real windy—real windy—and the old man wants me to keep working. I told him no, I'm not swinging any weights over people's heads, forty feet up. He says I have to do it. I just told him to shove it—if I wouldn't walk under it, I'm not going to do it. I walked off the job—I didn't give a damn if I was in Idaho or not. Next day before I left he called me back—they had to get the work done and there was nobody else. Things were better after that. Always remember it: if you respect yourself it all comes home.

Sometimes a work stoppage over a firing, speed-up or other grievance will turn into a regular walkout. In the spring of 1973, for example, a bus driver on a line in Queens was suspended. The other drivers simply walked out, leaving the buses behind.[2] In Detroit we saw a work stoppage which developed into the occupation of an auto plant. Grievances and conflict over poor and dangerous working conditions had been accumulating for some time at the Mack Avenue Chrysler stamping plant. In August 1973 several workers who had been involved in protesting conditions were fired. One of them, active in a radical organization, went back to the plant and demanded his old job. When he was ordered to leave, he sat down on the line. Plant guards tried to remove him and a fight broke out. Chrysler ordered the whole shift out of the plant, but at least two hundred workers stayed inside. We heard someone ask a worker inside why they were striking. The reply: "I don't work in the department that started it; I don't even know the guy that got fired; in fact, I don't even know what he got fired for—we're just taking care of business." (The next day, an official of the United Auto Workers organized a squad of several hundred union officials, cleared the pickets away from in front of the factory and policed the area for the next two days to allow Chrysler to resume orderly operations. Several dozen participants in the strike were later fired.)

The strike is the weapon workers most often use to get better pay and other benefits. Some strikes are official union actions, which we will discuss in the next chapter. Others are wildcat strikes, occurring independently of or even against the official union structure. For example, we talked with workers in Cleveland who were on strike against Seaway Food. About 350 warehousemen and drivers were maintaining a picket line twenty-four hours a day. They were unsatisfied with a proposed contract and wanted increased medical benefits, a better pension and a contract running only one year instead of three. They had already voted down two proposed contracts: "The union keeps coming back with a little less here and a little more there."

The basis for cooperation was the fact that they all knew each other, even though they worked in several different terminals. When we asked who was organizing the strike, we were told: "We're all together. . . . We don't have any organization. We just keep the line going. We have no official strike sanction. People are solid 1001 percent."

They had no idea how long the strike would last; their objective was to force the union and the company to come back with something acceptable to them. They emphasized that the strike was a wildcat:

> Don't believe what you read in the fuckin' papers. The union's trying to claim they've got it under control. The company is shooting its mouth off, the union's shooting its mouth off, and you can't believe any of it. This is a wildcat. . . . The union had plenty of time to take a strike sanction vote, but they didn't want to do it. I hear there's a meeting tomorrow, but none of us got any notices about it.

Walkouts can also be used to affect conditions off the job. In Houston, Texas, in April 1973, for example, six hundred longshoremen walked off their jobs to protest the beating of four fellow longshoremen by police who were arresting them.[3]

Wildcat strikes can spread far beyond a single workplace. In 1971, letter carriers struck in New York City. Postal workers all over the country shared the same grievances, and within a few days several hundred thousand were on strike, despite the complete opposition of the national union leadership. An example on a smaller scale occurred in New York City at the Nathan's restaurant chain in March 1972. The shop steward at the Times Square restaurant was fired when he objected to a kitchen worker making a pizza at the counter. Thirty-five Times Square workers pulled a lunch-hour work stoppage, demanding his reinstatement. Workers at the Greenwich Village restaurant joined in sympathy. The company then fired those who had taken part in the work stoppage. Next day not only the fired workers at Times Square and Greenwich Village, but also workers at the Coney Island restaurant, were on the streets picketing for the reinstatement of all those fired. On the restaurant doors were pasted copies of a telegram from the union headquarters ordering the members ''to return to work forthwith.'' As the president of Nathan's explained, the walkouts violated the company's contract with the union, which called for arbitration of dismissals.

Work stoppages, sitdowns and wildcat strikes challenge the power of the employer directly and openly. When workers refuse to obey orders or refuse to work altogether, they are brought into serious confrontation with management. Such confrontations involve the risk of firing and other reprisals. They therefore require a high degree of solidarity on the part of the workers. Once workers go on a wildcat strike, they face the situation Ben Franklin described among the initiators of the American Revolution: ''We must all hang together or we shall all hang separately.'' But if workers can effectively stop production and keep it stopped, they have a gun pointed at the employer's head, which may be enough to prevent reprisals and force substantial concessions.

THE SIGNIFICANCE OF WORK RESISTANCE

We found a considerable variation in the extent to which workers used direct action techniques to improve their jobs. There are still some places where workers compete with each other to give the employer their last ounce of energy. For example, we found garment shops where workers on piece rate even worked through lunch hour to make a little more money. Such situations are exceptional, however. In most places, there seems to be, at the least, general cooperation in regulating the pace of work, whether through quotas or simply through general understandings. In many places, labor-reducing techniques are intricate and sophisticated. Less wide-spread but not uncommon are situations where workers have taken the offensive, trying to win substantial amounts of time or consider-able control over their labor for themselves.

Direct action on the job is significant for a number of reasons. Most obviously, it is a very practical means by which workers can combat the worst aspects of work and gain a little freedom and pleasure for themselves. It is a type of tactic which almost any group of workers can apply to improve their own situation. But it has further implications which many who use it may never consider.

As individuals, workers have little choice but to turn the time of their lives over to those who have the wealth to employ them, to use as they see fit. But once they do so, workers cease to be merely isolated individuals; they become part of a social group. However they may differ, they have one thing in common—their relationship to their employer. The employer himself established that connection by hiring them, and he organizes their cooperative labor through his plans and orders. But when workers use the kinds of direct action we have described, they establish cooperation among themselves with-out having to go through the employer or anybody else, and are thus able to coordinate their activity in their own interest.

Such direct cooperation gives workers tremendous potential power. As individuals, workers may be dependent on employers. But employers are dependent on their workers as a whole. Unless workers work, all the employer's offices, factories, machinery, expertise and union contracts are useless. As we have seen, em-ployers go to great lengths to prevent workers from getting together to cooperate in their own interests—to keep the group they have created from acting like a group. But to the extent that workers can overcome their divisions, they can begin winning back control over the time of their lives.

Of course, what such on-the-job action can achieve in itself is extremely limited. It cannot improve conditions on a job beyond the point where it seriously interferes with profitability—for at that point the company is likely to close down or move. Neither can it eliminate the basic subordination of working people, the need to go to work for someone else. As long as such action does not involve sustained cooperation among workers in many different workplaces, and as long as its purpose remains limited to minor improvements, it will remain a weak and primitive tool.

But at many times in the past, workplace struggles have broken through these limits. The history of the American working class has seen a series of giant mass strikes, in which millions of workers in thousands of companies and dozens of industries supported each other not only on the job, but in sympathetic and general strikes and even in armed battles with the employers and their supporters. These mass strikes are often passed over as quickly as possible in official history books, for they indicate possibilities for challenge to the status quo that many would prefer to forget. They show that the day-to-day struggle of workers on the job can, under appropriate conditions, develop into struggles on a far more massive scale. The basic processes of mass strikes

> begin in the cell-unit of industrial production, the group of those who work together. . . . It is in these groups that the invisible, underlying process of mass strike develops. They are communities within which workers come into opposition to the boss, begin acting on their own and discover their need to support each other and the collective power they develop by doing so.[4]

Resistance on the job can thus be the starting point for developing a far more powerful challenge to those who control the time of our lives.

Overcoming the limitations of present patterns of on-the-job resistance requires a deliberate effort to turn sporadic actions into a continuous, organized force. The range of issues contested, the number of participants and the extent of their involvement need to grow. Workers who are affected by common problems need to establish regular means for considering and conducting action. Even for small groups this requires ways to ensure free discussion and democratic decisions—for example, a mutual understanding that when certain types of grievances or issues arise, people stop work and gather to discuss them. Where appropriate, such assemblies might well decide to meet regularly, as an organized expression of the workers as a group. Where larger numbers are affected by problems in common, they may have to coordinate their decisions and actions through delegates. By such means, workers can strengthen their organization, and thereby develop the power that is already potentially theirs.

As work groups begin to take control over their own actions, they reverse the process by which employers have established more and more power over their activity. In a group of workers who cooperatively control their struggle against the employer can be seen the seeds of a social group which controls its own labor completely. To achieve such control would require a strategy far different from any workers use today. We will return to the elements of such a strategy in Part IV of this book.

Tom Coffin/Liberation News Service

5. THE UNION

One of the basic structures on many jobs is the union. About 20 percent of all jobs are covered by union agreements, including the great majority of those in large industrial companies. Unions are more significant than this statistic suggests, because they are at present the most important kind of formal organization to which workers belong. Whenever workers get together to consider doing something to change their conditions, one of the possibilities is to change the union if there is one, or bring one in if there is none.

Historically, trade unions often developed out of the kind of informal cooperation among workers we described in the last chapter. They started as a means by which workers in different workplaces could establish direct relations among themselves on a lasting basis.

The first combinations of workers often did not accept their complete and permanent subordination to employers. In some cases, unions of skilled craftsmen gained the kind of power over the production process we have described in the case of the skilled steelworkers at Homestead (see page 31). (Even today, vestiges of this nineteenth-century pattern persist among workers in a few industries, notably construction, whose craft unions still largely control who can enter the trade and how the work is done.) In other cases, early unions challenged the whole idea that some people should have to work for others.

But as time went on, a strategy of unionism developed that was far more limited. It did not challenge the employers' right to direct the labor of others; rather, it sought to strike a bargain that would be beneficial to both. Employers, at least in periods of prosperity and growth, could afford to provide a slowly rising standard of living to their workers. They could also afford to give up some of their more authoritarian practices—favoritism in hiring and laying off, for example. At the same time, they could reap great advantages from being guaranteed a stable, satisfied work force which could be counted on not to disrupt production or strike unexpectedly. The essential strategy of unionism was to exchange workers' ability to strike and disrupt production for certain concessions from employers over wages and working conditions. This exchange was embodied in the union contract. As one labor lawyer put it:

> Collective bargaining as it has developed in the United States since the nineteen-thirties is premised on the existence of a "settlement range" within which both labor and management feel that it is in their interests to reach an agreement rather than resort to economic pressure in the form of slowdowns, strikes, lockouts or boycotts.[1]

Since employers initially had little desire to deal with unions at all, unions had to use militant tactics—strikes, occupations and violence—to raise the cost to management of not accepting unionization. Such struggles were often successful—not because the unions were more powerful than management, but because they could make enough trouble so that it was cheaper for management to recognize and deal with them than to resist them. From the point of view of the unions, such recognition was the objective of militant tactics. Once companies were willing to "bargain in good faith," strikes and violence became generally unnecessary.

Once recognized, the unions began fulfilling their side of the bargain—providing a stable work force and seeing that it did not disrupt production. William Serrin, a journalist with the *Detroit Free Press,* sums up the contribution made by the union to the functioning of the auto industry today in a recent book on the 1970 General Motors strike:

> What the companies desire—and receive—from the union is predictability in labor relations. Forced to deal with unions, they want to deal with one union, one set of leaders, and thus they have great interest in stability within the UAW and in a continuation of union leadership. They also want to have the limits of bargaining clearly understood and subscribed to.

Serrin quotes a former negotiator as saying that "GM's position has always been, give the union the money, the least possible, but give them what it takes. But don't let them take the business away from us." The union, Serrin concludes, "has come to accept this philosophy as the basis of its relationship with the companies."[2]

As the function of unions narrowed, their organizational character changed to match. Many unions originated where workers simply met and decided to form a union. If officers were elected, they remained at work alongside those who had elected them. Union officials had little power of their own; the power to decide and act lay with the workers themselves as a group. Gradually, however, the balance shifted. More and more of the real power came into the hands of union officials who evolved into professional ''labor leaders'' with a daily life far different from those they represented. Labor leaders became essentially politicians, organizing affairs primarily to maintain their own power. Under them there developed a bureaucracy of lawyers, economists, organizers, publicists and other professional experts not even subject to election; these union bureaucrats became the real, permanent managers of the unions—often surviving when elected leaders were thrown out. The union ceased to be an expression of workers' direct relations with each other; it became another external group to which they related one by one.

This change was not necessarily the result of corrupt or malicious leaders; it grew out of the basic function of unionism. If unions were to sign contracts with employers, they had to develop means to enforce those contracts, even against the will of their own members.[3] To bargain effectively with management, unions had to develop a structure of power centralized in the hands of expert negotiators. While there may be much show of democracy, the elected bargaining committees and other representatives of the rank and file generally have little power. In the UAW, reputedly one of the more democratic unions, journalist Serrin found that once negotiations reached the crucial stage, the elected bargaining committee did not even know what was going on. As UAW secretary/treasurer Emil Mazey explained: ''The basic decisions were not made by the committee; we make the decisions, the top leaders of the union. And the decisions are conveyed to the committee and they agree.''[4]

The result, as *Business Week* wrote, is that ''today, a union is very much like a business set up to serve as legal agent for workers.'' Union leaders have little choice but to act like the managers of such a business, lest they lose out to other leaders or unions who would perform that function better.

This process has repeated itself many times in the course of history. Unionism enters most workplaces when discontented workers get together to try to improve their conditions. Most unions have a militant struggle somewhere in their past, in which workers cooperated directly with each other against the employer. The last

How Much the Top Labor Leaders Earned in 1972

Union officials have become a social group distinct from the rank-and-file workers they are supposed to represent. Their incomes, as this chart indicates, are often closer to those of corporate managers than to the unions' working members. Union officials don't face the same daily life conditions as regular workers and therefore naturally develop interests different from the rank-and-file.

Rank	Salary	Allow-ances	Ex-penses	Total
1. Frank E. Fitzsimmons, pres., Teamsters	125,000	2,745	3,736	131,481
2. Murray W. Miller, sec.-treas., Teamsters	100,973	4,295	8,960	114,228
3. Hunter P. Wharton, pres., Operating Engineers	80,833	22,200	—	103,033
4. Joseph Curran, pres., National Maritime Union	85,257	5,200	1,636	92,093
5. C. L. Dennis, pres., Railway Clerks	70,000	—	21,069	91,069
6. John H. Lyons, pres., Iron Workers	48,000	15,120	18,071	81,191
7. James T. Housewright, pres., Retail Clerks	60,000	13,000	8,082	81,082
8. Peter Fosco, pres., Laborers	75,000	—	5,599	80,599
9. Edward J. Carlough, pres., Sheet Metal Workers	50,000	19,490	8,166	77,656
10. George Meany, pres., AFL-CIO	72,960	—	1,816	74,776
11. Terence O'Sullivan, sec.-treas., Laborers	70,000	—	3,410	73,410
12. Ed S. Miller, pres., Hotel & Restaurant Employees	49,999	12,810	8,841	71,650
13. David S. Turner, sec.-treas., Sheet Metal Workers	45,000	19,490	6,345	70,835
14. Jos. D. Keenan, sec., Electrical Workers (IBEW)	55,000	—	15,640	70,640
15. I. W. Abel, pres., Steelworkers	60,000	—	9,937	69,937
16. Patrick Gorman, sec.-treas., Meat Cutters	50,976	—	15,276	66,252
17. Martin J. Ward, pres., Plumbers	47,610	17,690	—	65,300
18. Chas. H. Pillard, pres., Electrical Workers (IBEW)	60,000	—	4,439	64,439
19. Paul Hall, pres., Seafarers	55,609	—	8,383	63,992
20. William T. Dodd, sec.-treas., Plumbers	39,675	22,310	1,211	63,196
21. Walter J. Burke, sec.-treas., Steelworkers	42,500	—	19,892	62,392

Source: *Business Week*, August 18, 1973, p. 63. Based on union reports to the U.S. Department of Labor.

22. Robt. Diefenbach, sec.-treas., Hotel, Restaurant Employees	43,000	12,810	5,520	61,330
23. Alvin E. Heaps, sec.-treas., Retail, Wholesale Workers	30,577	—	30,747	61,324
24. Newell J. Carman, sec.-treas., Operating Engineers	45,783	14,970	386	61,139
25. William W. Maguire, sec.-treas., Retail Clerks	47,500	10,400	3,753	61,082
26. Hal Davis, pres., Musicians	50,000	5,105	5,492	60,597
27. Thomas F. Murphy, pres., Bricklayers	40,000	14,640	4,552	59,192
28. David Selden, pres., Teachers	30,000	—	27,911	57,911
29. Newton W. Black, pres., Glass Bottle Blowers	37,500	18,200	—	55,700
30. Juel D. Drake, sec., Iron Workers	35,000	17,525	2,679	55,204
31. S. Frank Raftery, pres., Painters	44,223	5,975	4,806	55,004
32. Max Greenberg, pres., Retail, Wholesale Workers	38,221	—	16,783	55,004
33. Lane Kirkland, sec.-treas., AFL-CIO	46,878	—	8,052	54,930
34. William Sidell, pres., Carpenters	48,140	5,443	1,311	54,894
35. Thomas W. Gleason, pres., Longshoremen (ILA)	40,000	13,099	1,732	54,831
36. W. A. Boyle, pres., Mine Workers*	47,917	—	6,912	54,829
37. John T. Joyce, sec., Bricklayers	33,333	14,640	6,173	54,146
38. Alexander J. Rohan, pres., Printing Pressmen	39,022	6,940	7,970	53,932
39. William DiSilvestro, sec.-treas., Painters	33,167	7,325	12,902	53,394
40. Frank Bonadio, pres., Building Trades Dept., AFL-CIO	39,167	10,722	2,052	51,941
41. George Hardy, pres., Service Employees	49,585	—	2,338	51,923
42. Al H. Chesser, pres., Transportation Union	46,706	—	5,118	51,824
43. Robert Georgine, sec.-treas., Building Trades Dept.	34,167	11,061	4,789	50,017
44. Charles E. Nichols, treas., Carpenters	39,000	5,460	3,669	48,129
45. James B. Cole, treas., Iron Workers	30,000	17,820	113	47,933
46. Leonard Woodcock, pres., Auto Workers	38,134	—	9,315	47,449

*The UMW reduced salaries after Boyle lost office.

85

big wave of such union building was in the late 1930s and early '40s. But even at its militant height, experienced observers could predict accurately the "maturation process" the new unions would follow. Benjamin Selekman, for instance, writing in 1937 when CIO militance was at its height, was able to predict the unions' changing role. During their initial phase, they were regarded by management as a dangerous threat to be suppressed. The negotiation of the first agreement would establish a modus vivendi, allowing for the development of supplementary union activities, but at the same time decreasing identification of members with the organization. A period of building joint relationships would follow, marked by further union bureaucratization and the development of a set of consistent attitudes by both management and the union. Still later would come acceptance of the union as a permanent fact, and the development of a joint administrative channel for the handling of grievances and the regular reopening of negotiations.[5] John L. Lewis, founder of the CIO, foresaw the evolution from recognition struggles to labor peace more succinctly: "A CIO contract," he said, "is adequate protection against sit-downs, lie-downs or any other kind of strike."[6]

At the beginning of many unions it would have been difficult to separate the activities of informal work groups from the enthusiastic support their members gave to the newly organized unions. Many workers felt that the unions were truly their own organizations. John Sargent, a local leader of the union at Inland Steel, gave a picture of what unionism in the steel industry was like in the early days of the 1930s:

> Without a contract, without any agreement with the company, without any regulations concerning hours of work, conditions of work or wages, a tremendous surge took place. We talk of a rank-and-file movement: the beginning of union organization was the best kind of rank-and-file movement you could think of. John L. Lewis sent in a few organizers, but there were no organizers at Inland Steel, and I'm sure there were no organizers at Youngstown Sheet and Tube. The union organizers were essentially workers in the mill who were so disgusted with their conditions and so ready for a change that they took the union into their own hands.
>
> For example, what happened at Inland Steel I believe is perhaps representative of what happened throughout the steel industry. Without a contract we secured for ourselves agreements on working conditions and wages that we do not have today, and that were better by far than what we do have today in

the mill. For example, as a result of the enthusiasm of the people in the mill, you had a series of strikes, wildcats, shut-downs, slow-downs, anything working people could think of to secure for themselves what they decided they had to have. If their wages were low there was no contract to prohibit them from striking, and they struck for better wages. If their conditions were bad, if they didn't like what was going on, if they were being abused, the people in the mills themselves—without a contract or any agreement with the company involved—would shut down a department or even a group of departments to secure for themselves the things they found necessary.

This approach went far beyond the strategy of trade unionism. Far from recognizing the legitimacy of management power and the employers' need for hard work and steady production, it assumed that the workers' needs were the only legitimate criterion for action. A struggle between unbridled workers' militance and the employers' need for a pacified labor force was inevitable. In this struggle, the union leadership, especially at the national level, soon became the employers' ally. John Sargent continued:

What happens to a union? And what happened to the United Steelworkers of America? What makes me mad, and what makes thousands of other people in the mill mad, is that the companies became smart and understood that in order to accommodate themselves to a labor organization they could not oppose that labor organization. What they had to do was recognize that labor organization. And when they recognized a labor union they had to be sure they recognized the national and international leadership of that labor union and took the affairs of that labor union out of the hands of ordinary elected officials on a local scale.

The result was that the union became

a watchdog for the company. The local union has become the police force for the contracts made by the international union. If a local union tries to reject a contract in the Steelworkers Union, the contract is put into effect and the local union acts as the police to see that the men live up to the contract.[7]

As this account indicates, what really happened is that groups other than the rank-and-file workers grew to have more and more power over the actual functioning of the unions. Even at the local

87

level, the union leadership, no longer personally affected by conditions in the workplace, began to emerge as a separate group with an
interest in maintaining their own power position. The International,
now firmly in place, no longer needed to rely on rank-and-file
militance to secure its acceptance by the corporations. The great
powers given it to lead coordinated struggles—control of union
funds, authority over contracts, ability to appoint officials, power to
suspend or take over locals, even the right to discipline and ensure
the firing of workers—were now focused on getting workers into
line, ensuring that their action did not overstep the bounds of the
strategy of unionism.

The contract itself, a legally binding document, introduced the
courts as another determinant of what the unions could do. The
complex grievance procedures established by the contracts created a
whole bureaucracy of lawyers, company and union officials,
mediators and arbitrators to administer them, by whose decisions the
unions were bound. Through a mass of labor legislation, the
government has similarly become an important factor in labor
relations, defining by law exactly what unions may and may not do
and regulating their activity through the National Labor Relations
Board, the Labor Department and a vast mediation bureaucracy.
More recently, wage controls and government pay boards have
limited the unions' range of action even more.

This legalism makes fairly simple disputes into complex ones by
removing them from the shop floor. They become legal debates over
what management can and cannot do, not what workers need. It is
common for management to do something workers object to, and
then bring in the union to say that management has the right to do it
because it isn't forbidden in the contract. The use of worker action to
deny a management "right" is taboo with most unions since it is
extralegal—something that an organization which bases its existence on the legality of court-enforced contracts does not want. This
legalism is supported by an almost magical belief in the beneficence
of the law. Like a magician who simply pulls cards from his sleeve
but distracts the audience's attention by making mysterious and
unnecessary movements, legal obscurities can make conflicts between workers and employers into issues comprehensible only to
legal professionals. A shop steward and aspiring union politician
described to some militants his experience in negotiations with
management:

> Have you ever dealt with these people? Well I have. I've been
> on the contract negotiation committee and I've gone with the

B.A. to solve some beefs. Well, I used to be like you; I would argue with anybody. But now I see how complicated things are. When you negotiate with the boss he comes with lawyers; not a lawyer, but lawyers. And they sit down with big stacks of papers and it gets complicated and detailed.

This legal rigmarole turns union business into a mystification workers are supposedly incompetent to understand, let alone control.

Finally, the employers themselves wield vast power to influence what unions actually do. They can offer jobs in management to those lower level union officials who are cooperative. They can help make or break the careers of top union leaders by allowing them the appearance of victories or pressing them to defeats. For the unions as institutions they can offer easy cooperation or perpetual harassment—or downright unionbusting. And in the end, their superior power assures that they have the knockout punch, should it ever be necessary to slug it out to the end, a fact which does much to keep union leaders "reasonable." A local union official at the Lordstown Vega plant told journalist Emma Rothschild that during the negotiations with GM, he had a recurrent fear that "if they had a strong desire they could just evacuate the buildings and leave." And a GM official said of auto workers: "They complain and yet, if we closed Lordstown down and then reopened, we'd get 50,000 applications."[8] In short, rank-and-file workers have become only one of the many groups able to shape what unions can and will do.

In our travels, we found one shop where the union's role was reminiscent of John Sargent's description of early unionism. It was a large plant in an industrial town outside a major midwestern city. A microcosm of industry, the plant made its own rubber and had a foundry, machine shops and assembly operations. The plant dominated the landscape as we drove past small houses on steep hillsides, into the downtown area (railroad tracks ran right through its center) to the union hall. We talked for several hours with the elected Business Agent, who had been a scrappy militant in the strikes of the 1940s, and four young shop stewards he had recruited to become active in the union.

Conditions at the plant were exceptional, because the union supported and even encouraged workers to settle complaints right on the shop floor. If a grievance got bogged down, they stopped the unit where it occurred. The B.A. told us: "They don't leave, they just sit down by the machines. The bosses say get to work and they just sit there. Pretty soon the company gets someone who can settle the thing."

When we asked for an example, he turned to one steward and said:

> We had one in the machine shop two-and-a-half weeks ago, didn't we, Tony? A supervisor was doing a production job. He'd been warned about it over and over. No one would have objected if he'd asked the steward was it okay for him to try to straighten out this particular job, but he maintained he had the right to do anything he wanted. So we closed down the department. The company will squall, but I tell 'em, "What the hell, we let 'em let off a little steam."

The plant was largely on piece rates, and the B.A. told us: "We control the rates. When rates are readjusted, they always move upward, never downward." The result, according to the workers we talked with, was that they were able to "make out" in five-and-a-half to six-and-a-half hours, using the rest of the eight-hour day for themselves. The B.A. boasted:

> If there is no conflict here, it's because we're on top, not because we're too weak. I called up the plant personnel man the other day about something and asked him how he was. "Terrible," he said. "What's the matter?" "I don't hear from you with complaints enough, and when I don't hear from you, I know we're taking it too easy and you guys are stealing the plant."

It was clear, though, even to the B.A., that these conditions were based in part on this particular management's tolerance. "I've got to give a lot of the credit to this company," he said. "They believe a flexible policy is in their long-run interest." Perhaps, too, the union was tolerated because it had only called one contract strike in the last thirty years, and it lasted for only two weeks.

Needless to say, workers preferred working where the union made a real effort to maintain decent working conditions. People who left this company and went to work at other plants often tried to get back because conditions were better. As one worker there told us:

> I worked in a steel mill for six months and the only reason I knew what a steward was is that my father knew them and introduced me. Over there, you'll get a foreman on your back, and if you don't do something about it yourself he'll just keep on you, because there is no steward around.

Yet even though the workers in the plant considered the union exceptionally good, they still viewed it largely as something external to themselves, not as something for them to participate in, let alone an expression of their own activity. When we asked the stewards about the workers' attitude toward the union, the answer was:

> Well, there are always some people who gripe if you don't get a hundred percent of what you go for, but mostly people are pretty satisfied. We try to get them involved in politics and things, but they are mostly pretty apathetic.

Perhaps most telling was the fact that they had to change from monthly to quarterly meetings of the union, because they were unable to get a quorum of fifty members to meetings. The union has 2500 members.

A union which will regularly close down departments over grievances is rare, even archaic. (So is a company which will tolerate it without disciplining workers or retaliating against the union.) Indeed, the usual pattern is just the opposite. When we asked a crane operator whose department had just been flooded with noxious gas and extreme heat, produced by a newly installed process, why they didn't just close the job, his reply was simple and direct: "That would be a wildcat, and the union and company wouldn't allow it."

When union officials prevent groups of workers from acting—even to protect their own health—they clearly have become something separate from the workers on the job. They have instead become part of the apparatus which makes workers work. This is often explicitly recognized by union officials themselves. For example, a UAW committeeman at the Ford plant in Wixom, Michigan, generally regarded as an "outstanding" committeeman, told a *Wall Street Journal* reporter:

> The committeeman is finding himself more and more doing a foreman's work, because they say they're too busy, and they know we'll do it for the people. . . . The main function of a committeeman is to settle problems right on the floor. I'm a mediator, a foot-soldier out there. Without the committeeman, Ford couldn't run this plant.[9]

The extent to which the union may take over the task of enforcing "work discipline" would surprise even a hardened cynic. This committeeman, who carried his own stopwatch, described how he took over the role of that most-hated of management officials, the time-study man. He recalled that a man "was working a job installing back-window trim. He said he didn't have enough time to do it, but I timed him, and he did. When I told him, he accused me of not doing my job."[10] The image of a union official standing over a worker with a stop watch telling him that he had to do his job in less time than the worker considered reasonable tells much about the current role of unions.

Another story told by the same committeeman shows the role of the union in breaking up workers' resistance at the lowest level. A worker was switched out of his regular job to one that was considered less desirable. The foreman contended the change was the result of the man's poor attendance record; the worker claimed it was really a retaliation because he had left early one day to take his wife home from the hospital. The committeeman worked out a compromise with the company. Meanwhile, however, the worker had staged a one-man strike on his new job. Far from backing him up, the committeeman, furious, berated the worker and allowed the company to forego the compromise and send the man back to the undesirable job.[11]

Of course, most unions don't do management's work in quite this direct a way. But unions can be resented as much for what they fail to do as for what they do. One worker at U.S. Steel in Gary told us:

> I was there for a year and I never knew my griever. The union does absolutely nothing. I hate it worse than the company.

A worker at Republic Steel said:

> There's a steward appointed for every hundred or so men and they're under four grievers. The stewards don't know the law, though. All they can do is file a grievance. The grievers know more but you can never find them.

A young auto worker in Detroit was totally disillusioned with the union:

> I once took a grievance to my chief steward. He said, "Look, I'm not going to file a grievance for you, quit bothering me."

Even a group of workers at U.S. Steel and Inland Steel we talked with, who believed in the union and were trying to reform it, agreed that it was hardly a presence on the job, and that it was almost universally hated by the workers.

In some places, we found the union riddled with petty corruption. Many people had little stories to tell from their own experience. A UAW committeewoman in Detroit reported:

> The lower levels of the union have gotten increasingly corrupt over the past—say five—years. Chief stewards go in and out

of the plant with company permission, and get all kinds of other privileges. That's a real change in the union.

A worker in an electrical shop in Cleveland described how, after many other people were turned down for the job, the son of the union president was promoted from assembly to the tool-and-die department. In many plants, union positions are a regular steppingstone to foreman and other management jobs. Many union officials are able to make private gain off pension funds and other powers of their office. While such corruption is not the core of the problem, it certainly adds to the distaste with which unions are viewed.

The core of the problem is the assistance the unions render to management. It would be a mistake to underestimate its extent, for labor stability is extremely important to management. In 1950, when the UAW agreed to a five-year contract with General Motors after more than a decade of short-term agreements, *Fortune* wrote:

> General Motors has regained control over one of the crucial management functions . . . long-range scheduling of production, model changes and tool and plant investment. It has been so long since any big U.S. manufacturer could plan with confidence in its labor relations that industry has almost forgotten what it felt like. The full consequences of such a liberation of engineering and production talent can as yet only be guessed at, but one estimate from Detroit is that in planning freedom alone the contract is worth fifteen cents per man per hour to the corporation.

Fortune concluded that "GM may have paid a billion for peace [but] it got a bargain."[12]

The unions serve as a buffer, heading off workers' own attempts to use their strength directly against the employer. The union presents itself as a channel through which workers' problems can be solved without taking matters into their own hands. The whole apparatus of the grievance procedure is designed to keep workers at work when a dispute arises, so that production will not be disrupted. When workers pull a work stoppage or a walkout, the union makes it its business to try to work out a compromise to get them back to work. And when dissatisfaction with more general conditions arises, the union sees that it leads to a strike only when the contract expires, and in an orderly way that the company can plan for. The union thus protects employers from the one real weapon workers have: their ability to control or stop production.

Unions have not become identical with employers; they are a third force, standing between workers and management and pursuing interests of their own. Since their only real power lies in their claim to represent their members, union leaders, like any politicians, have to try to retain the support of their constituents. They make a great show of leading a militant struggle against the employer, especially at contract time. Gus Tyler of the ILGWU told Wilfred Sheed that it never hurts to seem tougher than you are:

> When Mike Quill, the New York transit workers' leader, would stand up at those Garden meetings and really lace into Lindsay and let the other guys have it, the members would stand there and cheer and yell. He didn't have to call a strike. And he didn't. If they didn't have a chance to ventilate, he'd get the strike and it'd go wildcat.[13]

A Detroit labor lawyer explained the cynicism appropriate to interpreting the language of union demands:

> *Our Members Demand Establishment of a Company-Funded Day Care Center So That Our Members' Wives Can Work*— This or any other similar, seemingly revolutionary, concept broached as part of a union's initial package of demands is probably a trade-off item that the union will give up in return for something else, such as money.
>
> This demand may have been something bandied about at a meeting held by the union's negotiating committee with the rank and file. The committee incorporated it into its demands to placate the employees and to serve as the basis for the refrain throughout negotiations that the company doesn't pay a living wage.
>
> *This Item Is Critical to Our Members*—This can be and often is applied to almost any type of union demand. It often signifies that union politics require that management offer something in a specific area to preserve the credibility of the negotiating committee in the eyes of the rank and file.
>
> This frequently occurs where a dissident element has arisen within the union to oust the present leadership. The union will often accept just a small part of the proposal in the contract or possibly just a promise by management to study the matter. . . .
>
> *Any Agreement We Reach Is Subject to Approval by the Membership*—This is a standard union refrain. . . . Often rank-and-file approval is a foregone conclusion, especially when the contract is heartily endorsed by the union leadership. On occasion, however, the union anticipates membership rejection and then returns to the bargaining table for something additional for the membership.

In reaction, management often holds something back for just such a situation. Every so often, though—and with greater frequency in recent years—rank and file rejection of an agreement comes as a surprise to both the union leadership and the management. This creates extremely difficult problems and in some cases may unravel everything to which the parties previously agreed.[14]

Such negotiations, in short, are an attempt to establish the basis on which workers can be gotten back to work.

Even strikes themselves, when controlled by the union, can be a means of manipulating workers to return on terms they might not otherwise accept. Emil Mazey, secretary/treasurer of the UAW noted:

I think that strikes make ratification easier. Even though the worker may not think so, when he votes on a contract he is reacting to economic pressures. I really believe that if the wife is raising hell and the bills are piling up, he may be more apt to settle than otherwise.[15]

And labor journalist William Serrin of the *Detroit Free Press* observed:

A strike, by putting the workers on the streets, rolls the steam out of them—it reduces their demands and thus brings agreement and ratification; it also solidifies the authority of the union hierarchy. . . . "A strike," explains a man who has intimately observed automobile negotiations for two decades, "does not have to be a stress to be avoided. It can be a tool for agreement."[16]

Most unions still hold that the power to strike remains necessary to ensure their survival, but a number of unions are taking the logical last step in union/management cooperation and giving up the right to strike altogether. The United Steelworkers of America, for example, had an agreement with the steel corporations not to strike when contracts expired in August, 1974; any issues they could not settle between themselves were to be submitted to binding arbitration. Such plans are spreading, amidst much fanfare about a "new era of labor peace." In the steel industry, the plan has met relatively little rank-and-file opposition for the simple reason that many workers feel they have not won much through such official strikes anyway. A worker at U.S. Steel in Gary said of the last national steel strike: "Nineteen fifty-nine—everybody knows they lost that strike."

When we asked Andrew Korenko what his fellow workers felt about the steel contract, he replied: "Nobody liked it. They didn't like the money and to a lesser extent they didn't like the no-strike deal. But there is stockpiling anyway, so you probably couldn't get much through a strike."

Andrew Korenko also pointed out the distinction workers sometimes make between the national level of the union and their own local: "People have *some* feeling about the local, but the international is just a monolith." It is common for workers to feel that the local to some extent still represents them, or at least is led by people they know and on whom they can put pressure. The same people may view the higher levels of the union as just another alien bureaucracy. At times locals may support or even lead strikes that the national leadership is opposing, as in the 1970 postal workers' wildcat. These union grass roots in turn help keep workers from rejecting unionism decisively.

The development of the union into something separate from workers themselves, though inevitable, did not become apparent all at once, either to management or to workers. For workers, it has been a gradual realization. One older radical in Detroit, an auto worker since the forties, told us:

> The separation of workers from the union has steadily moved further and further down. There was always conflict in the UAW between locals and the International. During World War II it often came down to the stewards versus the local, when it came to supporting wildcats and the like. For a long time now most workers haven't had any use even for the lowest levels of the union. In the mid-fifties one really powerful rank-and-file leader I knew who was steward in his plant said that during a strike the barrier between workers and lower-level union officials would dissolve, but that within a few days the old distrust, suspicion and sense of separateness would return again.

Today, the attitudes of many workers, especially younger ones, have moved from distrust to bitter hostility, largely as a result of the factors we have described. When we went on a late-night call-in radio show in Detroit, just as the night shift was coming off, antagonism to the union was the common theme of the auto workers who called in. Indeed, there were more complaints about the union than about the work itself. The sentiment of many younger workers was expressed by a phrase we heard over and over again, not only among auto workers but among many others as well: "I don't like to say it, but I guess I hate the union as much as I hate the company."

Many people recognize that this reflects a sharp change in attitude. As we sat in the call-in show, an older woman phoned in to complain:

> The young people don't know about the union. I remember when we would walk four miles to bring food to my daddy when he and those men were inside the Chrysler plants during the sitdowns. We'd hand it up to them on long poles to the second floor. My daddy was a strong union man. Now he's retired and has a union pension and a good life. The young people just don't understand what it was like before the union. The men had to give gifts to the foremen to keep their jobs. They should appreciate all the union's done for them.

Many a younger worker has received a similar lecture from older workers and union officials.

Unions still retain a degree of support for several other reasons besides this lingering loyalty among older workers who remember the "bad old days" before unionization. Many lower level union officials—like many foremen—are personally known and liked by workers. Many people recognize that conditions are generally better where there are unions and support them for that reason. Sometimes the union will maintain credibility by supporting the demands of part of the workers, often those with the most seniority. Like any political machine, unions perform a great many small services, pushing selected grievances, fixing some things up with the employer, getting a worker off a bad job or even helping to solve problems off the job. As a worker in a small electrical factory in Cleveland told us:

> People hate the union worse than the company. It's nothing but a private clique of leaders. But it has done enough favors so that if their back was pushed against the wall, a lot of people would probably support it.

Many more workers consider themselves "union men" or "union women," but mean by that a commitment to something far different from the unions as they now exist. They are the inheritors of a social and even moral tradition that workers should stick up for each other and not let themselves be pushed around. That tradition existed before modern unionism and it exists today outside of it, but because unions are the most visible form of workers' organization, loyalty to workers as a group often goes under the name of unionism. The paradoxical result is that even militants who attack the unions are often known as ''strong union men.''

In many unions there are reform and ''rank-and-file'' caucuses and movements which attempt to restore greater democracy and militance to the union structure. Such an aim is a natural response to the ''maturation'' of unions. Even the Gary steelworker who told us, ''I hate the union more than I do the company,'' also felt that ''maybe the first step for changing anything has to be taking over the union.''

Yet the cynicism about such efforts is quite general. Many of today's distrusted officials were yesterday's militants. Even personally honest union officials find they have to play by the rules or be defeated by them. In Detroit we had described to us a young black worker, unconnected with any political organization, who got elected chief steward in an auto plant.

> He was gung ho to do a good job and be different from all the other stewards. The job defeated him. There was nothing he could do. Within eight months all his enthusiasm was gone and he was convinced it was impossible to do anything with the union.

Not all officials who start out honest remain that way. Once they enter the union structure their own interests become different from those they represent. They enter a world of offices, lawyers, cocktail parties and negotiations. They no longer share the income level or the working conditions of the workers on the job.

But the social separation of union officials from ordinary workers is not primarily a problem of the personal qualities of individuals; it has its root in the nature of unionism itself. The crux of a union is its ability to bind its members to an agreement with management. This is what distinguishes it from any other form of workers' organization. All its institutional characteristics are devoted to this end. The goal requires that workers' relinquish their right to determine their own action. The actual authority to initiate action in a union resides in its officials and bureaucrats, not in its members—and this top-down organization of power is essential if the union is to prevent its members from violating its agreements with management. It is this, far more than their sheer size or the need to coordinate large numbers of people, that makes top-down organization a nearly universal characteristic of established trade unions.

In a very profound sense, there is no way that the rank and file can take over a union. The structure of unions is top-down—the best that can happen is that a new and perhaps better group will take power at the top. That group, in turn, has to oppose itself to the rank and file at a certain point if it wants to maintain its agreements with management.

This was vividly illustrated by the recent take-over of the United Mine Workers by a rank-and-file reform organization, the Miners for Democracy. Arnold Miller, a retired miner, stricken with Black Lung disease from his years in the mines, was elected president of the union in 1973. Miller was as close to the rank and file and as free of corruption as any major union reform leader in many years. With his election, the UMW was changed from a corrupt and dictatorial racket to a progressive union with democratically elected leaders. Yet the UMW has continued and even improved its role in limiting workers' direct action and holding them within the limits of the contract with management. The reform leadership has launched a campaign against wildcat strikes and other forms of direct action which miners had developed over such issues as safety, health and pensions. When West Virginia coal miners struck on a massive scale to protest the lack of gasoline for getting to work in early 1974, the union reform leaders organized the effort, including substantial radio appeals, to get them back to work. Conflict between miners and the U.M.W. came to a head in late summer, 1975, when the firing of a participant in a local wildcat led first to a regional strike and then to a walkout which closed 80% of the bituminous coal industry demanding the right of local miners to strike. The union executive board — controlled by the reformers — ordered the miners back to work, and union opposition to the movement was so pronounced that miners closed down "their" union headquarters with picketlines. It took nearly a month from the strike's beginning for union officials and court injunctions to get the miners back to work.

Workers are usually better off with honest unions than with corrupt ones, but efforts to reform unions, like the unions themselves, serve to channel and contain discontent. Instead of using their direct power over production to change their situations, workers are urged by such reform movements to support efforts to "take over" the union from unsatisfactory leaders. But as the example of the mine workers indicates, even with reform leaders, the union remains a power separate from and often even opposed to the groups of people who actually work side by side on the job. If workers are to gain more control over the time of their lives, they will have to do it themselves.

6.THE BIG PICTURE: THE BIG RIP-OFF

So far we have looked at work from the viewpoint of the individual and the workplace. The fundamental patterns we have found reveal much about the organization of our society as a whole.

Every day, hundreds of millions of people throughout the world go to work. At the workplace they produce goods and services that are considered useful. But what is produced by no means belongs to those who produce it—when workers go home from work, the products they have spent their previous hours creating remain behind, the property of the employers who have hired them. This is hardly hot news; most people realize they're working to fill someone else's pocket.

Often the workings of society seem complex and mysterious. The newspapers are filled with the gyrations of the stock market, the complexities of diplomacy, the speeches of politicians. But the foundation on which all such activities rest is the labor of those who produce society's wealth; without their activity, the stockholders would be reduced to eating their stocks and the politicians their words.

No matter what kind of society people live in, they have to work. This might not be true in the imaginary world of hobo song, where

> you never change your socks
> and little streams of alchohol
> come trickling down the rocks. . .
> There's a lake of stew
> And of honey, too—
> In the Big Rock Candy Mountain.

But in the real world, most things we need do not spring from nature ready to use. We have to make the things we need by applying human labor, and the tools and materials created by past labor, to the resources provided by nature.

The way these elements are organized has varied greatly from society to society. In some, the available resources and the products of each individual's labor have been shared among all the members of the tribe; in others, work has been done by slaves who were owned by and labored for their masters, or by serfs, who worked part of the time on their own land and part of the time for their lord; at times, people have owned their tools and materials and produced either for their own needs or for exchange with the products of others; and in certain contemporary societies, productive property is owned by the state, by whom all workers are employed.

What we experience every day at work reflects the particular way work is currently organized throughout our own society. A small group of wealthy people owns the natural resources and products of labor which are necessary for production. The rest of the population have no way to meet their needs except to sell the time of their lives to those who possess the productive wealth of society.

The difference between what all workers produce and what they are paid for their labor is the total profit—that which ends up "in someone else's pocket." Profit is the goal for which production is organized in this society. It is the reason that the workplace is organized to squeeze as much work out of workers as possible. It is also the reason, as we shall see in Part II, that production is not organized to meet the life needs of those who perform it.

The productive wealth of the world is owned by many different individuals and companies. They share the total profits that workers produce. But they do not share them without conflict. On the contrary, the companies and even the nations of the world are engaged in a continuing competition to get control of an ever-larger share of what is produced by the labor of humanity. The share each gets is its profit.

Employers have little choice about whether or not to increase their profits as much as possible—at least, if they want to stay in business. Each company's survival in the general competition is largely determined by its ability to make production cheaper by producing more "efficiently." To do so it must have profits to reinvest in improved techniques and larger-scale production. If employers fail to accumulate profits for this, they lose out to the competition. Thus, the drive for profits isn't just the result of employers' lust for money or power; it is something they must do if they are to remain in business. As in the days of economist Adam Smith two hundred years ago, so today businessmen are faced with the alternative: "accumulate or perish!"[1]

The actual organization of production is not necessarily performed by those who own the means of production. With their wealth, they are able to hire large numbers of professional managers to do that for them. Whether businesses are run by their owners or by managers, they still have to try to accumulate profits, which belong to the owners. The point therefore is not that the owners of wealth run society, but that society is run for the owners of wealth.

Many workers, instead of working for private employers, work for the government. A certain proportion of what other workers produce goes in the form of taxes to support them. The government performs functions essential for preserving the system of production for profit. First, it guarantees the property rights of those who own the means of production—by courts, police, even the military if necessary. Second, it maintains the social conditions necessary for profit making to go on. When social problems arise, it intervenes to keep them from getting out of hand. When difficulties in profit making occur, it tries to create solutions through economic, diplomatic or military means. And it tries to maintain conditions under which the population will continue to accept the existing system of society—even if this at times brings it into conflict with the short-range interests of some owners of productive wealth.

Most people recognize that in practice, the most powerful influences on government are usually important businessmen and their lawyers. But even if this were not so, government would still have little choice but to try to preserve business profit, for the government itself as an institution depends for its continuation on the existing organization of society.

Everyone recognizes the power of the great institutions of our society—the giant corporations and the government. But less often do people stop to think that this power is nothing but the joint capacity of the individuals whose labor they control and coordinate. With no workers, General Motors, the White House and the Pentagon would have no more life or power than an Egyptian pyramid standing in the midst of the desert. These institutions are powerful only because millions of people turn over to them their own power to labor and create.

The power of these institutions is the powerlessness of the rest of us. All those who do not own the means of producing wealth are, reluctant as they may be to admit it, in the same essential predicament. They have to work for those who own the means of production; they can change their employers but not their position as employees. No matter how hard they work or how much they produce, they do not produce what they need for themselves; they create wealth which belongs to their employers—wealth with which employers can hire them again, wealth with which they are controlled. The result of workers' work is that the rich get richer and the rest of us have to go back to work for them.

Yet this very organization of work creates an organization of workers. They share common interests and a common predicament. They are connected by the cooperative nature of their work and their need for each other's products. They often join together in struggles to improve their lives. If these struggles and their goals could be sufficiently expanded, they could abolish a social organization in which some people have to work for others, and lay the basis for a society in which people could directly coordinate their own work to meet their own needs.

II

LIVING

Laurie Leifer/Liberation News Service

"Whether people feel off-the-job life is getting better or worse
probably determines, more than any other single factor,
whether they adopt strategies that accept the status quo or try to
change it. . . . If the benefits offered by the existing
organization of society continue to fade and the costs of accepting
it continue to grow, action to reorganize society will
become not just a feared or hoped-for dream, but the most
immediate self-interest."

Living

People don't live on the job. Indeed, many people think of their real lives as starting when they get off from work. The time clock seems to carve out work as a realm apart from the rest of life.

This apparent separation of work and nonwork realms is relatively recent. For an early American farm or artisan family, the relation between work and the rest of life was close. Work was carried on in and around the home. Work time and free time were interspersed. Work mates were usually family members as well. Much of the work was for the immediate needs of the family.

As production came to require the cooperation of larger numbers of people, and as it came under the control of employers, work moved away from the home and into factories, offices, stores and other workplaces. The job came to seem cut off from everything else.

But this is largely an illusion. Even when you leave the factory gate or walk out the office door, your life is still affected in a multitude of ways by what goes on behind them. The powerful institutions and forces which surround us, affecting us even inside the walls of our homes, gain their strength from the life they suck out of us at work. Far from escaping into a realm of freedom, people are faced with further consequences of their lack of control over the making and use of what they produce. A young worker overheard in a bar in Somerville, Massachusetts, put it eloquently:

> You go to work for someone and they rip you off all day. Then you drive a car some other company ripped you off for, go shopping and get ripped off at the store and go home and get ripped off by the power company, the gas company and the landlord. It seems like the only thing you can do without getting ripped off by them is sit in the park and shiver.

Only by gaining control over work itself would it be possible to shape freely the rest of life.

The importance of the nonwork realm was brought home to us by a discussion we had with a group of young steelworkers in Chicago. For several hours the talk had focused on what went on at work, when one of them broke in to chide us:

> Look, work isn't the whole story. I drive to work and maybe listen to the Watergate hearings on the car radio. I go home and face all the crap of the cities. Everywhere I go I have to breathe the air. Not so long ago we had a war going on.

Whether people feel off-the-job life is getting better or worse probably determines, more than any other single factor, whether they adopt strategies that accept the status quo or try to change it.

During the quarter of a century that followed the Great Depression, most people experienced dramatic improvements in their general conditions of life. The society as a whole likewise seemed to be growing, and growing better. There was a profound and widespread optimism that things would go on improving steadily. This sentiment underlay the widespread support for the existing organization of society and much of the hostility toward those who wanted to change it. Many people had indeed never had it so good.

Over the past decade, however, this situation has begun to change, first gradually, then more rapidly. Most people we asked agreed that living conditions were worsening. Few expected any rapid improvement. This change, its causes and results, are the main subject of Part II of this book.

We believe the feeling that things are likely to get worse may force many people to consider life strategies based on changing rather than just accepting the status quo. This has already been reflected in waves of consumer boycotts, wildcat strikes and truckers' blockades. If the benefits offered by the existing organization of society continue to fade and the costs of accepting it continue to grow, action to reorganize society will become not just a feared or hoped-for dream, but the most immediate self-interest.

Cidne Hart/Liberation News Service

7. HARD TIMES

People need goods and services that are created by human labor. Some of these products, like food, are necessary for biological survival. Others are needed for survival as a human being in a particular civilization—primitive bushmen may not need electricity, but modern city dwellers can hardly live without it. These products are what most people create every day at work.

But in our society, as we have seen, most people cannot produce directly for their own needs. They can produce only when they sell their time and creative abilities to an employer who owns the necessary means of production. As a result, production is organized first and foremost not to meet the needs of the producers but to increase the power and profit of those who own and direct productive wealth. Despite the amount of labor that working people do, and despite the tremendous amount workers can produce with modern technology, most people's needs for the products of labor are inadequately met.

This reality was masked during the decades that followed the Great Depression. The United States experienced sustained prosperity, during which incomes rose substantially, inflation was moderate and the occasional recessions relatively short and mild. It was widely asserted that America had become an "affluent society." While there might remain a few isolated "pockets of poverty," it was said, the good things of life were in general distributed quite equally, and all but a small minority had high incomes and a high standard of living. If anything, the problem was that people consumed too much, not too little; such affluence disturbed the natural ecology and left people's spiritual needs unmet in their endless acquisition of unnecessary gadgets and other consumer goods. Further, it was assumed that this affluence was bound to continue and steadily increase; the depressions, crises and "hard times" that had periodically struck the economy in the past could now be prevented through newly discovered government policies. In short, the economic problems of society had essentially been solved. As a result, the social movements that had addressed the economic needs of working people in the past were now largely obsolete.

This view has been rudely shattered by the realities of the past several years. "Hard times" are not only possible; they are upon us. They have substantially reduced the standard of living for most Americans and have led to protest actions on a massive scale.

AMERICA'S LARGEST PROTEST

Mrs. Ann Giordano recalls that she was never particularly conscious of food prices; her Staten Island kitchen didn't have enough shelf space for her to buy in large quantities. But one day when she had put the groceries away there was still space left on the shelf. She vaguely wondered if she had left a bag of food at the store. Next time she came home from shopping, she looked in her wallet and concluded that she had accidentally left a $20 bill behind. When she went back to the supermarket and found out how much her food really cost, she suddenly realized where the shelf space had come from and where the money had gone.

It was early spring in 1973. Food prices were soaring, and millions of shoppers were having similar experiences. Mrs. Giordano, who was thirty-three and described herself as "just a housewife," called some of her friends and discussed the idea of a consumer boycott—an idea that was springing up simultaneously in many places around the country in response to rising food prices. Soon a substantial grapevine of women were calling homes all over Staten Island, spreading word of the boycott. They called a meeting at a local bowling alley to which over one hundred people came on two days' notice, named themselves JET-STOP (Joint Effort to Stop These Outrageous Prices) and elected captains for each district. Within a week they had covered the Island with leaflets, picketed the major stores and laid the basis for a highly effective boycott.[1]

Mrs. Giordano and her friends were typical of those who gave birth to the 1973 consumer meat boycott, "a movement which started in a hundred different places all at once and that's not led by anyone." As a newspaper account described it:

> The boycott is being organized principally at the grass-roots level rather than by any overall committee or national leadership. It is made up mainly of groups of tenants in apartment

buildings, neighbors who shop at the same markets in small towns, block associations and—perhaps most typical— groups of women who meet every morning over coffee. All have been spurred into action by the common desire to bring food prices back to what they consider a manageable level.[2]

The 1973 consumer meat boycott was undoubtedly the largest mass protest in American history. A Gallup poll taken at the end of the boycott found that over 25 percent of all consumers— representing families with fifty million members—had participated in it.[3] Large retail and wholesale distributors reported their meat sales down by one-half to two-thirds.[4] The boycott was strongest among what the press referred to as "middle income" families— those with incomes around the national average of $10,000 or $12,000 a year. It represented, in the words of one reporter, "an awareness that, for a whole new class of Americans like themselves, push has finally come to shove."[5] In "low-income" neighbor- hoods, sales fell less during the boycott, largely, as retailers pointed out, because the residents, who can't afford much meat at any time, had been cutting back for weeks due to high prices. As one Harlem merchant said: "How much can these people tighten their belts when they don't have too much under their belts in the first place?"[6]

Some advocates of the boycott made the dubious argument that it would bring meat prices down by reducing the demand for meat. For most participants, however, the movement was seen as a protest, a way of making visible to politicians and others what they felt about the rising cost of living. President Nixon responded by putting a freeze on meat prices, but his move was met by scorn among many boycotters who felt that prices were already far too high ("They locked the barn door after the cow went through the roof," com- mented one housewife).

The boycott did not prove to be an effective tactic for combatting high prices, but it did show the tremendous capacity of ordinary people to organize themselves on a massive national scale around issues of mutual concern.

It also suggests that the development of society has made popular movements possible on a larger scale than ever before. The inter- dependence of the economy means that many problems, instead of just affecting one or another limited group, affect most people in common. Rapid and widespread communications allow word of proposed actions to spread almost at once to virtually everyone. Faced with similar problems in the future, people should be able to act on just as massive a scale, but with far more effective tactics.

111

GET POOR QUICK

Massive protest over rising prices should have come as no surprise. Inflation has steadily reduced the living standard of most working people over the past few years. Average take-home pay—adjusted to account for inflation—fell slowly but steadily from 1965 to 1970. After a brief respite in 1971–72 it began to fall again.[7] In 1973 and the first half of 1974, it fell nearly 7 percent.[8]

Inflation has had somewhat different effects on different groups of people. For better-off workers, it has often meant an end to the nonnecessities that made life more than just a struggle to get by. A butcher, shaking his head over meat prices, put it this way:

> People are just going to have to change their habits and what they expect. There are going to be fewer two-car families, fewer boat families, fewer vacation-home families and fewer snowmobile families.

A letter carrier in Gloucester, Massachusetts, illustrated this point:

> I work this job and then I work at a liquor store on the side. Even so, it gets harder all the time to get by. The bills keep piling up. You can do without a lot of things, but you can't do without food. I've got a vacation place up in New Hampshire, I'm really fond of it, but I don't have any money to do anything with it. It seems like something is always going wrong and I can't afford to fix it. Seems like I should sell the place if I can't keep it up, but then with prices going the way they are, you don't know what to do.[9]

A number of people we talked with whose incomes were near the national average wondered how people who made less than they did could even manage to survive. The question was very much to the point; inflation hits harder the less money you have to start with. The widow of a parking-lot attendent in South Boston, for example, lives with four of her children in a four-bedroom tenement apartment. She receives $220 a month from social security, about $216 from federal welfare funds, and nets about $16 a week baby-sitting for a neighbor; her total income is about $6000 a year. "I used to be able to go to the store with $50 and come back with six or seven bags of groceries," she stated. "Now I'm lucky if I come back with three." The family diet is now almost exclusively government-surplus macaroni and rice, canned spaghetti and frozen potpies, with chicken or cold cuts every other night and fresh vegetables about twice a week. She has no social life; she can't go anywhere "because there's nothing left after the rent and food."[10]

Such a living standard is not limited to those on welfare. A number of unionized hospital workers on a strike picket line in New York were interviewed by a reporter. One woman with three children who was a unit clerk at Beth Israel Hospital took home $106 a week after taxes: "Thank God my kids are not steak eaters. I buy stew beef sometimes and chicken and canned corned beef." Along with some bacon and hamburger once a week, that was what her children had for meat. Another woman took home $107.50 after taxes, which she referred to as a "bean-diet" salary. "I make kidney beans with rice. That's got protein, and I give my son plenty of milk. . . . I make beans and potato salad or greens and fresh vegetables. I seldom buy meat at all." She pays $120 a month for a one-bedroom "hole in the wall" in Brooklyn. Another hospital worker said she had about given up trying to support her family on $108 a week after taxes, and was sending her year-old son south to live with her mother. "That way, I know he'll eat all right."[11]

These families had after-tax incomes of more than $5500 a year. The conditions for those even poorer were indicated by a recent study of low-income families commissioned by a Senate committee. It found families with little or no food in their homes and little or no money to buy any; families with nothing to eat but Wonder Bread and hog jowls, and families that had switched to dog food as their source of protein.[12]

All this was before the fall of 1974, when the economic crisis moved into an acute downward spiral. By January 1975, unemployment reached its highest level since the end of the Great Depression. Millions of people, already staggering under the impact of inflation, were hit by layoffs, furloughs and plant closings. Millions more saw their hours sharply reduced. The result was a massive shock to the living conditions of the employed and the unemployed alike.

It is frequently pointed out that the impact of unemployment has been considerably softened by social reforms instituted since the Great Depression. The most important of these is unemployment insurance. It indeed makes a substantial difference; as an Oswego, New York union official in the construction trades (most of whose members were unemployed) put it, "If it wasn't for unemployment insurance, I don't know how they would eat."[13]

However, the level of unemployment benefits is set to tide workers over between jobs, not to maintain them in extended unemployment; under the impact of inflation, it is hardly even sufficient for that purpose. The average unemployment benefit is $65 a week, far less than half the average wage. Consider, for example, a worker recently laid off from a small auto parts plant in Detroit.[14] His take-home pay had been $125 a week; his unemployment benefits run $70 a week. After paying the rent on a five-room apartment and making payments on a stove, refrigerator and dinette set, there is $40 a week left to support a family of four. So far, the family has had to put off buying a new bed so that their young children can sleep separately; eat cheap greens and canned pork-and-beans in place of meat and ground beef instead of ham; and pass up a much-needed surgical operation for one family member. Despite these cutbacks, the future looks worse still: bills are piling up, savings have been exhausted and a company-paid health insurance plan is about to run out. The unemployment compensation itself will probably continue to be eroded by inflation—and it will not last forever. If mass unemployment persists, millions of workers may exhaust present benefits during the months ahead. If unemployment compensation provides a cushion, it is hardly a cushy one.

The other important new sources of income for the unemployed are employer-funded benefit programs established in union contracts. The most prominent of these is the United Auto Workers' Supplemental Unemployment Benefits (SUB's), established some years ago as a union ploy to head off demands for a guaranteed annual wage in the auto industry. Combined with government unemployment benefits, SUB's bring the income of an unemployed worker with seniority at a major auto company up to 95 percent of regular pay.

Such a program makes good sense—why should workers be penalized for the failures of their employers? But only a small minority of workers are covered by such programs. A few industries provide benefits for unemployed workers, but the major auto companies are virtually the only ones who come near to providing a worker's regular income. Even the auto industry's SUB fund is rapidly running out of money; payments have already been cut for low-seniority workers and one company's sub fund went completely dry in 1975.

A substantial proportion of the unemployed receive neither employer nor government unemployment benefits of any kind. They include new entrants and reentrants into the labor force, discouraged workers who have given up looking for a job, workers in occupations not covered by such programs and those who have exhausted their benefits. Millions of them aren't even counted in the official unemployment statistics, making these figures deceptively low. For these unemployed, the problem will be to survive at all.

While much is made of the factors that soften the effects of economic contractions today, less attention has been paid to a number of "cushions" that existed in the 1930s but have now largely vanished. During the Great Depression, prices fell by an estimated one-third, easing substantially the impact of falling incomes. Food was plentiful and food prices were extremely low, helping to reduce the extent of downright hunger. Many workers still had relatives with farms, to which they could return while unemployed. The greater national and international interdependence of today's economy means that particular regions and industries are less likely to escape the economic contractions of the economy as a whole. Finally, the greater complexity of society now makes it more vulnerable to disaster when aspects of economic production break down. In the 1930s, many people could substitute simple for complex ways of life: they could burn wood instead of oil; cool with ice instead of refrigerators; buy food from nearby farmers rather than through complex national marketing chains. For most urban Americans, such expedients are simply not possible today. The result may well be that normal life will become impossible to continue long before impoverishment has reached the levels of the Great Depression.

PROFIT VS. NEED

Even in times of general prosperity, people suffer the consequences of a system of production directed to making profits for a minority, not to meeting the needs of the majority. Detroit auto companies are notorious for producing cars that will have to be replaced in a few short years, even though they could build cars that would last for hundreds of thousands of miles. This is so well known that it has even been given a name, "built-in obsolescence." Similarly, studies publicized recently have shown that many companies have reduced the nutritional value of their food products, notably breakfast cereals, to a minimum; they can be made and preserved more cheaply that way, and are therefore more profitable.

Seeking profits, businesses often try to manipulate needs, rather than meet them as they freely develop. A blatant example is the effort to create "needs" for products which people otherwise might not buy through high-pressure advertising. Businesses may even try to shape people's very lives: For example, a notoriously powerful "highway lobby" of auto, gas, rubber and highway construction companies has successfully promoted huge national expenditures for highway construction. The effect in practice has been to destroy most public transportation through lack of available funds, making cars a necessity of life.

Many needs don't get met at all because it is not profitable to meet them. According to government estimates, the United States needs to build four million new housing units a year for the next ten years.

Housing Starts

Although unmet human needs increased, production to meet them fell. The annual rate for housing starts fell from 2.4 million in May 1973 to 880,000 in December 1974. By March 1975 U.S. industry was operating at less than 66 percent capacity, and more than 8 million workers were officially listed as unemployed. People needed homes and other products, but businesses found them unprofitable to produce.

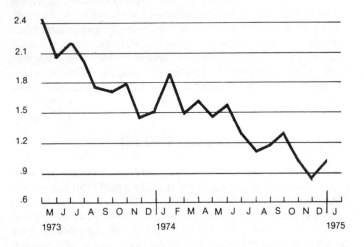

Source: *New York Times*, June 19, 1974 and February 20, 1975. Statistics from U.S. Department of Commerce.

But it has only been constructing them at half that rate, at a time when millions of people are unable to find suitable housing. There are plenty of unemployed people willing to work making houses and housing materials—but they can't because it is not profitable for employers to hire them for that purpose. Similarly, many people have had to wait days or even months to get needed medical care. This situation continues, not because people don't want and need medical services, or because there is nobody to build the facilities or to train to use them, but because the necessary resources have gone to other, more profitable purposes. Thus many people's most basic needs for housing and medical care go unmet.

During periods of prosperity, these deficiences often seem tolerable, a price worth paying for the rapid economic expansion and rising living standards that have marked the system of production for profit through much of its history. Unfortunately, however, such prosperity has been anything but constant.

Every period of economic expansion has been followed by periods of recession, stagnation or depression. In the twentieth century alone, the United States experienced depressions and recessions in 1903, 1907, 1911, 1914, 1921, the entire decade of the 1930s, 1949, 1954, 1957, 1961 and 1970.

These declines in production were not the result of floods, crop failures or other natural disasters. Nor did they occur because all of people's needs had been met, so that no more production was needed. Whatever their immediate trigger, they were part and parcel of an economic system in which things are produced only when it is profitable to do so. While other kinds of economic systems have crises of production due to planning errors, natural disasters or social disruption, only private market economies have produced business cycles and economic depressions.[15]

During such crises, the conflict between production for profit and human need becomes appallingly apparent. During the Great Depression of the 1930s, for example, one-quarter of all wage and salary workers were unemployed and living in desperate need, while workplaces stood idle, ready to produce. Yet people were prevented from going into them and producing; they belonged to the employers, who did not find them profitable to run. Similarly, while millions of people went hungry, large amounts of food were deliberately destroyed because they could not be profitably sold. John Steinbeck vividly described a common occurrence:

> The people come with nets to fish for potatoes in the river, and the guards hold them back; they come in rattling cars to get the dumped oranges, but the kerosene is sprayed [on the fruit]. And they stand still and watch the potatoes float by, listen to the screaming pigs being killed in a ditch and covered with quicklime, watch the mountains of oranges slop down to a putrefying ooze; and in the eyes of the people there is a failure; in the eyes of the hungry there is a growing wrath.[16]

Such descriptions may sound like something from the distant past. But in 1974, when, as we have seen, millions of families were forced to virtually give up meat, the following item appeared in the *Wall Street Journal*:

> In Springdale, Ark., Tyson Foods Inc., a major broiler
> producer, drowned 300,000 chicks and destroyed 800,000
> eggs that would have hatched broilers, as the first steps in
> phasing out a facility until broiler production becomes profita-
> ble again.[17]

American farmers destroyed thousands of chickens and sharply
reduced their production of beef in order to restrict supply and raise
profits. As housing grew harder and harder for families to find,
housing starts decreased from 2.4 million a year at the beginning of
1973 to 1.4 million in mid-1974, despite substantial unemployment
in the construction industry. As energy shortages reached crisis
proportions, domestic production of oil fell, and power companies
sharply reduced their planned investment in expanded nuclear and
conventional facilities.[18] As living standards fell and shortages
prevailed for many products, millions of workers were laid off,
instead of being able to produce the food, housing, energy and other
products people so badly needed. In short, the organization of our
economic system still makes it impossible for people to use the
available resources to meet their needs.

During periods of economic expansion, the idea arises that
economic crises and "hard times" are a thing of the past. During the
expansion that followed the Great Depression of the 1930s, this idea
was strengthened by the belief that the private economy could be
controlled through limited government intervention. New government policies—the so-called "New Economics"—would prevent
the swings between boom and depression that had marked the history
of economies based on production for private profit. The core of the
"New Economics" was the expansion of government spending,
budget deficits and credit whenever recession threatened. These
policies have been applied by every government administration
since World War II, whether Republican or Democrat.

For a considerable period of time, these policies seemed to ward
off economic contraction with some success. Unfortunately, however, the medicine began to reveal side effects which were not so
benign. The first consequence was a tendency toward a stagnation of
economic growth. In the past, depressions had served to create
conditions for renewed expansion by squeezing out less competitive
companies, enlarging more efficient ones, reducing claims on
capital and cutting wages. While the "New Economics" succeeded
in warding off depressions, it was unable to create the conditions for
a classical business expansion. Government continued to grow,
creating jobs for many of those who might otherwise be unemployed, but business itself could not achieve a steady expansion.

A second consequence of the "New Economics" was the rise of inflation. From the first, politically conservative economists had warned that budget deficits and other government attempts to stimulate the economy would lead to inflation. Whatever the validity of their arguments, their conclusion was evidently right, for every attempt to promote economic expansion through government stimulus has aggravated inflation. On the other hand, their proposals to abandon the "New Economics" have little better to offer; whenever government stimuli have been withdrawn, results have been rising unemployment and incipient recession.

The "New Economics," despite its claims, has not really found a way to overcome the historical processes of our economic system. No matter what "policy mix" has been applied, the American economy for the past decade has suffered continuously from unemployment or inflation or—increasingly—both at the same time. This last condition has even required the invention of new language—"inflationary depression" and "stagflation"—to describe it. Each attempt to stave off recession has aggravated inflation, and vice versa. The economic panacea, far from having cured the disease, has merely created a new set of symptoms. Doubt has finally set in about the belief that "every economic problem is amenable to solution if only the federal government will adopt the 'right' policy at the right time and execute it effectively."[19]

While our economic system continues to produce economic crises, the form they take today has changed as a result of increased government intervention. Inflation and shortages have joined unemployment and falling production as manifestations of the system's inability to adapt production to human needs. But most people rightly feel that the form "hard times" take matters less than the actual deterioration in their conditions of life. As an old-time radical tool and die maker told us:

> You do not need statistics to know what is happening in the economy. If you cannot afford to buy enough food, you will feel it in your stomach. If you cannot afford fuel and clothing, you will know what is going on in the economy because you will be cold.

WHO PAYS FOR THE SYSTEM'S FAILURES?

As long as the economy continues to expand, workers' conditions of life can improve at the same time that profits increase. But when economic expansion falters, different social groups come into conflict over who will bear the burden of the system's failures. Managers and owners try to restore profitability at the expense of workers. And government policies that are officially issued for the good of "the economy," "the nation" and "the people" inevitably result in benefit to some and loss to others.

As the role of the government in the economy has increased, its policies have come more and more to affect how the fruits of production are divided. This does not mean that the government has a free hand to divide the benefits any way it wants to. If it pursued policies that did not assure a continued expansion of profits, the result would be a general economic and social collapse, threatening its own stability. Thus, regardless of what individuals or party may be in office, the government has consistently striven to maintain the profitability of the economy—at the expense of workers if necessary.

As a result, those who are hurt most by the failures of the economy are the members of the nonaffluent majority. Inflation, for example, whatever its other effects, has reduced the real wages of workers. This directly benefits employers: When prices rise faster than wages, income that would have gone to workers goes to business instead.

This evident fact has been obscured by a barrage of propaganda designed to persuade the public that rising wages are the cause of rising prices. The effectiveness of this seemingly plausible line of argument is indicated by a recent survey of union members: 61 percent of them believed that excess union demands are the major cause of inflation.[20] The truth is quite the opposite. Every general increase in labor costs in recent years has followed, rather than preceded, an increase in consumer prices. Wage increases have been the result of workers' efforts to catch up after their incomes had already been eroded by inflation. Nor could it easily be otherwise. All a businessman has to do to raise a price is to get up in the morning and make an announcement; barring price controls, it will take at most a few weeks to go into effect. Wage rates, on the other hand, are primarily determined by contracts in the unionized sector, which usually run for two or three years. As long as they accept such contracts, workers are bound to lag behind inflation; they can't even try to catch up until the contract expires. Even the minority of workers covered by cost-of-living escalator clauses—about one-third of unionized workers and fewer than 10 percent of all workers—receive their increases after, not before, the rise in consumer prices. The attempt to blame inflation on workers' wage increases is hardly more than a justification for those who want to increase profits by decreasing real wages.

Wage/price controls, applied off and on over the past few years, similarly held down workers' incomes. It is relatively easy to control wages, since they are set by employers who generally have every interest in keeping them within official guidelines. But most experts on economic controls agree that it is almost impossible to police effectively the tens of thousands of constantly shifting prices in the economy. Companies have myriad techniques to raise prices by reducing discounts, cutting quality, selling on the black market, etc. Where there are flexible price controls instead of an absolute freeze, companies can generally present their cost and profit figures in ways that make price increases appear justified. And if all these techniques fail, they can withhold their products to create artificial shortages, thus pressuring the government to allow price increases—a tactic employed by both the gasoline and the beef industries during 1973. During the years when wages and prices were supposedly "controlled," wages in reality fell further and further behind prices. Nor was this result accidental; for as the *New York Times* reported when peacetime wage and price controls were first established in 1971, "the essential purpose of the whole complicated system of boards, commissions, and councils created to manage the drive against inflation" was to "tighten the knot on future wage settlements and increase pressure on unions to acquiesce in the arrangement."[21]

When employers are unable to expand their profits and therefore stop expanding production, it is working people who pay the highest price. Even in the relatively mild recession of 1961, the official unemployment rate was 10 percent for skilled workers, 12 percent for semiskilled workers and 20 percent for unskilled workers.[22] Unemployment also affects those who remain at work, eliminating overtime, cutting hours, putting a downward pressure on wages and forcing many people into low-paying, insecure employment. A severe depression can lead to misery on a colossal scale; even today, most people too young to remember it have heard stories about the terrors of the Great Depression and what it meant to those who lived through it.

Nearly a year ago, when this chapter was first being drafted, we wrote: "The social and political costs of recession and depression are so high that economic policy makers will no doubt seek to avoid them if at all possible. But as the amount of government spending and credit required to keep down unemployment grows greater and greater, and the rate of inflation consequently grows higher and higher, a point may well come when they find it necessary to choose between allowing recessionary pressures to take their disastrous course, or abandoning direction of the economy by private business."

Subsequent events indicate which choice they made.

HOW DO YOU FIGHT HARD TIMES?

Changing economic conditions exert profound though sometimes contradictory effects on the strategies people adopt for dealing with the problems of everyday life. When people expect general economic expansion, they may use strikes and other tactics to win a share of the benefit. (Strike waves for this purpose are common on the upswing of business cycles.) In general, however, steady economic growth makes it possible for people to achieve a rising standard of living using strategies of individual advancement—rising within a firm, looking for a better job, getting more education, moving to a different region or neighborhood. Only if high expectations for improvement are inadequately fulfilled are people likely to turn to more militant forms of action on a large scale during times of relative prosperity.

When "hard times" set in, real incomes decrease and unemployment rises. It becomes impossible for most people to continue living in the same way. At the very least, they have to restrict consumption, work longer hours or increase the number of breadwinners in the family. The rising threat of unemployment may lead people to avoid actions that might lose them their jobs. But such strategies can do little to arrest the deterioration of living standards most people experience at such times. Since a whole class of people are experiencing the same problems simultaneously, however, they often turn to strategies involving forms of collective action.

The effects of general economic conditions on people's feelings and action were evident during the period we worked on this book. At the end of 1972, the United States was just coming out of a period of considerable unemployment and relatively low inflation. With real wages rising somewhat and jobs scarce, strikes had been relatively few. In early 1973 there was a sharp increase in prices, especially for meat, followed by the massive consumer meat boycott.

That summer prices rose in all spheres. An organization of women workers in Chicago told us that its supporters—nonunionized office and store workers in the downtown Loop district—were falling further and further behind the cost of living, making pay increases the big issue for them. Industrial production was very high, however, and most of the industrial workers we talked with felt that with heavy overtime they were more or less keeping up with the cost of living. Indeed, one of the grievances we heard most widely expressed was compulsory overtime; there were many walkouts protesting this and it was the most talked-about issue in the auto negotiations that summer.

As the inflation rate continued to rise, it began cutting into living standards more and more. By early 1974, many people were finding themselves without money to pay their bills at the end of the month, and so had to cut back sharply on all family expenditures. The tone of discussions often changed to one of fear and anger. In Boston, we began hearing such comments as, "We ought to all go on strike, just to show them" and "If it gets so that you can't buy food, we'll just have to get down our guns and take it." The fuel shortages and fuel price increases greatly intensified this sentiment and led to massive strikes and highway blockades by the independent truck owner/operators. By the spring of 1974, we noticed a great increase of strikes; just driving around eastern Massachusetts, you would run into them frequently. By June, a nationwide strike wave was under way, with more strikes than at any time since 1946. Such a response was to be expected from the cumulative increase of prices over wages.

These various actions may well represent the beginning of an extended period of experimentation with a variety of collective strategies. Only through such experiments can people discover what forms are likely to be most effective. Some lessons are already evident, however.

It is often as consumers that people first experience and respond to "hard times"—witness the 1973 consumer meat boycott. Yet as that boycott showed, people really have only the most limited power in their role as consumers. They may be able to affect one or another company, but they have little control over the economy as a whole. Similarly, while the increasing number of people joining food co-ops and sharing living quarters may ease the hardship of falling incomes, their actions have little impact on general social conditions.

Where working people do have power is on the job. By halting production, they can force concessions from their employers. Thus it is natural that workers have turned to strikes on a massive scale to try to recoup what they have lost to inflation.

As we saw in Chapter 5, trade unions have been the main medium through which workers have negotiated for concessions from their employers. The strategy of trying to use the unions to cope with inflation has therefore been widespread.

One top union official reports that "workers are putting enormous pressure on their leaders to get more money."[23] The demand for cost-of-living escalators in contracts is particularly strong. Among nonunion workers, there has been a sudden interest in unionization. According to another union official, "there's greater interest in joining trade unions today than at any time since the Korean war. . . . If this inflation keeps going the way it is, every worker in the U.S. will be in a trade union.''[24]

But by and large, trade unionism has not been successful in combatting the decline in real earnings. Unionized workers, like others, have fallen further and further behind rising prices. Far from leading a fight to maintain workers' incomes, union leaders have generally done everything possible to limit ''excessive rank-and-file demands.'' They have gone along with government wage controls, even though their members' real wages were shrinking month by month. (The reasons union officials act so differently from the interests of their members have been explored at length in Chapter 5.)

Even the minority of unions with cost-of-living escalators in their contracts do not fully protect their members from inflation, since the escalators almost never provide one hundred percent of the increase in the cost of living and often have ceilings. For example, in the forty-month electrical workers' contract with General Electric which expired in May 1973, workers received four cost-of-living increases totalling 24 cents an hour. But even before the end of the contract, union sources estimated that GE workers had lost an additional 29 cents an hour in real wages as a result of inflation.[25]

The average worker covered under the Steelworkers' contract signed in April 1974 will receive about an 80 percent recovery for rises in the cost of living—better than many.[26] If consumer prices continue to rise at the 10 percent rate prevailing when the contract was signed, workers covered by it will find their incomes down 6 percent when the contract ends three years hence. Yet the contract itself—and the union bureaucracy standing behind it—would prevent them from striking even to save their incomes from such a reduction.

Because of these failures, many workers have had to turn to strategies of collective action on the job that are independent of , or even in opposition to, the union officialdom. The most effective action against inflation in recent years was the 1970 strike wave, particularly the Teamsters' wildcat. The Teamsters union had negotiated a national contract which did not adequately compensate workers for the rapid inflation of the late 1960s. It was all set to be signed, when drivers in sixteen cities, mostly in the mid- and far-West, refused to go along and went out on a wildcat strike which the *New York Times* described as ''a revolt against the national union leadership and a $1.10-an-hour raise that has been accepted in a national contract.''[27] After a bitter twelve-week strike, in which the union tried to get the drivers back to work and the state of Ohio called up 4100 National Guardsmen to escort strikebreakers, the strikers finally forced a wage increase two-thirds above that originally negotiated by their union—and far above federal wage guidelines. This set the pattern for substantial wage increases throughout industry, contributing to a brief respite from declining real wages during 1971 and 1972.

A more recent case was a spreading strike by government employees in Baltimore in July 1974. After six months of bargaining with the city, the garbage workers' union ratified a contract granting a 6 percent raise—far less than the increase in the cost of living. The garbage workers, whose take-home pay averaged about $90 a week, called a wildcat strike against the settlement. After they went out, the union leadership eventually endorsed the strike. Meanwhile, other groups of municipal workers joined the strike—jail guards, park employees, highway maintenance workers, keepers at the city zoo and, finally, about half of the police force. Amidst reports of burning and looting, the governor sent in state troopers to "maintain order" and serve as strikebreakers, while the courts threatened to jail strike leaders who ignored injunctions ordering the strikers back to work. The power of what had become virtually a general strike of municipal employees, however, quickly forced concessions. The city, which had absolutely refused any wage increases over 6 percent, agreed to raises averaging 19 percent over two years—just about enough for workers to keep up with inflation, instead of having a substantial cut in their real wages as the original settlement would have provided.[28]

The only way workers can keep from being left behind by inflation is to win wage increases that equal or exceed the increase in prices—and to win them as soon as prices rise if not before. If unions don't do this, workers can hardly accept their leadership unless they are also willing to accept a continuing decline in their standard of living. Thus it is not surprising that, as one union official pointed out recently, "a tremendously high number of proposed contracts are being turned down by union members these days."[29] The consequences are bound to be wildcat strikes and strikes which, while officially sanctioned by union leaders, are in practice opposed and even sabotaged by them.

Such actions outside official union structures require some kind of organization, if only an informal one. Sometimes this is provided by local union leaders or by a dissident caucus; these, however, remain separate from rank-and-file workers and subject to many of the same influences as the rest of the union leadership. For many contract rejections and wildcat strikes, the organization is created out of the informal, on-the-job organization of workers described in Chapter 4. For example, a Teamsters' contract rejection we know about developed out of various informal discussions in which a number of drivers concluded the contract proposed by the union was unsatisfac-tory. They then "passed the word" about their conclusion. A consensus was thus built up—and generally accepted by those who had not even been given a chance to see the contract. The vote against it was overwhelming. We have already described a wildcat strike for pay and benefit increases conducted by similar informal groups of co-workers (see Seaway strike, page 75). Strikes conducted along such lines are likely to increase in the coming days.

A good deal can be won by such a strategy in a period of inflation, as the 1970 Teamsters' wildcat and other examples show. Workers may be able to keep up with price increases or even get ahead of them if they simply refuse to work when their real incomes decline, wage controls and contracts notwithstanding. But this strategy is likely to be less viable in times of severe economic crisis, particularly in a depression with high unemployment. Under such conditions, employers can offer little in the way of wage increases, since their profits are low or nonexistent; wage cuts may be their only way to stay in business. Strikes are risky because in periods of high unemployment employers can often fill strikers' jobs. As the economy passes into recession or worse, workers must turn to other types of action.

The only way working people can protect themselves from the worst effects of depression is through concerted mass resistance to every encroachment on their conditions of life. Wherever people face a common problem, they will have to take immediate direct action to combat it. No doubt a great variety of tactics will be applied, but their effectiveness will depend largely on the threat to the existing social order posed by masses of people who are im-poverished and unemployed. To the extent that working people can wield that threat, they can force at least some concessions from those who control society's resources.

To do so effectively, struggles cannot remain limited to isolated groups; people will have to support each other's actions on the widest possible scale. In short, working people can only successfully fight the effects of hard times by creating a massive, continuing social movement through which they fight for the interests of all working people in every sphere of life.

People in groups which need to act together will have to use their imaginations to create tactics which can be effective in their particu-lar situation. There are some lessons that can be learned, however, from the immediate and the more distant past.

When employers decide to reduce work, they develop a plan to do so in the way most advantageous to themselves. Workers and unions have frequently tried to impose counterplans of their own. At the *Washington Star-News,* for example, management recently proposed to cut costs by eliminating 100 out of the 550 employees in the editorial and business departments. The union proposed that instead everyone work four days for four days' pay in exchange for a guarantee against layoffs. Workers supported the plan 9 to 1, and management accepted it. A committee reviews individual situations and allows a few workers to work full time in hardship cases. Similarly in the garment industry, the union has traditionally opposed layoffs and insisted that the available work be divided among all available workers. Workers can use strikes and other forms of direct action to demand an equitable distribution of work—or simply impose it by leaving work early, staying home on a regular schedule or systematically refusing overtime. They can also use forms of guerrilla resistance to ensure that as many workers as possible are necessary to perform the available work.

A method sometimes used to combat plant closings is the sit down strike or factory occupation. Since little economic pressure can be put on a company through the occupation of an unprofitable plant, the main purposes of such actions have usually been simply to protest the closings or to generate public pressure for measures to keep local employers in business. In 1974, for example, workers seized the Rheingold breweries in New York City when management decided to close them down. The occupation led to political intervention which successfully kept the company, something of a local institution, in business.

Such measures can only be effective in special situations. Usually workers have little power to ensure their employment when it is not profitable for employers. Government job expansions have rarely employed more than a small fraction of the unemployed. The unemployed and impoverished in past depressions have therefore turned to forms of direct action to meet their needs, often in cooperation with those still employed. During the early 1930s, for example, ''Unemployed Councils'' sprung up in dozens of cities around the country. A labor expert described them thus:

> The Unemployed Council is a democratic organ of the unemployed to secure by very practical means a control over their means of subsistence. . . . The Councils' weapon is democratic force of numbers and their functions are: to prevent evictions of the destitute, or if evicted, to bring pressure to bear on the Relief Commission to find a new home for the evicted family; if an unemployed worker has his gas or his water turned off because he can't pay for it, to investigate the case and demand their return from the proper authorities; to

see that the unemployed who are shoeless and clothesless get
both; to eliminate through publicity and pressure discrimina-
tions between Negroes and white persons, or against the
foreign born, in matters of relief; for individuals or families
and children of the unemployed who have no relief as a penalty
for political views or have been denied it through neglect, lack
of funds, or any other reason whatever, to march them down to
relief headquarters and demand they be fed and clothed.
Finally, to provide legal defense for all unemployed arrested
for joining parades, hunger marches, or attending union
meetings.[30]

Perhaps their most frequent tactic was the anti-eviction "riot";
when a family could not pay the rent and the sheriff put their
belongings out onto the street, local members of the Unemployed
Council would simply call a meeting of the neighbors, march en
masse to the site of the eviction and move the family back into the
house. They also used mass meetings, marches and disruptions to
press employers, government agencies, city councils and state and
federal governments to meet the needs of the unemployed.

Similar tactics have been used in recent years by impoverished
groups throughout America. The welfare rights movement, for
example, greatly expanded the availability of assistance for the poor
through demonstrations, occupation of welfare offices, disruption
of local government functions and similar tactics. Likewise, squatters' movements in a number of cities have found unoccupied
housing for homeless families, moved them in and protected them
from attempts at eviction. As hard times deepen, more and more
people may be forced to turn to such techniques to meet their
immediate needs.

Where food, clothing, housing, utilities and other vital necessities
are at hand, people can join together to make sure they are available
to all who need them without regard to "property rights," by
pressuring those in power, or, more directly, by occupying housing,
making their own utility connections and distributing the contents of
stores and warehouses to those in need—all techniques applied
during the Great Depression.

The essence of depression, however, is that people not only lack
things they need, but are unable to produce them. As we have seen,
the equipment and resources necessary to produce exist, but are not
profitable for owners to use. The result: The means of production
stand idle while those who could use them are unemployed. Under
such conditions, the rational way for people to meet their needs is to
ignore established rules of ownership and use the means of produc-

tion to produce the things they need. Sometimes small groups of workers try to do this by themselves. In the 1930s, for example, thousands of unemployed coal miners dug their own mines on company property, used the coal for themselves or trucked it to the cities and sold it below the commercial rate. When company police tried to close their mines, the miners frequently defended themselves by force, usually with strong community support. In France in 1973, workers occupied a watch factory that management had planned to close and began producing watches under their own control, which they sold through workers' organizations throughout the country.

There are usually strong odds against such attempts by isolated groups of workers to take over workplaces and produce for themselves. They usually lack the resources to compete with giant corporations; they generally have to accept conditions as bad or worse than workers elsewhere; and they are not likely to be permitted to use privately owned productive property for long without being violently attacked. Such actions still leave the participants at the mercy of those who control the rest of society.

Though such isolated attempts by workers to produce for themselves are almost bound to fail, they point the way toward a genuine alternative to the minority control of society. If people are to avoid the terrible and unnecessary suffering that accompanied the last great depression, they will have to produce the things they need, even though such production is not profitable for the owners. To do so, the majority will have to take over the productive resources of society as a whole for their own use. Such a strategy may appear radical and impractical in normal times, but under depression conditions it may well be the only practical alternative to impoverishment and endless misery for the great majority. Whether to adopt such a strategy or accept their suffering passively will be up to that majority to decide.

8. ENVIRONMENT: NATURAL AND SOCIAL

THE QUALITY OF LIFE

It may seem that when you leave work you are entering a realm of freedom where you can live as you like, at least within the limits of your income. In reality, however, everyone lives in an environment which includes other people, the things they have produced and nature as people have transformed it.

Most people have little control over the environment in which they have to live. They don't decide the quality of the air they breathe or the water they drink; they have little choice in what they hear and see around them. Yet it is their own labor that shapes that environment. In Gary, Indiana, steelworkers run giant mills that pour smoke and poison into the air they breathe when they go home. In Albany, New York, construction workers tore down housing to build a downtown mall, driving thousands of people into already overcrowded slums, and a few, reportedly, into living in the streets and parks. In Detroit, auto workers wait restlessly, ensnarled in traffic jams caused by the cars they have built.

Because people do not control their cooperative activity at work, they cannot control the environment it shapes. They create that environment, but in the interest and under the orders of their employers. Wherever you go, your surroundings are shaped by the interaction of powerful business and governmental organizations that control other people's labor. This situation underlies the powerlessness that many people experience even off the job.

To a limited extent, people can select the surroundings in which they will live. If you are wealthy, you may be able to have your own estate and shape it to your personal desires; if you don't have to work, you can avoid environments you don't enjoy. But if you aren't rich, you have to live someplace you can afford; and if you have to work, you have to go where the jobs are. The result is that for most people the choice is limited. For instance, recent surveys indicate that nearly 40 percent of Americans would like to live in rural areas, but less than 20 percent do so. Eight out of ten people living in cities would rather live in the country or suburbs.[1] America's cities are filled with homesick migrants who have had to leave the impoverished mountains and hollows of their birth in search of jobs in the city.

Nearly one American in five moves every year, the great majority in search of "economic opportunity." Such moves are voluntary only in the sense that hungry animals run a laboratory maze "voluntarily" in order to receive food. In truth, they are responses to employers' decisions about where to locate the jobs. As urban historian Sam Bass Warner concluded: "The magnitude of the corporate and federal effort has in large measure determined the national location of jobs; it has designated the industries and places where jobs would be plentiful and where they would be sparse."[2] It thereby largely determines where most people have to live.

In recent years, there has been a widespread feeling that the entire environment, social and natural, is deteriorating. This has often been discussed in terms of a declining "quality of life." This phrase, however undefinable, captures something very real that you experience as you move through a dirty, crowded city street, closed in by decaying buildings, assaulted by harsh noises and smells, surrounded by poverty and unmet needs. In part, it is the "urban crisis," the breakdown of facilities and opportunities that was dramatized by the massive riots of the mid-1960s. In part, it is the "ecology crisis," the destruction of the natural environment, brought to public attention by widespread agitation a few years later. In part, it is simply the endless hassle of trying to function in surroundings over which you have no control.

This deterioration of the environment has sometimes been blamed on excessive economic growth, but it would be fairer to attribute it to a social organization which prevents people from cooperating to meet their own needs. The shortage of housing, medical care and other urban facilities, and the failure to install nonpolluting technologies, result from the priorities of profitability. They are further aggravated by the onset of hard times, which have reduced the resources available for such purposes. The degeneration of the natural and social environment is part and parcel of the general decline in the conditions of life that most people now face.

HOW OUR ENVIRONMENT WAS SHAPED

The same forces that turned most Americans into workers shaped the environment in which they live. When the first Europeans visited

America, they found a continent of wilderness sparsely populated by tribes of Indians who hunted, fished and farmed. Over the next three hundred years, immigrants and their descendents settled much of it with family farms and artisan-based towns. But with improvements in transportation, the growing scale of markets and the increasing number of workers under each employer, the natural and social environment increasingly came to be formed by the drive to accumulate wealth.

The natural environment was developed with thought for little besides profit. Where such natural resources as timber, coal, minerals or fertile land were found, they were taken over by private enterprises and developed for their profit, regardless of the effect on either nature or society. As mechanization allowed an increase in the size of agricultural operations, vast numbers of farms were deserted or concentrated into large "factory farms," increasingly controlled by corporate "agribusiness," while many rural people festered in poverty or migrated to urban areas. In the past, forests were stripped and farmland turned to dust bowl in the search for profit. Today, it is coal land that is being stripped and oil-bearing shale land that will soon be strewn with rubble.

Even more devastating to the natural environment have been the polluting substances that have been poured into the air, water and land. While industrial cities have always been notorious for their foul air, pollution has reached crisis proportions since World War II. Between 1946 and today, environmental pollution levels have increased between 200 percent and 2000 percent. As professor Barry Commoner has convincingly shown, most of this increase results neither from rising population nor from increased private consumption; the effect of both these factors combined explains only a small fraction of the increased pollution levels.[3] Instead, as Commoner established, "the chief reason for the environmental crisis that has engulfed the United States in recent years is the sweeping transformation of productive technology since World War II."[4] Business has introduced hundreds of new processes which affect the environment, with little concern for the effects on the people who live there, let alone the rest of nature. Examples include fertilizers and pesticides, synthetic fibers, detergents, plastics, chlorine, mercury, concrete, lead additives for gasoline and high-compression engines. Most of the polluting substances released into the environment by these technologies are emitted in the production process: industry accounts for half of all air pollution and more than half of all water pollution.[5] But even when the environment is polluted by the auto exhaust, soft-drink containers or other wastes apparently generated by ordinary people, those people had no say in designing the high-compression and high-pollution engines, nonreturnable containers and other "advances" responsible for the pollution.

The consequence of environmental pollution is not merely smog-filthy air, stinking rivers and blighted landscapes. At the very least it means that a certain number of people will die before their time of cancer, respiratory ailments and other pollution diseases. At worst, it may have the results that Professor Commoner has soberly suggested:

> The present course of environmental degradation, at least in the industrialized countries, represents a challenge to essential ecological systems that is so serious that, if continued, it will destroy the capability of the environment to support a reasonably civilized human society.[6]

The same social forces that affected the natural environment have shaped and reshaped the patterns of urban and rural America. Where waterways and potential railroad routes made transportation profitable, cities were built. The population increased steadily in and around urban centers, as employers sought the advantages of being near markets, suppliers and workers. Such large agglomerations of enterprises and people required massive transportation and educational, medical and waste disposal facilities, which in turn increased urban concentration still further. The largest cities became diversified producers of many products, as well as commercial and financial centers, while smaller cities surrounding them specialized in a few products for which they provided a profitable location. A disproportionate number of all cities were located in three industrial belts, each about five hundred miles long, in the Northeast, Midwest and, more recently, southern California—each known today as a megalopolis. The accumulation of tens of millions of people in large urban belts destroyed the natural ecology of hundreds of thousands of square miles, while producing sufficient waste to poison much of the surrounding land and water.

Early American cities consisted of a thoroughly mixed collection of houses, workshops, small factories, stores, warehouses and other buildings, all standing side by side. But in the years following the Civil War, a new pattern developed which has lasted until recently. As cities grew, competition for space in the central areas became ever more intense, the price of land rose, and lucrative commercial and financial operations—with their skyscrapers and giant stores—came increasingly to dominate the downtown areas. Surrounding this core developed wholesalers, warehouses and multistory factories that required little land. Radiating outward from the center of the city were manufacturing sectors, built along the main lines of water and railroad transportation. As many industrial enterprises grew, they moved farther and farther out along the transportation lines from the central city, seeking cheap and plentiful land, and in some cases an escape from city taxes and labor movements.

Filling the spaces between the "industrial fingers"[7] were residential neighborhoods. In early American cities, most housing was not segregated by income. There might be an occasional small slum quarter or a fashionable street or two inhabited by the rich, but cities were mostly made up of mixed neighborhoods with prosperous homes, boarding houses, workers' cottages and shanties, all side by side with stores and small factories.[8]

About one hundred years ago this pattern changed sharply. In the 1870s, the middle classes began moving to suburbs beyond the fringe of the city, commuting to downtown offices and stores. Streetcars and other mass transportation soon accelerated this migration. By the turn of the century, most American cities were composed of concentric rings, strongly segregated by income. Around the central business district was a band of old, often decaying buildings into which immigrants, the poor and, later, blacks were concentrated. Surrounding this inner core was a belt of working-class housing—row houses, apartments, two- and three-family houses and small detached homes crowded onto tiny patches of land. Beyond this lay the suburbs of the middle classes, themselves considerably segregated by income.[9] There was often one exception to this pattern of concentric rings: If the inner city possessed a particularly attractive area of high elevation or unindustrialized waterfront, it might serve as a residential preserve of the rich.[10]

As part of the economic expansion that followed World War II, a new urban organization was laid on top of the old one, transforming how and where people live and work. The key to the new pattern was the high-speed highway cutting between, around and through nearly all major cities, often destroying and dividing whatever urban neighborhoods lay in its path. The most common pattern for these highways is a wheel with an inner belt surrounding the downtown area, an outer belt surrounding the city at the fringe of the built-up area, and spokes running from the center outward. In some of the largest cities, notably Los Angeles, the highways do not converge on any one center, but form a grid through a vast, decentralized urban area. We found in our travels that we could make sense of almost any city we visited, armed only with a freeway map and knowledge of these general patterns.

135

Living

The building of high-speed highway networks and the development of efficient diesel trucking freed industrial companies from the need for downtown and railroad locations. Since World War II, therefore, there has been a vast migration of industry from the center of the city to cheaper land in the surrounding areas, especially since cheap land allowed modern, one-story factories, parking lots and surrounding yard space. An old-timer in Detroit described how production had moved out of the city to the urban rim. "They haven't closed many plants," he told us, "but the ones in the city have far fewer workers than they used to. The new, modernized plants are in the suburbs."

Four-fifths of all new jobs in large metropolitan areas during the 1950s and '60s were in the suburbs.[11] Just from 1960-68, male employment decreased 3½ percent in central cities and increased 26 percent in suburban rings.[12] "Industrial parks" set in the middle of undeveloped land lined the superhighways. Older, less dynamic and profitable companies—paying lower wages—tended to stay behind in the inner city. Retailing likewise moved to suburban areas; by 1974, more than half the country's retail business was being done in some 14,000 shopping centers, mostly in the suburbs.[13]

The expansion of highways and the decentralization of jobs, combined with rising incomes, made it possible for millions of people to move from city to suburbs. In 1950, roughly one-third of Americans lived in central cities; by 1970 this proportion had decreased slightly, despite the great influx of rural migrants. However, the proportion of Americans living in metropolitan areas but outside central cities increased from less than one-fourth in 1950 to over one-third in 1970.[14] The cheaper land in the "urban fringe" allowed free-standing single family houses with larger yards and the other advantages of relatively low-density housing. They were occupied by managers, professionals and the better-off white- and blue-collar workers. An estimated 60 percent of AFL-CIO members, for example, live in suburban areas.

For many families, the ability to buy a home in the suburbs was the most dramatic improvement of living standards accompanying post-World War II prosperity. On the other hand, moving to the suburbs often meant leaving urban neighborhoods in which they had deep community roots based on ties of family, nationality and decades of informal social contact in stores, churches, schools and the street. Suburban life, for all its advantages, often lacked the interest and community of older inner-city neighborhoods. As Sam Howard explained:

Most of the white factory workers around Chicago live in the southwest. That's where you'll find the rows of ticky-tacky boxes. I grew up there. There is absolutely nothing for kids to do. At least up here on the North Side there are a few bars and places to go. When I see people from back down there, they all tell me the same thing. You might as well get in a coffin, pull down the lid over it and wait.

A number of factors, most associated with the end of the post-World War II era of prosperity, indicate that the period of residential suburbanization and upgrading has drawn to a close. It has grown steadily harder for many families with limited incomes to buy a house at all, let alone one in the suburbs. Despite the maturation of the "baby boom" generation, fewer housing units were started in the 1960s than in the 1950s.[15] More and more of these were apartments; single-family homes constituted over 80 percent of housing starts in 1959, but had dropped to 55 percent in 1969.[16] Overall housing costs nearly doubled in the last twenty years, rising even faster than most other prices. According to Senator Harrison Williams' calculations,

> far more than half of the families in this country cannot afford to buy housing. . . . The average family income in the United States is about $11,000 a year. If you take the rule of thumb that one should not spend more than 2½ times one's family income for housing, this means that half of all American families cannot afford to buy a home costing more than $27,500. And that is a full $7,500 below the average cost of a new home.[17]

The result, a *New York Times* article reported, is that "in nearly all areas of the nation rising home costs are slowly putting the dream of a family house out of reach of many young families."[18]

At the same time, the suburbs themselves have lost much of their appeal as an escape from the undesirable aspects of urban life. Herman Miller of the Census Bureau reports that "the suburban slum-ghetto is becoming a visible, though unmeasured, phenomenon in many large metropolitan areas, particularly those around older cities."[19] Nearly 10 percent of the suburban population was poor by the official federal standards of the 1960s.[20] In 1973, serious crime rose 3 percent in cities, but 10 percent in the suburbs, according to FBI statistics—part of a continuing trend.[21] Many suburbs have become, in effect, "outer cities," barely distinguishable, except for a somewhat larger lot size, from the large tracts of single-family housing for workers that marked traditional cities.

With the migration of jobs and homes to the suburbs came the rise of the auto and the decline of public transportation. The number of urban transit riders decreased yearly after 1945, until by 1973 it was barely more than a quarter of its wartime peak.[22] Today, thirty-six of the forty-seven million Americans who work in metropolitan areas get to work by car, while only five and one-half million get there by subway, streetcar, bus or railroad.[23] The distance between home and job averages between five and six miles.[24]

Many workers will commute anywhere in their metropolitan area, sometimes sixty miles or more each way, allowing access to a wider range of jobs but tying up larger amounts of time getting there and back. The migration of jobs and the atrophy of public transit have made car ownership a ticket of admission to most of the urban job market. Workers without cars—usually those with low incomes living in inner cities, especially women—are thus largely excluded from the better jobs on the urban rim, and are thereby locked into chronic unemployment, underemployment or low-paying inner-city jobs.

The decisions which have shaped the social and natural environment have rarely if ever been controlled by those they have affected. Nor have they been made by any single authority. In general, the environment has been shaped by the often contradictory actions of conflicting companies and agencies. While attempts at city, regional and environmental planning have frequently been made, the planners have rarely had sufficient power to control private interests, and in many instances have simply furthered the objectives of those interests. The result has been to compound powerlessness with chaos.

In the period of general economic growth following World War II, many people experienced an apparent improvement in their surroundings. But the unplanned consequences of that growth actually contributed greatly to the deterioration of the environment. As "hard times" reduce the resources available to improve the natural and social environment, that deterioration becomes an ever-greater threat to people's desire for pleasant and healthy conditions of life.

COMMUNITY ACTION

Over the past few years there have been many and various attempts by people to affect their natural and social environment. Community movements have used tactics ranging from lobbies to mass demonstrations, sit-ins in government offices, blockades of construction sites, occupation of vacant buildings by squatters, rent strikes and riots. Their objectives have included preventing the destruction of neighborhoods by highways and urban renewal, controlling neighborhood social institutions, closing down local polluters, affecting the location of schools, airports and other public facilities, turning vacant land into neighborhood parks, protesting police brutality, preventing evictions—in short, they have tried to deal with almost every aspect of the environment that impinges on daily life. While many of these actions have failed, there have been some notable victories as well.

A number of factors make it more difficult for people who live in the same area to get together than it is for those who work in the same workplace. Neighborhoods often include a greater mix of social groups with conflicting interests—renters, owners and landlords, blue- and white-collar workers, businessmen and professionals may live within a few blocks of each other. Neighbors are not together continuously in the same way they are at work, making informal coordination more difficult. People do not face the same kind of immediate enemy they do at work; their life is structured not by a clearly identifiable employer, but by an often-mysterious "they" which may include dozens of private and governmental power centers. At the same time, life is freer, so that the need to fight back often does not seem so pressing. Finally, people do not have the direct counterpower at home that their ability to stop production gives them at work. The main tactics available to them, therefore, are either working through established channels or direct physical disruption.

Nonetheless, when compelled by an immediate need or by an act of government or business that clearly affects the residents of an area in common, people can often organize themselves to act quite effectively. An example has been the continuing confrontation between East Boston, an old, stable, low-income community, and the nearby Logan Airport, run by the Massachusetts Port Authority. The airport over the years has destroyed more and more of the community's parks and housing. Planes have knocked down TV antennas and stripped trees of their leaves; airport electrical signals have disrupted TV reception; land use regulations have prevented needed residential construction in the vicinity of the airport. Most devastating of all has been the noise. A resident reported: "I have two children at high school, they say the noise is so unbearable teachers have to stop talking at their classes. It happens all day."[25]

Neighborhood organizations lobbied the state legislature for bills to ease the impact on East Boston, but with little effect; the only one to pass was a bill prohibiting the Massachusetts Port Authority from collecting bridge tolls from vehicles bearing the remains of deceased veterans. The failure of legislative remedies, the destruction of a beloved local park, the eviction of families and the destruction of their homes to make room for airport expansion led many in the area to turn to more militant tactics.

In September 1968, the residents of Maverick Street, tired of having six hundred trucks a day use their street going to and from the airport, decided to conduct a "baby-carriage blockade." A group of women and children parked themselves on the street and physically blocked the trucks for a week. Police were called, but turned out to be in sympathy with the blockaders. Under pressure from the mayor, the Massachusetts Port Authority finally agreed to construct a new road on airport property to relieve the traffic on Maverick Street.

Direct action tactics were next applied to oppose further airport expansion. In early 1969, residents conducted a series of coordinated slowdowns and blockades on bridges and tunnels leading to the airport. "Telephone trees" linked residents in various neighborhoods, allowing quick phone communication for such actions. The once-insular "Easties" joined city-wide antihighway demonstrations with their own anti-airport signs, and formed a coalition with other communities affected by the Massachusetts Port Authority. Demonstrations, mass attendance at hearings and other direct action techniques were used to oppose a proposed runway expansion, finally forcing the governor of the state to intervene against it. The noise and threat of Logan Airport still hang heavily on the people of East Boston, but so far at least they have succeeded in preventing the Massachusetts Port Authority from destroying their community altogether.

In nearby East Cambridge we saw an example of how rapid and massive community self-organization can be.[26] The traditional, quite decayed neighborhood includes people of Italian, Portuguese and Irish backgrounds and a few blacks; even the newspapers regularly refer to it as "working class." A high school student: "Most of the kids here drop out of high school. They take factory jobs, get bored in a week and quit. Then they just hang around here, drink and do downs, and sometimes do rip-offs."[27]

One Saturday night in October 1972, Larry Largey, a local boy who worked at a Macy's warehouse, got drunk and on his way home smashed the window of a Portuguese bookstore. A police paddy wagon arrived and Largey was put in the back by two policemen, one of whom was notorious throughout the city for his harassment of young people. (He had arrested two friends of ours at different times.) A family that lived across the street described how the two officers followed Largey into the wagon and closed the door: "We saw the wagon shake. The wagon was rocking like a roller coaster. . . . When the door opened, I looked into Largey's face and it was covered with blood."[28] Largey was taken to jail; a few hours later he was found unconscious in his cell and was dead-on-arrival at the hospital.

Police and press gave the impression that Largey had died of an overdose of alcohol and barbiturates, but his friends in East Cambridge felt that he had died as a result of a police beating. In the courtyard of the Roosevelt Towers housing project, center of the neighborhood, the kids talked about Larry's death. That night to protest, they set a fire in the street, waited for police to come, and then threw stones and bottles at them from the project roof. The next day they went over to a local community organization and asked them to put out a leaflet demanding the jailing of the policemen involved. That night they blockaded the main street of the neighborhood with a fiteen-foot wall of flaming wood and trash soaked with gasoline. The next night they set an aging Chevrolet on fire. The police chief arrived, got hit on the head by a bottle and offered a meeting the next afternoon.

There then began a curious pattern of action through government channels during the day, alternating with riots at night. At the meeting, various city officials explained to hundreds of kids from East Cambridge the various bureaucratic procedures that would be required to suspend the policemen. When the city manager admitted they were still drawing pay, the hall broke into loud booing. As one of the eyewitnesses of Largey's arrest put it, after an emotion-charged account of what he had seen: "I just want to ask one question. If I had a fight with a police officer, and he died the next morning, where would I be today?"[29] The East Cambridge kids were unimpressed by the politicians and officials on the stage. One of them summed up their strategy in a short speech before they left the hall: "We'll keep doing what we've been doing until they're suspended." That night the rioting continued, with two cars burned.

Next day, hundreds of kids marched on the Cambridge police station from housing projects in different parts of the city, while another contingent came in from the projects in neighboring Somerville. The crowd moved on to a special city council meeting, attended by an estimated 2000 people, mostly from East Cambridge. The mayor announced that two of the policemen had been placed on leave of absence without pay, and that the city government would begin an independent investigation. That night, for the fifth and last evening, there was substantial rioting in East Cambridge.

The gains won by this movement were modest at best—the policemen in question were never suspended, let alone tried, despite a finding by the city's investigator that at least one had used force "wholly unwarranted and without legal justification."[30] Perhaps more important, it gave the neighborhood some sense of its potential power. It showed possibilities for uniting groups that at other times had been quite antagonistic. The neighborhood has a reputation for severe racism, but we saw blacks and whites rioting happily side by side in the streets. Nor was the movement limited to young people, although they clearly led the way; hundreds of older East Cambridge residents were in the streets as well. The attitude of the older participants was illustrated by a middle-aged woman in the midst of a milling crowd who pushed into the street and began acting more aggressively than any of the kids around her; she yelled threateningly at the policemen standing there, cursing them roundly, then returned to the curb and shook her head, saying: "I can't blame these kids for what they're doing."

Since colonial times, riots have been a chronic feature of urban life—in the American Revolution they were known to political theorists as "the people out of doors." The reorganization of urban areas since World War II may have somewhat limited this type of action—riots are not too common in the suburbs. But for the more impoverished groups in the central city, they remain one of the few potential sources of power.

The restructuring of American cities has affected the kinds of collective action people can take in other ways. For example, it has widened the gap between work and neighborhood. At one time, many of the people in a particular urban neighborhood were likely to work for the same company or at least in the same industry. Working class communities often provided considerable support for workers engaged in strikes and other industrial conflicts; indeed, strikes sometimes became community struggles as well. Today, workers may not even work with anyone who lives in the same community. A union official at a plant outside Pittsburgh told us that their 2500 members lived in many dozen different towns, including semirural areas and even farms spread throughout two counties. Such a pattern makes community support for workers' action on the job far less automatic. In contrast, community support has been of great importance in a number of strikes, such as those by sanitation workers in Memphis and hospital workers in a number of cities, where the workers' homes are concentrated in inner-city ghettos.

The breakup of older urban neighborhoods may have another effect as well. A large proportion of urban American workers have been immigrants or the children of immigrants. To a considerable extent, their cultural roots and personal identification have been with their own nationality. Many workers felt that they belonged more to a particular ethnic community than to the working class. This feeling was reflected and strengthened by the fact that older urban neighborhoods were often defined more along ethnic than class lines. With the migration out of inner-city areas, these traditional ethnic distinctions often fade. As a team of sociologists studying newer working-class areas put it in the jargon of their profession:

> The residential areas where elements of older ethnic concentrations have regrouped into secondary ghettos . . . are characteristically far more homogeneous—they are *working class* ethnic communities—communities which need not be even ethnically homogeneous. The shattering of the old ethnic ghettos finds the resettlement area containing similar social class levels of differing ethnic groups. While there is a substantial continuing commitment to ethnic identification, there is also greater social and even physical distance between different social class groupings of the same ethnic groups. . . . Increasingly, even kinship identification fails to take precedence over social and physical distance. Thus, one can already begin to observe trans-ethnic class values taking on increased importance, particularly for the youth of these communities.[31]

While the impact of these changes is impossible to predict, they may make possible a far broader and more unified cooperation among working people of different backgrounds than has ever existed in the past.

The restructuring of the city may well have weakened the informal communications links among different groups of workers. For example, we were told that during World War II, the streetcars served as the nerve network by which workers throughout Detroit kept in touch. Morning gossip was the primary way people found out about job openings; it was also the way news of the almost daily sit-down and wildcat strikes was spread. Driving to work in your own car puts an end to that. Similarly, the dispersion of older urban neighborhoods dissolved many informal networks of friends and relatives through which workers supported each other. We found, however, that such networks still exist, spreading through entire metropolitan regions. A steelworker in Cleveland told us: "People have friends and relations all over the area in steel and auto plants." And an assembler in Cleveland reported: "The kids still know their high school friends. There are definitely networks that exist."

In general, these networks aren't used to coordinate any kind of action, or even to communicate what's going on at different places. A steelworker in Detroit observed: "The guys where I work are from the down-river area, around River Rouge. They don't seem to know much about what is going on in other plants or in the auto industry, although they do have friends and relatives that they see." Nonetheless, such networks could still be used for informal coordination on a metropolitan-wide basis, if there were a need or desire to use them that way.

Faced with a deteriorating social and natural environment, people may find large-scale community action more and more necessary. We have described several examples in which people organized themselves quickly to act on a massive scale. Most efforts were shortlived and relatively ineffective, however, reflecting the limitations of such community action.

Yet there are situations in which "the people out of doors"— large-scale mass action—may be a very effective tactic indeed. During the Great Depression, for example, unemployed workers halted thousands of evictions and forced improvements in welfare through mass actions that continued for months. In such times of social crisis, the community may be as much a focus of social struggle as the workplace.

Indeed, at such times the artificial separation between work and the rest of life may begin to break down. People at work may use their abilities to organize themselves and to halt production as means to support community struggles. In Italy, for example, it has become common in recent years for workers to strike over transportation issues and to pour out of their factories to defend squatters in nearby apartments from eviction attempts by the police. Community action, such as mass picketing or disruption, may likewise be used to support strikers, as was common during the great strikes of the 1930s. Such a merging of action at work and in the rest of the environment reveals the truth that it is above all the labor of people at work which shapes all social reality—and that they are the same people, whether at work or away.

Ultimately, the problem of the environment is that most people are excluded from control of the labor that shapes their surroundings. The decisive power to apply natural resources and labor—and thereby to shape the world we live in—lies in the hands of those who own the resources and direct the labor. As we have seen, they have little choice, as our society is organized, but to strive to accumulate power and profits before all else. The result is an environment that is poorly adapted to human needs at best, injurious to life and health at worst. Only by taking control of their cooperative labor can people gain the power to shape the environment. Even then, the creation of an environment adapted to their needs and desires will remain a monumental task—but one that they will at last be in the position to undertake.

Anne Dockery/Liberation News Service

III

THE WORKING CLASS

"Most current members of the working class, whatever their race,
sex or occupation, have shared two important historical
experiences. First, they have shared the expanding aspirations that
made a steady job and an adequate income no longer a
sufficient definition of a good life. Second, they have shared the
deterioration of real incomes and general social
conditions of the past few years, which have made it harder and
harder just to get by."

The Working Class

As we have seen, the great majority of Americans neither own the means of production nor control the production process, and therefore have to work for those who do.

The bulk of the profits produced by the working population belongs to those who own the natural resources, raw materials, machines, workplaces and other means by which wealth is produced. They form a social class that has been known as the ruling class, the wealthy or the capitalist class. By profession they are most often executives, businessmen and professionals, but they are wealthy enough to live without working should they so choose. We have already seen how small the class that owns the basic productive resources of our society really is: Such resources are held primarily by corporations, and 1.6 percent of the population owns four-fifths of all privately held corporate stock.

With the growing size of business enterprises and the growing complexity of society, the actual organization and direction of productive activities have largely been taken over by a class distinct from the owners of wealth.[1] This group has variously been called the managerial elite, the middle class and the new class. Its members are primarily managers, professionals, officials, supervisors and bureaucrats of all types. The widest definition of the managerial class might include the nearly 25 percent of the workforce who are classified in government statistics as managers, administrators, professionals and technicians. A narrow definition was given by *Fortune* magazine, which took this 25 percent and eliminated all those with incomes under $25,000 a year and all those who, like preachers, actors, athletes and funeral directors, did not have business decision-making authority. *Fortune* concluded that there were 250,000 managers and 50,000 scientists, engineers and professionals, who constitute the real managerial elite.[2] At the top, the managerial class fades into the capitalist class; at the bottom it fades into a broad group of lower level professionals and technicians, skilled workers, working foremen and others who share some characteristics with the managerial class and others with the working class.[3].

Most members of the managerial class are employees, but profoundly privileged ones. The income received by the best-paid 10 percent of the population—mostly managers and professionals—is substantially more than that received by the entire bottom half of the population.[4] Three-quarters of them own stock, though few own more than $10,000 worth.[5] In most cases, they have far more job security and far less reason to fear unemployment than other employees. While the objectives for which they work are usually set by others, they are likely to have far more chance to exercise autonomy and creativity in their work than most employees—indeed, it is precisely the fact that their work involves something more than the rote following of orders which makes them the organizers of social production.

In many cases, the labor of the managerial class involves directing the labor of others, and their jobs give them authority over other workers. Sometimes they make decisions that affect other workers, even though they do not give the orders personally. They are, in short, bosses. And yet they are in an ambiguous position, because they are also themselves employees with bosses, whom they may hate and fear as much as do other workers. This contradiction was dramatized in a conversation with a supervisor at a large computer company just before his Christmas vacation. He complained at length about the laziness of the workers under him, their lack of interest in their work and their desire to escape it. Then, toward the end, he turned to his wife and said, "Well, dear, only two more days at work and then—liberation from oppression."

These two highly privileged classes remain quite small in comparison to the overwhelming majority of the population whose labor actually produces and distributes social wealth, but who neither own nor direct the equipment and materials they use in that labor. This majority has been called the common people, the laboring class, the proletariat, the masses and the working class.[6] They must work to live; their jobs have little scope for autonomy or creativity; they work under the more or less constant direction of a boss; their physical conditions are often unpleasant and frequently unsafe. Their job situations are defined, not by their individual potentials, but by their position in society.

The core of the working class is the three-quarters of the employed population (and their families) who are either manual workers or low-level clerical, sales and service workers. As we have seen, there is also a broad group on the fringe who share some characteristics with the working class and some with the managerial class—technicians, "mass professionals" like teachers and nurses, working foremen and the like. Depending on where the dividing line is drawn, the working class might include anywhere from 75 percent to 90 percent of the population.

Manual and low-level white-collar workers are, roughly speaking, the three-quarters of the population with the lowest incomes. Their family incomes, even counting second breadwinners, averaged around $8000, about a third of the average income of the best-paid quarter of the workforce.[7] Individual incomes for nonsupervisory workers averaged $146 a week in January 1974—$7592 a year, assuming a worker was employed all year.[8] The highest paid 5 percent of manual workers earned about 80 percent more than the average manual worker, or less than $14,000 a year in 1974. Incomes of clerical workers fell below those of skilled manual workers. In short, most members of the working class make enough money to survive, but few make enough to live high.

Most workers are at the mercy of sickness, accidents and changes in markets, technologies and general economic conditions, over which they have no control. Most face lives of chronic insecurity. Sam Howard told a common story:

> My father worked for a paint company. He injured his back at work. The company refused to put him to work because of his injury; they refused to fire him. When he got a lawyer to start suing them they fired him outright. . . . Now he's left without a job.

Even the wife of a highly skilled front-end mechanic with a top working-class income and with skills in great demand told Joseph Howell:

> Everything is okay now with us moneywise. But if anything was to happen to Sam, like if he was to lose his job or something, we'd be back in the poorhouse. So I try not think too much about it. . . .[9]

For most working people, poverty is a constant and realistic threat. Contrary to widespread opinion, most poor people are not part of a social class separate from the working class, but are workers suffering hard luck or bad times. One large-scale study recently found that 40 percent of Americans had incomes so low that they qualified for welfare, food stamps or public housing, for at least one year between 1968 and 1973.[10] Similarly, a presidential commission discovered that one-third of households considered poor by government standards in 1966 had not been classified as poor the year before. As the Commission commented nonchalantly: ''This flow indicates that the risk of poverty is considerably more pervasive than has been imagined.''

Were the working class nothing but passive and isolated victims of social oppression, their conditions might signify little more than a collection of private miseries. But the working class is also a group whose members are capable of getting together and taking action. We have seen a variety of such cooperative efforts: guerrilla actions on the job, the early stages of trade unionism, strikes, boycotts and "the people out of doors."

Not surprisingly, such actions generally take the form of a struggle against employers and those who support them. For as we have seen, the conditions of working people on and off the job are shaped by the power of employers and the policies that reflect and protect that power. A struggle to change those conditions must be a struggle against those who determine and benefit from them.

Individually, members of the working class have little power. But their situations give them a strong incentive to join together. Particular groups of workers face the same immediate conditions and the same immediate enemy; all workers share the same general problems and the same relation to employers as a whole. By joining together, they can become stronger than those who oppose them.

The Division of Wealth

This chart shows the distribution of wealth among consumer units in 1962, the most recent year for which government figures are available. The richest 20 percent of Americans own three-quarters of all privately-held wealth. The poorest 60 percent own less than one-tenth. Such realities belie the myth that we live in a classless society.

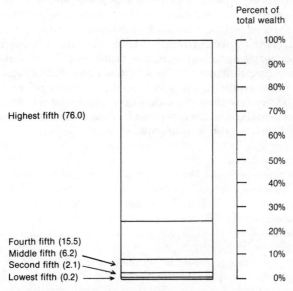

Source: *Social Indicators, 1973.* U.S. Department of Commerce, Washington, D.C., 1973.

Many divisions within the working class impede such cooperation. We have already seen some of them, such as the job classifica-
tions that often divide workers. In Part III, as we examine the
different parts of the working class, we will see many more—
differences of nationality, skill, income, occupation, race, sex and
age. Different groups within the working class experience their
subordination in their own particular ways, which seem to set them
apart from the rest of the class. If workers are to develop the power of
united action, they must deal with the problems of such groups and
dissolve divisive hostilities. A Boston truckdriver put the issue
sharply:

> The problem with having a revolution is that there are too
> many different kinds and groups of people. The country's full
> of different people—blacks, whites and everyone else. That's
> why in *this* country you won't have any big change. People are
> at each other's throats. . . . Of course, come to think of it,
> maybe it could happen if everyone had the same beef.

Overcoming the divisions among different groups of workers and
building cooperation among them is a historical process. It has its
roots in people's day-to-day cooperation at work, in neighborhoods
and in the other social spheres in which they live. In certain historical
periods of mass strike and social upheaval, such actions have spread
to all parts of the working class, making visible the ability of working
people to direct their own activity in their own interest, their capacity
to cooperate on the widest scale, and the enormous power they
possess when they do so. If a society of people cooperating directly
to meet their common needs is possible, these actions are the seeds
from which it is most likely to grow.

9. BLUE COLLAR

Factory workers, teamsters, railroad workers, construction workers, mill hands, miners, lumbermen, sailors—manual labor from the start has included a wide range of occupations with differing conditions and patterns of work. Into these jobs have been drawn European peasants and American farmers and sharecroppers driven from their lands; urban artisans squeezed out of their trades; migrants from all over the world seeking to escape poverty and oppression. Yet despite their diversity of occupation and background, blue-collar industrial workers until fairly recently formed a distinct social group and were often felt to comprise the entire working class.

The first wage workers in America may well have been artisans reduced to the status of employees and young women from farm families coming to work a few months or years in the cotton mills of New England. But by 1887, a clergyman was able to report: "Not every foreigner is a workingman, but in the cities, at least, it may almost be said that every workingman is a foreigner."[1]

Immigrants have come to the United States from every country in the world. Up to 1880, nine-tenths of all immigrants came from England, Germany, Scandanavia and Ireland.[2] In the decades following 1840, famine drove 1.25 million destitute Irish to the United States. They furnished much of the unskilled labor for canals, railroads and other public works, and settled in the eastern cities, where they became construction or factory workers. Industrially experienced German and British immigrants provided much of the skilled labor.

After 1880 there began the "new immigration" of people from southern and eastern Europe—Italians, Hungarians, Poles, Jews, Russians and others. Most came from peasant backgrounds and started as unskilled workers in the United States.

World War I and the restrictive immigration laws passed in its

153

aftermath severely reduced the flow of workers from southern and eastern Europe. Mexicans and later Puerto Ricans became the main foreign source of labor. Meanwhile, the introduction of farm machinery forced large numbers of farmers and their children into the industrial work force, especially white and black farmers from the South. Where 90 percent of Americans worked in agriculture in 1800, the proportion fell to 53 percent in 1870, 21 percent in 1930[3] and 3.8 percent in 1972.[4] Over 20 million Americans have left farms since 1940.[5] Those leaving the farm swelled the industrial labor force; 5.75 million of the 30 million blue-collar workers in the United States in 1958 were born and raised on U.S. farms.[6] A recent easing of immigration restrictions allowed nearly half-a-million foreigners to enter the United States in 1968 alone, primarily Italians, Greeks, Portuguese, Chinese and Filipinos.[7]

Because of its diversity of backgrounds, the American working class never developed a common class culture like that of many European countries.[8] The life possibilities of American workers were limited in the same ways by their common class position, but their life styles were more likely to be determined by ethnic and religious background than by any common working-class culture. From the last quarter of the nineteenth century until recently, neighborhoods, churches and associations were organized along ethnic far more than class lines.[9]

Virtually from the start of immigration, employers exploited the divisions between native and immigrant to prevent workers from combining. Harriet Martineau's account, *Society in America*, reported that in the 1830s employers hired foreigners as their "only safeguard" against workers' attempts to improve conditions through strikes.[10] A labor paper in Massachusetts complained in 1845 that the capitalists of Danville protected themselves against "disorderly strikes" by importing surplus help from England,

> whose abject condition in their own country has made them tame, submissive, "peaceable and orderly citizens," that is, ready to work fourteen and sixteen hours a day for what capital sees fit to give them.[11]

Similarly, different immigrant groups were used as strikebreakers against each other. In 1846, a large number of Irish laborers in New York struck for 87½ cents a day. The New York *Weekly Tribune* reported that the contractors hired

> a cargo of freshly landed Germans to take their places and ordered the old laborers to quit the premises, which they

refused to do and resorted to the lawless and unjustifiable step of endeavoring to drive the Germans from the work by intimidation and violence. Of course the military was called out, the Irish overawed, the Germans protected in their work, and thus the matter stands.[12]

As the working class expanded, it also became a permanent fact of American life. The frontier moved ever further from the centers of population, and the new industrial workers lacked the capital, skills and often the inclination to take up farming. The result was a class dependent on the ability of employers to make a profit from their labor, and therefore subject to unemployment and economic insecurity. Even in "good times" there was often unemployment; in the summer of the prosperous year of 1845 there were an estimated 20,000 unemployed in New York City,[13] and there have been few times since—except during wars—when unemployment has been negligible. But "hard times" were frequent, for the new system was marked by periods of stagnation and depression in which hundreds of thousands of workers were laid off and unable to find other work.

Though all workers faced the same economic insecurity and subjugation to the employer, their particular conditions varied enormously. Some were able to maintain a stable and even prosperous life, either through possession of needed skills, through organization or through the good fortune of having a fairly secure job with a prospering employer. Others, unable to establish themselves in these ways, faced chronic unemployment and jobs of short duration, low pay and substandard conditions. The differential among various working-class jobs resulted from a number of factors: the deliberate policy of employers, the power of certain well-organized groups of workers, the shortage or excess of certain skills and the sheer random chaos of the labor market. The result was, in effect, an "occupational ladder," up (or down) which an individual worker might move.[14]

Disadvantaged groups tended to be concentrated at the bottom of the industrial hierarchy: recent immigrants, those without skills or education or those living in underdeveloped parts of the country like the South, older workers past their physical prime, and later such discriminated-against groups as blacks, Puerto Ricans and Chicanos. The better jobs generally went to those groups which had had the longest chance to accumulate seniority, develop skills and "learn their way around." Many times it was a matter of sheer luck; one worker might arrive at the factory gate just in time to be hired for what proved to be a steady job, while another who had applied there the day before might remain part of the chronically unemployed.

Many workers were gradually able to climb the "occupational ladder" and achieve a more secure place for themselves or their children. Nonetheless, even the most favored workers were vulnerable to being cast among the unemployed by hard times, business failures or changing technology.

Conditions varied greatly between the relative prosperity of the better-off parts of the working class and the poverty of those at the bottom.[15] Throughout the history of the American working class, many workers lived in solid working-class districts—the predecessors of today's working-class suburbs—or at least avoided the severe overcrowding of the slums. A piano in the home and a business suit on the street were common symbols of respectability, if not affluence. A visitor to the United States wrote in 1837:

> On entering the house of a respectable mechanic [skilled worker] in any of the large cities of the United States, one cannot but be astonished at the apparent neatness and comfort of the apartments, the large, airy parlors, the nice carpets and mahogany furniture and the tolerably good library, showing that the inmates are acquainted with the standard works of English literature.[16]

For the impoverished part of the working class, the picture was quite different. Many were migratory workers, floating from job to job in lumber camps, mines and farms. More—the urban poor—were forced into sweatshops, general labor, service work and other marginal jobs with low pay, terrible conditions and no chance for permanent employment, let alone advancement. They were crowded into unhealthy urban slums with poor health and atrocious sanitation. A report of the Committee on Internal Health in Boston described conditions in a house in Half-Moon Place in 1849, where dozens of people lived in a triple cellar:

> One cellar was reported by the police to be occupied nightly as a sleeping-apartment for thirty-nine persons. In another, the tide had risen so high that it was necessary to approach the bedside of a patient by means of a plank which was laid from one stool to another; while the dead body of an infant was actually sailing about the room in its coffin.[17]

Many workers did not at first accept their new position as a permanent wage-earning class; they looked for alternatives to the new capitalist control of production. But capitalism did not go away, and as it continued to expand, the hopes that the growth of wage labor could be prevented gradually faded. In their place came three broad types of action through which workers and groups of workers have striven to survive and improve their condition. First, workers have tried to win out in individual competition—the struggle to "get ahead" or at least to keep your head above water when others are going under. Second, particular groups of workers—organized along ethnic, craft, sex, industrial or other lines—have tried to monopolize parts of the labor market and thereby gain partial control over their conditions of labor. Third, workers have tried to use their potential social power—their great numbers, concentration and critical position in the functioning of society—to force changes in their condition. No doubt many individuals tried more than one of these strategies at the same or different times.

The existence of an industrial hierarchy meant that workers or their children could hope to advance as individuals. Many tried to rise to positions as skilled workers or foremen through seniority, skills, "connections" and loyalty to the employer. As industry expanded, newcomers poured into the unskilled jobs, creating a genuine opportunity for many of those who had seniority to rise. Some workers tried to save enough money to go into business for themselves, escaping wage labor and perhaps even becoming employers, but this became ever harder as the amount of capital needed to compete successfully grew larger and larger. For many, the attempt to get a good education for themselves or their children was seen as the key to a better job, and the sacrifices made by working-class parents to educate their children from the early 1800s to the present have often been little short of heroic.[18] These possibilities for "getting ahead" helped keep alive the idea of "economic individualism" that had arisen in the far different society of individual proprietors of early America.

An alternative approach was adopted by many workers who had a skilled craft or trade. This was the attempt to create a protected market for the labor of a limited number of workers through closed shops and apprenticeship regulations. If only union members could work at certain jobs and membership was kept small, good wages and conditions could be maintained through trade agreements with the employers, albeit at the expense of those excluded. (In practice, most craft unions excluded women, blacks and the unskilled, and often restricted membership to particular ethnic groups or even particular families.) Craft unions following this strategy made up the American Federation of Labor, and were increasingly successful within their limited spheres, particularly in construction and other high-skill, competitive industries. Their members composed a "labor aristocracy," the most advantaged section of the working class. With the rise of industrial unionism in the 1930s, skilled workers still tried to protect their privileged position through wage differentials, separate seniority lists and "skilled trades" divisions within the industrial unions.[19]

A third type of action was based on the power of workers to disrupt or halt the normal functioning of industry or even society through such direct action techniques as strikes, general strikes, occupations, mass picketing, demonstrations, riots and even virtual armed uprisings. These movements often involved solidarity and simultaneous action among workers of many occupations, industries, regions, nationalities and races—at times approaching general movements of the entire working class. Although such movements have been pointedly ignored in many history texts, millions of workers have repeatedly participated in them throughout the past hundred years.[20] At times workers have taken such action in retaliation against wage cuts, speed-ups or attempts to break strikes. At other times they have used it to force employers to recognize unions and thereby establish "a sort of equilibrium in the power of the conflicting classes." And occasionally workers have seen such actions as part of an effort to abolish their subordinate position altogether—not to replace it with a return to the precapitalist world of the independent proprietor, but with a new organization of society in which workers would control their own labor and share its fruits. Thus, for example, participants in the Seattle General Strike of 1919, who managed most of the city's essential activities for the days of the strike, saw their activity as a preparation for the day workers would run the whole of society for themselves. Their newspaper stated:

> We see but one way out. In place of two classes, competing for the fruits of industry, there must be, eventually ONLY ONE CLASS sharing fairly the good things of the world.[21]

The Industrial Workers of the World, a union federation whose members were largely drawn from the more depressed migratory and factory sectors of the working class, saw strikes and direct action on the job as a preparation for a general strike through which workers would take over social production for themselves. These were only the more conscious expressions of a general striving for more power over their lives and over society that many workers revealed in thousands of strikes and upheavals.

One of the widespread social myths that accompanied the post-World War II prosperity was that blue-collar industrial workers were becoming an ever-smaller and less significant part of the population.[22] Official statistics were widely quoted to show that America had changed from a nation of blue-collar goods producers to one of white-collar service producers. These figures reflected two important trends—the great decrease in the number of agricultural workers and the great influx of women into office, sales and service jobs. But among male workers, the proportion in blue-collar industrial work has remained impressively high. Here are the figures:

PERCENT OF BLUE-COLLAR WORKERS IN MALE LABOR FORCE

1930	45.25
1950	48.4
1972	47

There are, in fact, more blue collar workers today than at any time in American history.

With the current deterioration of wages and living standards, industrial workers are again becoming recognized as a group. Their strikes are part of the daily news. Politicians publicly court their vote. Popular music, especially the recently resurgent country music, speaks straightforwardly of the workingman. These phenomena reflect a new awareness that many blue-collar workers have of themselves. Where that awareness will lead, time will tell.

Minton Brooks/Liberation News Service

10. WHITE COLLAR

Until the beginning of the twentieth century, the great majority of employees were manual wage workers. But with the growth of corporate business to gigantic size and the great expansion of record keeping and communications, there has been a tremendous expansion in low-level white-collar work, especially for women.

By far the fastest-growing group in the labor force has been clerical workers—they have increased from 3 percent in 1900 to 15 percent in 1960.[1] There were fifteen times as many secretaries, stenographers and typists in 1960 as in 1900.[2] Other swelling clerical occupations included bookkeepers, cashiers, office machine operators, bank tellers, ticket agents, telephone operators and shipping and receiving clerks. Similarly, the number of workers in finance, insurance and real estate has more than doubled since World War I, and the number of workers in trade has nearly tripled.[3] More than 30 percent of the manufacturing work force is now "white collar."[4]

At one time there was a great social gulf between "manual" workers in industry and "non-manual" workers in offices and stores. It was often assumed that this was the great division within society. In their classic study, *Middletown,* Robert and Helen Lynd found that the most important division within the population of the typical midwestern town whose life they examined was that between a "working class" who worked with things and a "business class" who dealt with people.[5] Every aspect of daily life, from where you lived to what time you got up in the morning, was determined by which of these two classes you belonged to—and there was no doubt in their minds that clerical and sales workers were on the "business class" side. Even today, the main division in government occupational statistics is between white-collar and blue-collar employees.

Today there is more difference within than between these categories. White-collar work has separated into two very different kinds of work. On the one hand, there is an elite of managers and professionals in business and government, drawing high salaries and generally commanding the labor of others. On the other, there is the great majority of clerical, sales and service workers whose incomes, working conditions and life prospects are far closer to those of blue-collar workers.

These two white-collar groups have been drawing apart in much the same way that journeymen and masters drew apart into workers and capitalists in the early nineteenth century. The result is to bring the lower-level white-collar workers ever closer to the position of industrial workers.

At one time, white-collar workers had higher incomes and far more job security than blue-collar workers. In 1929, for example, salaried employees earned 28 percent more than wage earners; in 1939 the figure was 30 percent. By 1944, however, wage earners were actually making more than salaried workers, and the two groups have been fairly close ever since.[6] White-collar workers once had substantial health, pension and vacation benefits, while blue-collar workers had few; today, blue-collar workers have almost caught up.[7]

White-collar workers were not subject to seasonal layoffs, and generally remained on payrolls even during the massive unemployment of the Great Depression. Today, layoffs of white-collar workers have become common, from either economic slowdowns or replacement by machine. In late 1973, for example, a Wall Street reporter described automation-related layoffs at Merrill Lynch, Pierce, Fenner & Smith and other brokerage houses in New York:

> Gone are the dozens of miniskirted young high school graduates who had flooded into Merrill's back offices in recent years to tend the clattering Teletype machines that once fed orders out. In their place sit a handful of seasoned employees, most of them middle-aged, quietly tending the computer outlets that allow each of them to do the work of two or three people.[8]

White-collar workers are often discharged with a callousness once reserved for their blue-collar counterparts. In late 1974, for example, the Macmillan Company, a big New York publisher, abruptly dismissed nearly one-sixth of its office employees, ranging from editors to maintenance staff, in response to poor business conditions and a union organizing drive. Those dismissed received a letter which began:

> The corporation has adopted a plan for curtailment of certain business activities in whole or part; consolidation of certain departments and divisions; and overall reduction of work force. We regret that we must inform you that your services will not be required beyond the close of business today.[9]

Blue-collar workers have achieved more job security through unions, while white-collar workers, according to *Work in America,* are viewed by management as "expendable": "Because their productivity is hard to measure and their functions often non-essential, they are seen as the easiest place to 'cut fat' during low points in the business cycle." The report went so far as to claim that "today, low-level white-collar workers are more likely to be sacrificed for the sake of short-term profitability than are blue-collar workers."[10]

Finally, the educational advantage of white-collar workers has decreased greatly, because of the increasing educational levels among blue-collar workers. The median number of years of school for clerical and sales workers increased only from 12.4 in 1948 to 12.6 in 1969. For craftsmen and foremen, the increase was from 9.7 to 12.1, and for operatives from 9.1 to 11.1.[11] These figures mean that a typical clerical or sales worker had 2.7 years more education than a skilled industrial worker or foreman in 1948, but only half a year more today.

Office work itself has grown steadily more factorylike as it has expanded, although it generally remains cleaner, quieter, safer and less arduous than most blue-collar work. It is largely built around machines—typewriters, adding machines and, more recently, computers. Jobs have become increasingly specialized as the work has been divided among a larger number of workers. Time-and-motion studies have been applied to office workers as greater use of machines has made production more subject to measurement and regulation. Computers have done little to make most clerical jobs more interesting; punch cards hold little more inherent fascination than file drawers.

There remain significant cultural differences between white- and blue-collar workers. Indeed, they may be the most significant differences left. White- and blue-collar workers often hold different conceptions of "respectability" and desirable life styles. However, even this cultural division has grown less, as the lower white-collar work force has been recruited increasingly from blue- as well as white-collar backgrounds.[12] Blacks have always been severely underrepresented among white-collar workers, but even this has begun to change; blacks increased from 5 percent of clerical workers in 1960 to 8 percent in 1970.[13]

White-collar workers have yet to reflect in action these changes in their conditions. Like impoverished aristocrats, many white-collar workers still cling to a degree of status based on the past, although it no longer corresponds to their real social position in the present. They often emphasize the status differences between themselves and blue-collar workers, and their closeness to management, even when this undermines their ability to struggle for their own interests. Their declining economic standing and their rapid approach to the position of blue-collar workers have even led at times to what one sociologist labelled "status panic."[14]

The white-collar workers' ties to management have also been maintained by a greater chance for advancement within the management hierarchy—at least for males—than that of blue-collar workers. Male clerical workers are about three times as likely to join management as their blue-collar counterparts.[15] To nurture such a carrot, as well as to keep clerical workers from completely goofing off, many business and government offices have an incredible proportion of supervisors—about one for every three-and-a-half workers.[16] Generally they are working supervisors who, while given responsibility for the work of others, must still continue to perform their own. While issues of favoritism in promotion have become a great source of resentment in many offices, the hope of "moving up into management" remains a potent lure for many white-collar workers. While most blue-collar workers think of themselves as holding jobs, many white-collar workers think in terms of having a career.

Although there have been many indications of growing white-collar discontent,[17] management has so far been able to defuse most of it. Office workers have raised to a high art the transformation of working time into reverie or socializing time, but they have frequently been less willing to stand up for their own interests than blue-collar workers. A young woman we talked with in Detroit who had worked in factories and now was working in the office at Chrysler summed up both the similarities and the differences this way:

> Of course, the people I work with now aren't as militant as the people on the line. For one thing, they come from the suburbs and think of themselves as a little more middle class—though

everyone knows they're a worker in that they are working to fill someone else's pocket. For another, the conditions aren't quite as bad—it's in an office, the heat doesn't go up to 120 degrees, and the supervisors are a little more polite. Nobody likes the bosses, but they're not hated the way they are in the plants. Every once in a while a production worker shoots a foreman, but the people I work with aren't going to kill any bosses.

The current rapid rise in the cost of living may give a fatal blow to much of the passivity of low-level white-collar workers. While many blue-collar workers have won some degree of compensation for inflation through strikes, unions and cost-of-living escalators, unorganized white-collar workers have little protection beyond the beneficence of their employers. Continued inflation may well lead them to try strikes and organization on a wide scale. For example, in the summer of 1974, employees at Harper & Row conducted one of the first strikes in the history of the book publishing industry. Workers in the publishing industry are highly stratified, but under the pressure of inflation, Harper & Row employees from lower level editors to stock clerks united in an independent employees' organization and stuck together until the strike was won. Such action, should it become widespread, would do much to dissolve the remaining distinctions between the white- and blue-collar sectors of the working class.

Laurie Leifer/Liberation News Service

11. FROM SLAVE TO WORKER

The historical experience of Americans of African origin—forced immigration and slavery—was far different from the experience of those who came from Europe. Even after the Civil War and the abolition of slavery, the position of black Americans was distinctive. As the black abolitionist Frederick Douglass, himself an ex-slave, pointed out:

> [Emancipation] left the freedman in a bad condition. It made him free and henceforth he must make his own way in the world. Yet he had none of the conditions of self-preservation or self-protection. He was free from the individual master, but the slave of society. He had neither money, property, nor friends. He was free from the old plantation, but he had nothing but the dusty road under his feet. . . . . He was turned loose, naked, hungry, and destitute to the open sky.[1]

Blacks faced the same fundamental situation as white workers—separation from the means of producing what they needed to live—but in a far more extreme form. T. Thomas Fortune, a black editor, wrote in 1884:

> To tell a man he is free when he has neither money nor opportunity is to mock him. To tell him he has no master when he cannot live except by permission of the man who monopolizes all the land is to deal in the most tantalizing contradiction of terms.[2]

Fortune's emphasis on the land was appropriate. Because the South remained primarily agricultural, most of the former slaves had little choice but to work for those who owned the land. In the decades following the Civil War, three out of five black men were employed

in agriculture.[3] While their labor took various forms—
sharecropping, tenant farming and wage labor—the reality was
generally the same poverty and lack of freedom. W.E.B. DuBois,
after the first serious sociological studies of the subject, concluded at
the turn of the century that "the keynote of the Black Belt is
debt. . . in the sense of continued inability of the mass of the
population to make income cover expenses." His detailed statistical
study of one county in Georgia found that with average agricultural
conditions, "the majority of tenants end the year even or in debt,
which means they work for board and clothes."[4] As late as the
mid-1930s, an observer of an Alabama cotton county could write:
"The plantation technique . . . has survived more or less despite the
formal abolition of slavery."[5]

A large proportion of those not engaged in agriculture were
concentrated in such largely rural work as lumbering, coal mining
and railroading, with many workers shifting back and forth between
those and farming. The small proportion who lived in cities worked
in what came to be labelled as "Negro jobs," such as domestic and
personal service, porters, draymen, laundresses and seamstresses.
Black artisans—more common than white ones in the South before
the Civil War—were increasingly excluded from the skilled trades.
Blacks were excluded from the burgeoning textile industry, except
for such jobs as sweeping and scrubbing.[6] In all areas, they were
forced into the worst jobs and the worst living conditions.

Until World War I, blacks remained overwhelmingly concentrated in the rural South. But in 1915 there began the "great
migration" which was eventually to lead to a complete transformation of blacks from predominantly southern rural farmers to predominantly northern urban workers. The initial trigger for this
change came primarily from the labor shortage created in northern
industry when European immigration was cut off by World War I.
A government report, *Negro Migration in 1916–17*, found:

> Employment managers and the higher executives of Northern
> industry are sadly worried by their labor problems. They feel
> that things are going from bad to worse; that even wage
> increases can avail little. . . . The majority of executives
> interviewed were favorable to the experiment with Negro
> employment in the North, and were sympathetic to sugges-
> tions concerning selection, training, housing, and recreation
> for the newcomer.[7]

Railroad and steel companies sent labor agents south to offer jobs
and transportation subsidies, while blacks already working in the
North wrote home about the new chances for employment. A survey

of major Chicago employers of black workers found that "inability to obtain competent white workers was the reason given in practically every instance for the large number of Negroes employed since 1914."[8] Between 1910 and 1920, the black population of Chicago more than doubled; that of Detroit increased sevenfold. This mass migration, slowed by depressions and rapidly accelerated by wars and other industrial labor shortages, has continued through today.

The pull from the cities was reinforced by a push off the land. Cotton prices collapsed early in the Great Depression, average acreage was cut in half and landowners converted tenants to wage workers or dismissed them entirely in order to take advantage of New Deal agricultural subsidies. Between 1930 and 1940, the number of black farm operators and laborers decreased by one-third.[9] Forced migrations began again after World War II, when the introduction of tractors and herbicides changed cotton production from year-round to seasonal labor. During the 1950s, cotton harvesting was further mechanized, and black farm workers, left with no employment on the land, had little choice but to migrate to the city or to starve. A tenant farmer in Humphreys County, Mississippi, indicated why:

> There used to be a whole lot more people on the plantation than there are now. The machines started long back in '50. I believe it really started back in '53, '54. Then every year they begin to get more and more, more and more, and that begin to cut people down out of the pickin', you know. In other words, before that they were pickin' all the crop. Then after machines got in, they started pickin' ends, see. And so now, the biggest of 'em not pickin' none.[10]

Since 1940, four million blacks have left the land. Their largely forced migration forms the background for many of the racial problems of today's cities.

Within the cities, there developed a separate labor market for black workers, which remains today. Only certain industries and particular firms within those industries normally hire black workers. A survey sampling companies in Chicago, for example, found that seven out of ten small firms, one out of five medium-sized firms, and one in thirteen large firms did not hire nonwhites, even in the late 1960s.[11] These patterns are perpetuated not only by employer prejudice, but by the geographic concentration of blacks in ghetto areas, and by the fact that many companies fill jobs with the friends and relatives of their own workers.

Further, there usually exists a racial hierarchy within each com-

169

pany. As two authorities on the Chicago labor market put what everybody knows:

> A good rule of thumb is that the lower the pay or the more disagreeable and dirty the job, the greater the chance of finding a high proportion of Negroes.[12]

Howard Kalado described to us the way this worked at the U.S. Steel plant in Gary, Indiana:

> Blacks are concentrated at one end of the mill with the furnaces and coke ovens—the hottest, dirtiest work. At the other end, where they finish the steel, the whites mostly work. In between it's mixed.

Blacks were practically excluded from the skilled trades as well. Even at the height of the civil rights movement and the tight labor market in 1965, a survey of forty companies by the National Industrial Conference Board found that "Negroes, generally, still are being hired for low-paying, low-status jobs. The number being employed in non-traditional Negro jobs is very small."[13]

Limited so often to such inferior jobs, black workers inevitably are subject to chronic poverty and frequent unemployment. Black unemployment rates normally run around twice that for whites, but even this understates the problem, since a large number of blacks, despairing or refusing to work under such dehumanizing conditions, drop out of the labor force altogether and vanish from the official unemployment statistics.

Long after the abolition of slavery, black Americans continued to be treated as a despised caste. The prejudice of many whites forced blacks to live in segregated ghettos, attend segregated schools and accept only those jobs whites themselves disdained.

Such "pariah groups" exist in many societies. In Japan, for example, a hereditary group called the *Barakumin* are segregated into special rundown ghettos, attend segregated schools, face discrimination in jobs and colleges, are discouraged from marrying other Japanese and face an unemployment rate of 35–50 percent— although they are identical with all other Japanese in appearance, language and race. Their status was established in the feudal period, on the basis of their performance of such religiously "unclean" occupations as leatherworking and butchering.[14] In the United States, the racial characteristics of skin color and physical features associated with it became the basis for such hereditary caste distinctions. From the early days of slavery, myths of black inferiority were created to justify inequality; an irrational amalgam of hate and fear was added, often as a means to rally all whites behind a racial domination that benefited the ruling white minority.

Once established, racial identification and the emotions that went with it—however irrational—tended to perpetuate themselves. Howard Kalado described to us the way such attitudes were adopted by those who grew up in his white neighborhood in Gary, Indiana:

> There is a deeply ingrained racism. I remember when I was young—every game was "catch a nigger"; if you smoked your cigarette funny you did it in a "nigger way"; everything was nigger this, nigger that.

Blacks have fought their oppression in many ways. Slave revolts began in the United States almost as soon as slavery—they could not be victorious only because slaves remained a minority, even in the South. Since emancipation, black strategies have reflected changing social conditions, different interests among blacks of different classes and varying responses among different groups of whites. Some strategies have involved alliances with the white upper classes; by such means, blacks at the turn of the century won financial support for black education and entry into many industries as strikebreakers. Some strategies have involved alliances with liberal whites to challenge discrimination through legal and political action; such were the civil rights movements of the 1950s and early '60s. Some attempted to build up the economic and social power of the black community itself through cooperatives, black businesses and nationalist organizations; this was the strategy of the massive movement led by Marcus Garvey after World War I, and of the "black power" movement of the late 1960s. Some involved using the mass power of black ghetto dwellers to disrupt urban life as a means of protesting their condition; the riots of the late sixties were largely such a protest. And some have involved cooperation with working-class whites against their employers and other shared enemies; the Populist movement at its peak in the late nineteenth century, the industrial union movements of the 1930s and a number of recent attempts at militant direct action at work exemplified this approach.

Antagonism between whites and blacks has often been exploited by employers to divide workers along race lines and prevent their recognition of common interests. As early as 1877, for example, a coal company imported four hundred black workers from Kentucky and West Virginia to break a strike by coal miners in Braidwood, Illinois.[15] In the great 1919 steel strike, the employers imported

30,000 to 40,000 black workers as strikebreakers. And in the 1930s, Henry Ford tried to use his black employees to organize a rival union to split the United Auto Workers. Hundreds of similar examples could be found before and since; use of black strikebreakers, in fact, became a standard element of employer strikebreaking strategy.

The reactions of white workers to the entry of black workers has been marked by two conflicting tendencies. Often white workers have seen the entry of blacks as a direct threat to their security and living standards, and have acted along racial lines to exclude blacks from their jobs and neighborhoods.

This reached its most organized form in the skilled craft unions, many of which to this day exclude all but a token number of black workers. It has also involved sporadic violence. During the peak migration periods of World Wars I and II, for example, dozens of blacks were shot and stoned to death by white crowds in such cities as Chicago, East St. Louis and Detroit. Desire to "get away from blacks" has been one, though by no means the basic, motivation for the migration of many whites to the suburbs. Steven Harper, who was working at a tool-making shop in the solidly white Detroit suburb of Warren, told us: "Everyone who's there is white, and they'd like to keep it that way out in Warren."

Yet there has also been a strong tendency in the opposite direction. As black workers became part of the general labor force, it became apparent to many workers that, whatever their personal racial feelings, they were cutting their own throats and playing into the hands of their employers if they allowed themselves to be divided along racial lines. The following atypical, but by no means unique, statement came from a business agent of the Carpenters and Joiners Union in Savannah, Georgia, in 1902:

> In Georgia they [Negroes] must be organized. I was born and raised among them; my father once owned some of them, and I know them. . . . We are always in competition with them. The contractors prefer them because they can get them cheap. . . . So I say we must organize them; for if we can afford to work all day on a scaffold beside them, then we can surely afford to meet them in the hall for an hour or so once in a while. . . . The mere fact that all of the boss builders in the South are advocating leaving the negroes out of the union is a good reason why we should organize them. . . . Let the good work go on, and let us hope for the day when there will be equal rights for all and special privileges to none. . . .[16]

The United Mine Workers and the industrial union movements of the 1930s and 1940s represented on a massive scale just this kind of interracial cooperation along class lines. Even in the deep South, instances of such unity across race lines can be found from the New Orleans General Strike of 1892 to the Mississippi pulpwood cutters' strike of 1971.

In the social context of such movements, individual racial attitudes proved subject to change as well. A black woman named Sylvia Woods described one example from her experience as an assembly-line worker and union activist in a Chicago war plant during World War II. She told how another black woman's seniority rights entitled her to enter a department where no blacks had ever worked before:

> Selma was a fiery little thing and she was single minded that she would go in there. . . . They [white workers in the department] said that if Selma came in, they would walk out.

Sylvia and a white woman active in the union told them that if they walked out, their jobs would simply be filled:

> They stayed. Nobody left. About two weeks later, there was an opening for a steward and they nominated Selma to be steward. Selma was elected.

Sylvia Woods described one of the men in that department, whose job they had saved on another occasion:

> That guy changed and he worked for Selma. He became one of the best union members in the shop. We threw a party one night and he came—this southerner who didn't want a black to do anything—he brought his wife and children. We used to call him Tennessee. I danced with him that night. It was really something.

The conclusion she drew:

> You have to tell people things that they can see. Then they'll say, "Oh, I never thought of that" or "I have never seen it like that." I have seen it done. Like Tennessee. He hated black people. A poor sharecropper who only came up here to earn enough money to go back and buy the land he had been renting. After the plant closed he went back there with a different outlook on life. He danced with a black woman. He was elected steward and you just couldn't say anything to a black person. So, I have seen people change.[17]

The most impressive interracial cooperation we have found anywhere in America is that which has been created by black and white workers at work, especially in the day-to-day struggle with the employer.[18] Over and over in our discussions and interviews we heard the same pattern described to us: Individuals may harbor racist attitudes in private or away from work, but at work they treat each other as individuals, irrespective of race, and cooperate fully across race lines. A steelworker in Cleveland summed it up: "Cleveland is a racist city, but that doesn't impede cooperation at work." Perhaps the most striking statement of this pattern we heard was made by Jerry Sands, a black auto worker we talked with in Detroit. He worked at the Pontiac, Michigan, General Motors plant, a plant which is notorious for having been closed down by white workers when an anti-school-busing group put picket lines around the plant. He told us:

> Don't get me wrong; I'm not saying that race is not a factor—all you have to do is look at what's written on the walls in the bathroom to know it's there.[19] But it has no effect on how people act. Our plant is one-third black, one-third white and one-third Chicano, but when it comes to the way we organize ourselves on the job, everybody works together pretty well.

In most of these situations, people continued to socialize along racial lines. Jerry Sands told us, "Blacks eat with each other or with Chicanos." And a Detroit steelworker likewise reported that blacks tended to eat and socialize with blacks and whites with whites, although young blacks were friendly when he was with them. But everyone we talked with agreed that these divisions had little effect on action.

There seemed to be significant differences in racial attitudes among people of different ages. A Detroit steelworker told us: "Older white workers will make racist comments, but I never heard a younger white make one." Jerry Sands said: "The very old whites and the young ones are the least racist—the in-between age group is the worst." And an assembler at a factory in Cleveland told us:

> About 60 percent of those at my shop are black or third world people. Everyone gets along all right. The young guys socialize; it's considered square not to. Blacks and whites go to parties at each others' homes.

He also brought up a theme we ran into often:

Whites admire the solidarity of blacks against the company.
When I first started working here, I saw the black guys sitting
down when they finished working, so I sat down too. A white
kid came up to me and said, "Don't sit down, the boss will get
on you." I said, "What do you mean, those guys are sitting
down." He said, "Well, they're afraid to do anything to the
blacks." So I said, "Shit, we should all sit down and let them
be afraid of all of us."

Andrew Korenko expressed a similar admiration:

They've got a good attitude toward the work—they just aren't
very interested in it. They stick together better than the rest of
the workers, and they get away with a lot more. The bosses are
really scared of them. I never heard a boss yell at a black man.
One guy came in six days out of the past two months and they
still couldn't fire him.

"Why can't they?" we asked. "He's got too many friends," he
replied.[20]

For most people, whether or not they act on the basis of race
depends largely on the situation they are in and the people they are
with. Racial identity is one of the frameworks within which people
see themselves and others—but only one. When this racial
framework is applied, it can lead to the most outrageous acts,
ranging from lynching and murder to the subtlest humiliations.
When the framework is not applied, people who might well be
labelled "racist" in other contexts can treat people of different races
as genuine friends, and cooperate with them in pursuit of common
goals.[21] To the extent that people feel the need to stick together on the
basis of their common interests as workers, they will find that the
entire framework of racism is one of the obstacles they must—and
can—overcome.

During the late 1950s and the 1960s, many blacks turned to direct
action on a massive scale to improve their social position. This action
occurred at a time when most white workers experienced rising
living standards and a relative satisfaction with the status quo. The
result was that black militance was often viewed as a threat to the
established well-being of the white majority. With the rise of
widespread discontent in that same white majority, however, the
relation between white and black could change radically. A renewed
militance among blacks might well come to be seen by white workers
not as a threat but as an ally in efforts to change a system from which
they both suffer.

12. WOMEN AND WORK

The early American family, as we saw in Part I, was largely self-sufficient. Within it, work was usually divided by sex, with the particular tasks assigned men and women varying with traditions, conditions and the inclination of the particular family. Most often men did the field labor and building, whereas women tended cattle, gardened, doctored, cooked, kept house, cared for children and conducted such household industries as soapmaking, weaving, spinning, clothesmaking, dairy and other food processing—the list could go on and on.[1] Within such a family the ancient common-law assumptions that women were not independent individuals but rather subordinates to male authority met with little challenge. As Blackstone's authoritative *Commentaries* on the common law put it:

> The husband and the wife are one person. . . ; that is, the very being or legal existence of the woman is suspended during the marriage, or at least is incorporated . . . into that of her husband.[2]

The transition from an economy of individual proprietors to one of employees affected women quite differently from men. The first factory workers, as we have seen, were young women who planned to work for a few years before getting married. Most women married late in their twenties, and it gradually became common for them first to go out to work—the majority in domestic service, factory work or teaching. By 1890 an estimated half of all women worked for pay outside the home for part of the eight to ten years between leaving school and getting married.[3]

Almost all women stopped working when they married. While reliable figures are hard to come by, Robert W. Smuts estimates that in 1890, only about 5 percent of all married women worked for money outside their homes.[4] The work required of most wives in the home remained great. Women gave birth to many more children than today, and therefore spent much more time either pregnant or caring for their offspring. The social belief that "a woman's place is in the home," while no longer considered so applicable to unmarried women, continued to serve as a block to the employment of those who were married. If family income was too small for survival, women might sew or perform other work at home for an employer on a piece-rate basis. But only in cases where their husbands were unable to work because of illness, unemployment or alcoholism were married women likely to work outside the home. As late as 1940, only 15 percent of married women were in the labor force.[5] Raising children and keeping house remained the main labor for most women.

The picture began to change with World War II. The extraordinary shortage of labor led employers and the government to undertake a massive campaign to recruit women for work—even for jobs in heavy industry and other male preserves. Work suddenly became a mark of patriotism, not disgrace, even for married women. Just between 1940 and 1944, the percentage of wives in the labor force increased nearly 50 percent.[6] Massive daycare facilities were set up to allow mothers to work. Centuries of belief that "women's place is in the home" went by the boards in a few short months. Polls of women war workers at the beginning of the war indicated that 95 percent wanted to quit when the war was over, but a similar poll near the end of the war showed that two-thirds wanted to continue at work in permanent jobs.[7]

After the war, women were pushed out of many jobs by men returning from the military; many others voluntarily quit to start families they had delayed for the duration of the war. Magazines again began to extoll the virtues of women in the home. But a return to the prewar pattern proved not to be in the cards. By 1950 a higher proportion of wives were in the labor force than at the peak of the war in 1944, and the proportion has continued to rise steadily, until today almost half of all wives work during any given year—and the overwhelming majority work at some point during the course of their marriage.[8] This constitutes a dramatic change in the lives of women and the worlds of both work and family.

Several factors have contributed to this change. The ages at which women marry and have children have dropped by roughly seven years, and women have generally had fewer and fewer children, except for the "baby boom" decade following World War II. Since, on the average, women marry before they reach twenty-one and have their last child by the time they are thirty, they have many more years of reduced child-rearing responsibilities during which their children are in school or grown up.[9] The advent of such new technologies as running water and central heating has lightened many traditional household tasks; backyard agriculture and kitchen industries have been taken over by commercial processing; and hospitals have replaced much home nursing. These developments made house-keeping potentially less time-consuming. The economy provided growing employment for women, particularly in low-level clerical occupations and part-time and semicasual jobs in retail stores and services. Under these conditions, older social beliefs about the proper place of married women in the home lingered, but had less and less effect on whether women actually worked. Today, about 60 percent of women work during the course of a year.[10]

The main reason women take jobs was put succinctly by the U.S. Department of Labor:

> Most women in the labor force work because they or their families need the money they can earn—some work to raise family living standards above the level of poverty or depriva-tion; others, to help meet rising costs of food, education for their children, medical care, and the like. The majority of women do not have the option of working solely for personal fulfillment.[11]

In 1970, barely one-third of all women in the labor force were married to husbands who made $7000 or more a year. The other two-thirds were either single, widowed, divorced or separated—usually supporting themselves and often children as well—or mar-ried to men who made less than $7000. These women were hardly working for "pin money." Their work was either an economic necessity for their survival, or the difference between a family life of deprivation and one of relative comfort.

Of course, dire necessity is not the only reason women want to work. A student at a Boston commuter college said: "I think both husband and wife should work so they can travel around some before they start having kids." But more typical was a licensed practical nurse in Cleveland who told us:

> Most of the nurses I work with are working simply because they have to. A large proportion of them have children but no husbands—they're divorced, they have illegitimate kids or they've lost their husbands. And most of the rest need the money almost as much.

Most married women, whether they work or not, have a full-time job at home as housekeepers and often childkeepers as well. A steelworker, describing the pressures that changing shifts at work put on families, said: "A lot of guys have traditional family lives where the wife stays at home most of the time. Taking care of the house almost has to be a full-time job for somebody when you're working this way." (Nonetheless, his own wife held down a full-time job herself in an auto plant on the far side of Cleveland.)

Many women find the boredom and social isolation of housework worse than having to take a job: "I just can't imagine sitting around home all the time knitting and doing nothing." We met Linda and her husband Larry, a pipefitter, when we camped one night in a parking lot next to their house in an aging suburb of Steubenville, Ohio. They were about thirty, and Linda told us she had two kids, one five, the other two. A few years before she had started studying to be a nurse, got trained as a lab technician and worked at the local hospital—until she got pregnant. When Tim said he was on a layoff, she said bitterly:

> I've been on a layoff too—for the last six years. I wish I could
> go back to work at the hospital, at least in the afternoon, but
> Larry here won't baby-sit for the kids. It gets on your nerves
> after a while, the little monsters. I go stir crazy sitting at home
> all day.

A young woman we met from Pittsburgh gave us a fairly typical account of what the women she worked with in a garment factory did with their children while they worked:

> Their kids either stayed with grandmother or other relations,
> or in either legal or illegal daycare. Often a neighbor took care
> of ten or twenty kids. The going rate was somewhere around
> $10 per week per kid, so that women with three kids were
> paying half their income for daycare.

After describing conditions in the factory that rivaled the horrors of a nineteenth-century sweatshop, she added: "When women told me they were working there to get out of the house, I figured things had to be pretty bad at home."

Women by no means enter the labor force on equal terms with men. From the beginning they have been concentrated in low-paying and insecure "women's jobs" and underrepresented or excluded altogether from those with better pay and job security. As early as 1829, a Boston newspaper editorialized:

> Custom and long habit have closed the doors of very many
> employments against the industry and perserverence of wo-
> man. She has been taught to deem so many occupations
> masculine, and made for men only that, excluded by a
> mistaken deference to the world's opinion from innumerable
> labors most happily adapted to her physical constitution, the
> competition for the few places left open to her has occasioned a
> reduction in the estimated value of her labor, until it has fallen
> below the minimum and is no longer adequate. . . . [12]

The job segregation of women was borne out by a government
study of the payroll records of 150,000 employees made in 1885–
86. It found only 800 instances where men and women were employed in the same job classification by the same employer, and in
600 of these, the men's wages were higher than women's by an
average of one-third.[13] Nor has this segregation disappeared; recent research indicates that it has declined little since the turn of
the century.[14]

In 1970, women who worked full time all year round made only 60
percent as much as men.[15] Far from getting better, this "income
gap" has been growing worse—back in the mid-1950s, women
earned 64 percent as much as men.[16] And in reality the "income
gap" is far worse, since 60 percent of women workers were
employed either part time or, even more commonly, only part of the
year.

Part of the "income gap" is the result of employers simply paying
women less than men for the same work. A Department of Labor
study in 1963, when such discrimination was still legal, found many
job orders even at public employment offices

> offering men higher wages or salaries than were offered to
> women for the same job. The orders covered a variety of
> occupations and industries. One offered $3,600 a year for a
> male clerk-typist and only $3,000 for a woman. Another,
> seeking an accounting clerk, quoted a rate of $1.80 for a man
> and $1.45 for a woman. Over one-half of the orders listed had
> wage differentials ranging from 11 to 25 percent of the men's
> rate.[17]

Even more significant than such unequal pay for equal work is the
problem pointed out in the Boston editorial 145 years ago—the
crowding of women into a few, low-paying occupations. Between
1947 and 1968, the number of women in the labor force increased by
75 percent, while the number of men increased only 16 percent.[18]
Yet, as the National Manpower Council concluded:

> The growth in the employment of women appears to have been accomplished more through increased employment in occupations held by women and by the emergence of new "women's" occupations than through the entrance of women into occupations formerly considered exclusively male.[19]

The most important growth in women's employment has been in clerical work; since 1940, women have increased from one-half to three-fourths of all clerical workers.[20] Today, one-third of all women workers are clerical workers[21] and their earnings have declined dramatically relative to male clerical workers since World War II.[22] The next most important growth was in nonhousehold service work—one of the lowest paid of all job categories.[23] More than 70 percent of working women were employed in these two categories or in low-paying operative and sales occupations.[24] Women were severely underrepresented among the higher-paying professional, technical and managerial jobs, and barely 1 percent of women were craftsmen or foremen.[25] One woman, who had been working at low-paying garment and waitress jobs, described this exclusion to us as she experienced it. She loved carpentry and had tried over and over to find work as a carpenter; she had also tried to break into other skilled trades or some of the better-paying industrial jobs in the Pittsburgh area; in every case, she told us: "I ran into a stone wall."

Needless to say, employers do not willingly make available information which documents women's inferior jobs and pay. But as a result of a Pentagon Papers-style exploit on the part of an unknown office worker, we can see exactly what it meant at one company. In 1973, a group of women passed out leaflets protesting discrimination against women in the downtown Loop district in Chicago. A few days later, to their surprise, there arrived the entire salary list for the General Office of Kraft Foods, one of the companies they had leafletted—evidently passed on by a worker in the office. When the women made known the salary information, Kraft evidently panicked. We were told:

> The result was a massive security drive. Overtime was cancelled for secretaries. Four approvals were needed to get material out of the files. It probably put them months behind. In fact if that happened everywhere, the Loop might close down without our doing anything.

An analysis of the salary list showed the extremes the "earnings gap'' could take: The 572 men employed at Kraft averaged $19,000 a year, while the 442 women averaged only $8000 a year. Women were severely underrepresented in professional positions and were paid less in most of them—even if they had been on the job a longer time. Women held 80 percent of the nonprofessional jobs—and earned $7400 a year compared with $12,300 for the men in such jobs. Some examples of job discrimination:

DUPLICATING MACHINE OPERATOR
Three women hired in 1971 make less than a man who started at the same time.
INTERMEDIATE CLERK
Two men hired since 1972 earn more than any of the women in this category even though 70 women have greater seniority.

A man hired in 1973 makes an average of $3,000 more than any of the women hired that year (9 women).

A man hired in 1972 makes an average of $2,500 more than any of the women hired that year (36 women).
MAIL CLERK
Of twelve employees in this category (three women and nine men), no women are senior mail clerks.[26]

Finally, women are concentrated in industries with small, competitive, marginal companies. Three-fifths of women work in the distribution of goods and services.[27] The 20 percent engaged in manufacturing are overrepresented in light industries such as apparel, textiles and food processing.[28] An analysis by Mary Stevenson of the University of Massachusetts at Boston indicates that about one-third of the ''wage gap'' for semiskilled occupations was due to the fact that

men are in the more profitable and powerful industries. The labor market assigns women to those industries which are not capable of paying higher wages because of the economic environment in which they operate.[29]

There are a number of reasons women are concentrated in inferior jobs. One is sheer prejudice about their capacities. Another pilfered document which came into our possession by entirely illegitimate means indicates how strong the stereotypes about women remain. It is a section of the *Supervisor's Manual for State Employees of the State of Massachusetts,* dealing with ''Women in Government,'' in use at least until 1968. It was prepared by a professor at the Bureau of Business and Industrial Training at Northwestern University. Among the ''Facts'' it listed about women were:

Finger dexterity far superior to man.
Women 10 times more nervous than men.
Women more patient in repetitive jobs.
Well suited for work involving exactness.

The Manual gave this description of ''The Female Mind'':

Women are identificationists.
Women are subjective.
Women are intuitive.
Women indulge in fantasy.
Women have fuller emotional lives than men.

It stated that the

role of achievers still belongs to men. . . . Women as a rule
don't seek job promotion—their emotions are secure in a
limited job.

And perhaps most devastating of all:

Women sometimes think Government and industry is silly.

With such attitudes prevalent, it is little wonder that women have
found it necessary to protest male chauvinism.

A second reason for discrimination against women has been the
policy of those professionals and skilled workers who can control
their own labor markets. Doctors, lawyers and other predominantly
male professionals have held the number of women allowed to
practice to a minimum through control of professional education and
training. Similarly, craft unions have excluded women almost
entirely from skilled trades through closed shops and apprenticeship
provisions, as part of their general policy of narrowing the competition for skilled jobs as much as possible. An attitude of male vanity
and scorn for women has at times accompanied this approach.

Another reason women are excluded from better jobs is the
work/life pattern most women share. Many young women enter the
labor force at first for only a few years, then leave to marry or to have
children. When they return to work, many still feel free to quit,
believing their main responsibility is at home. This, combined with
traditional prejudice, makes many employers reluctant to take on
women, no matter how qualified they may be, for jobs involving
extensive training or responsibility.

Employers are more than willing to perpetuate and exploit the
casual character of the women's labor market. One ''highly placed

executive in a mammoth insurance company,'' for example, told researchers from Columbia University that ''tender-minded academics'' were ''downright naive'' in their concern about worker turnover. It was his ''informed opinion'' that clerical personnel

> are easily trained for their jobs, that if they stayed on in large numbers they would become wage problems—we'd have to keep raising them or end up fighting with them; they would form unions and who knows what the hell else. It's better to hire girls who are too well educated to *stay* happy with the jobs we assign them to do. That way they get out before it's too late. [30]

Because of the discrimination against women in other spheres, those companies which do hire women find a tremendous labor surplus, and therefore are able to hold wages to a minimum—if one woman is dissatisfied with conditions, an employer can count on finding another who will put up with them. Substandard wages for women allow many marginal employers to survive and permit other employers to make extra profits.

From the point of view of business as a whole, those women who are not working constitute what a U.S. Labor Department publication calls a ''labor force reserve.''[31] The government's *Handbook on Women Workers* put it neatly: ''Women 16 years of age and over who are not in the labor force make up a womanpower reserve—a potential source of additional workers who might be needed in an expanding economy or in time of national emergency.''[32] In the meantime, this reserve of unemployed potential workers shows up in no unemployment statistics, receives no unemployment compensation, and doesn't walk the streets requesting or demanding jobs. It represents a hidden unemployment which holds down the wages of the employed without generating the social disruption that usually accompanies massive unemployment.

Women have long struggled against their subordinate position in the labor force and in society. They have conducted many of the most militant strikes in the history of the American labor movement. At the same time, they have had to organize to fight their subordination within male-dominated unions. In the first decades of the twentieth century, a strong feminist movement won the right to vote and an end to the legal inequalities under which ''the very being or legal existence of the woman is suspended. . . .'' During the late 1960s, a new woman's movement developed, attacking the unequal position of women in every sphere of life and trying to overcome the willingness of women to accept that position. The struggles of these movements, combined with the actual transformation of women's position in the home and the work force, have created a social recognition that women are separate individuals rather than mere appendages to men, but they have yet to abolish the real inequalities with which women are faced.

Women at times have been less willing to organize and fight back at work than men. One reason for this is that the tremendous surplus of women workers makes it easy for employers to fire women who make trouble, or to maintain conditions so bad that most women leave before they have time to organize. A second reason is that many women consider work secondary to their main activity in the home, rather than as a permanent situation they will either have to change or endure for life. As a young woman who had been involved in union organizing efforts among women in Portland, Oregon, put it to us: "Women workers are less willing to struggle because they see themselves as only working for short-term or supplemental incomes, even when it isn't really true." Finally, the traditional subordination of women in all spheres of life may sometimes lead to a greater willingness to tolerate subordination at work. The Massachusetts *Supervisor's Manual* stated, in its condescending way, that women show a "tremendous degree of loyalty if supervision is fair."[33] A case in point was a young woman we met who worked in a small jewelry shop with six other employees in downtown Pittsburgh. She painted fluorescent watch dials, and after four years she was making only $2.30 an hour. She wanted to quit but didn't because she felt an obligation to the company. She told us: "The boss is there, and I feel I have to come to work—it's just a feeling I have that it wouldn't be right not to."

But how well women fight back on the job generally has less to do with their sex than with the industry and conditions in which they work. Most women work in either white-collar occupations which have little tradition of overt resistance or in backward industries with small, highly competitive companies, where organizing is often most difficult. Thus, a woman who had worked in garment shops in Portland, Oregon, described the complete failure of women to stick together: "People would compete to get the good jobs on the piece rates." We heard similar stories over and over again from women in the garment and other competitive industries. But there were also many counter-examples. One woman who worked in a plant in Chicago that made washing machines told us:

> It's mostly women working there. It's all piece rates. The workers set their own top rate—125 percent of the company's

minimum. There's social pressure not to produce more and it's very effective. The company restudies the jobs often to try to speed up. But if the jobs get too fast, people just go slow and fail to make production. Once in a while some people will break the rate and at the same time accuse others of breaking it, but generally people stick together pretty well.

An electrical worker in Gloucester, Massachusetts, described the greater militance of women workers when the heating system of the plant broke down one winter day:

Everyone got colder and colder, more and more disgusted. Finally, most people agreed we should just walk out. When we got up to go, the women all put on their coats and left, but the men wouldn't walk out, they just kept on working.

The ancient division between women and men can cause conflict and division among workers. Sometimes this can be at the level of simple irritation. Sally Maxwell, a skilled printer, told us:

I've noticed quite a difference in the way men and women will teach you a job. The men are a lot more competitive. They tend either to assume you are stupid and incapable of learning, or they act as if you should already know the job and don't tell you what you need to know. The whole process is designed to show how much more than you they know and can do. I've never had that kind of problem with women.

The conflicts can involve far more overt hostility as well. A worker at Great Lakes Steel in Detroit reported:

There are a few older women at the steel plant left over as crane operators from World War II. They are now bringing in women for the first time since then. They are constantly whistled at and generally hassled. They're very young—like eighteen. The white women are really intimidated; most of the black women will talk back. If they talked back more, the men would probably lay off. Anyway, things should get better when they get more of them in there. It should humanize the place, too.

The reality today is that women are workers—after all, nearly 40 percent of all workers are women.[34] Attitudes on the part of men who treat women as anything but fellow workers are obsolete. They hurt male workers themselves, by maintaining a pool of low-paid competing labor, by ensuring low wages for their own wives, daughters and mothers, and by undermining solidarity against the employer on the job. The assumption of many women that they are working only temporarily and therefore need not organize to fight back on the job guarantees inferior conditions for themselves and all women. Until people accept these realities, they will be victimized by them.

13. THE SHARED EXPERIENCE

American workers are divided in many ways: by ethnic background, skill, job classification, collar color, sex, religion, age, values. It often seems natural to think in terms of these divisive factors rather than in terms of the working class as a whole, despite the basic problems, conditions and interests that all members of the working class share. But much of the recent historical experience of all kinds of workers cuts across these divisions, creating the basis for a new kind of cooperation along class lines.

By and large, the American working class was recruited from groups for whom survival itself was not secure—peasants and urban workers who immigrated from Europe, and native-born economically squeezed farmers, sharecroppers and artisans. Their conditions of life in urban industrial America, however brutal, impoverished and oppressive, were rarely worse than those they had left behind. They took for granted having to work hard at unpleasant tasks while living in want; the fact that they could survive, and that their children might even some day know something better, was cause for thanksgiving. Karl, a tool and die maker who had immigrated from Germany in the 1920s, had been a Wobbly and then an organizer of the unemployed, described for us the attitude characteristic of workers in the twenties and thirties:

> Back then if you had a good steady job, that was it—you felt you were set for life. That was what you needed for a good life, and if you had it you were satisfied.
>
> This was even more so because a large part of the workers were immigrants who came over from Europe, from countries which were poor or had been impoverished by the war. When they got to the U.S. they were able to get jobs and make a living—they felt it was a wonderful country.
>
> And even those who weren't satisfied with their current situation felt that they could get ahead. After all, the son of the Jewish immigrant garment worker was going to college.

The Great Depression of the 1930s shattered such hopes at the same time that it destroyed living standards. The willingness to work and work hard became by no means a guarantee of survival, let alone well-being. Under these conditions, workers who might have been satisfied with quite modest living standards had to turn to dramatic forms of mass struggle—anti-eviction riots, sitdown strikes, mass picketing, general strikes—to win enough to live on and a faint hope of security. Those who lived through the thirties often retain a tradition of militance, combined with a preoccupation with job security and economic survival.

World War II marked the end of the Great Depression. For most people, despite long hours, rationing, shortages and the draft, it meant a great improvement in conditions of life. Moreover, there was a widespread sense that if everybody would pull together to win the war, they could hope for prosperity and improving conditions when it was over.

The decades following World War II were indeed marked by a substantial improvement in living conditions for most people. Rising wages, relatively full employment and an increasing proportion of working wives caused the real income of American families to increase by about one-third between 1946 and 1968.[1] Living standards rose even faster than real income, as consumer debt grew from $6 billion to $86 billion in the twenty years following World War II.[2] Work became far less seasonal, allowing steady employment to groups that before had been chronically unemployed. Seniority provisions and union grievance procedures likewise increased job security substantially. Social security, unemployment insurance, workman's compensation, pension plans and welfare programs created an at least partially guaranteed basis of survival for those who were not at work.

These conditions represented a tremendous contrast to the recent past. For a worker who had expected impoverishment and insecurity, life may well have turned out far better than expected. A study of auto workers who had moved to a San Jose suburb in the mid-1950s gave an apt description of the way many of them regarded their recent experience:

> Here I am the son of a sharecropper with a ninth-grade education and no really saleable skills, and look at me: I'm paying off a nice new home, have a good car (often two), my kids and my wife are decently dressed; she has a washing machine, I have some power tools; what more do I have a right to expect?[3]

This did not mean, of course, that workers liked being workers and adored their employers and their jobs. But it did mean that they accepted the status quo and would even fight to protect it. Harvey Swados, who had worked intermittently in various factories since the 1930s, wrote, after a stint in an auto factory in 1956:

> The worker's expectations are for better pay, more humane working conditions and more job security. As long as he feels that he is going to achieve them through an extension of existing conditions, for that long he is going to continue to be a middle-class conservative in temper.[4]

Peter Waller, a skilled worker in Detroit, observed the declining militance at work that accompanied the new conditions:

> I first came to work in the auto shops right after World War II. It was only a few years after the sit-downs, and many of the workers still had that kind of militance in them, though there were also a lot of workers who had come in during the war. From there it's been downhill all the way. The unions became steadily worse and the workers less militant and united.

In part, he felt, this was because "the company systematically picked off the militants and fired them. There was a general atmosphere of fear—there was McCarthyism even in the plants." But the underlying reason he felt was the fact that "there were no economic crises—the economy continued to grow and things were pretty stable."

The trauma of deprivation during the Depression, combined with the new opportunities of the postwar years, shaped an entire generation. As sociologist Lee Rainwater put it: "The central life goal of the stable working class is the creation of a comfortable and secure place for oneself and one's family."[5] Tremendous sacrifices were made to that goal: Husbands worked fifty or sixty hours a week or took second jobs; wives went to work while retaining their other family responsibilities. The result was that many working class families were able to buy—albeit on credit—suburban tract houses, new cars and many other products they may never have expected to own.

The implications of post-World War II prosperity were far different for those who had not lived through the Depression. Most young people experienced the opportunity to make a living by working in a factory or office as a fact of life, not as anything to celebrate. Some degree of economic security was taken for granted; it became less and less of a preoccupation for most people.

On the other hand, the price their parents' generation had paid for a rising standard of living became forcefully clear to many young people. It had meant, in many cases, a life in which most forms of pleasure, satisfaction and self-fulfillment were sacrificed to endless hours of onerous and unfulfilling labor. What had seemed like a good life to one generation appeared almost a nightmare to many members of the next.

Young people's expectations were further raised by the great postwar expansion of education and the belief that a good education would allow practically anyone to escape from working-class status. By the 1960s, nearly four-fifths of all young people were graduating from high school, and half the graduates were starting college. By comparison, most people in 1940 left high school after less than two years. Throughout the postwar decades, those who received academic credentials often found employers eager to hire them for well-paid professional, technical and managerial jobs.

The new conditions made possible for young people a higher range of expectations. These generally included an adequate material standard of living, but often went far beyond it. Among widespread new objectives were time for personal pleasures and satisfactions, a safe, clean and aesthetic environment, freedom from the arbitrary authority of other people and institutions, and work that was interesting, expressive, creative and self-directed.[6]

These aspirations were often reflected in the attitudes younger workers took toward work. A young steelworker in Detroit told us:

> The younger guys want to work as little as possible. They have lots of free time at the steel plant. One guy punched in, climbed over the fence, went out to a party with some friends and climbed back in just to punch out. "That's where my head's at," he said, "getting paid for going to a party."

A group of young steel-union rank-and-file reformers we talked with in Gary agreed:

> The kids' heads are not in the work—older people are more involved in the work; kids are not interested. Most kids are not interested in moving up in the mill—most don't expect to be there too long.

Young shop stewards we talked with at a large factory outside Pittsburgh, where many younger workers had just been hired, said that the big difference between these workers and the old timers was that the latter would pound out the work for a full eight hours, while the young guys would refuse to. One of them told us:

I'll be cleaning up forty-five minutes before the end of the
shift, and he'll still be working five minutes before we're off.
The young guys won't tolerate that—if they can't make the
rate in five or six hours, they'll go up and make the company
adjust the rates.

Younger workers were generally considered more militant and
less afraid of authority. This was brought out strikingly when we
talked with foremen and other management people from General
Motors, Chevrolet and Chrysler, who were taking a course at the
University of Detroit. One woman said:

My son is working in production, and it's completely different
from what it used to be. People used to be afraid of the foremen
and fawn on them. Now there's no fear of them at all. If people
don't like what they say, they argue right back at them.

A black foreman added:

The new kids are more intelligent. They won't just take an
order like in the old days. You've got to watch it—if they don't
like something you do, you're likely to end up with a wrench
on your skull.

Old-time labor militants seemed to have very much the same impression. One veteran of the 1936–37 sitdown strikes in Flint,
Michigan, said:

The younger workers today are more advanced in some ways
than the workers of the 1930s. Back then, nobody would walk
off the job unless the thing was extremely well organized—
they were too much afraid of losing their jobs. Today, workers
are just much less afraid in general—they are willing to take
risks and fight back in ways that would have been exceptional
in the 1930s.

Peter Waller agreed, though with balancing reservations:

Younger workers are good in that they are not afraid—they
don't know what it is to be hungry. They are bad in that they
have no sense of their own power.

He saw this weakness as a result of their limited experience.
"They'll get that sense of power in the course of time and expanded
struggles," he added confidently. His wife, who works in another

auto plant in Detroit, added that young workers are much more likely to walk out over such issues as heat, speed-up and firings than are the older workers.

Another expression of new attitudes was the dramatic rise of absenteeism during the latter 1960s. A woman who had worked in a small auto parts plant in Detroit for twenty years, herself an old radical, told us:

> The present absenteeism represents something very different from past forms of resistance. In the past, workers have generally tried to make everyone act the same way, do the same things, out of a sense of fear. Today, there is no longer such a pressure for conformity among workers. Through absenteeism, the kids have won something that could potentially revolutionize life in the auto industry—part-time work. We know one kid, Steven, who works just Mondays and Fridays, and makes enough to get by.

Someone broke in to say, "Of course, he missed three days in the first four weeks—he just couldn't bring himself to get up that early in the morning." "Oh well," someone else chimed in, "I guess they'll just have to hire a part-time part-timer for the days when the part-timers don't come in."

Stories about absenteeism, whether real or apocryphal, were often told with glee. Perhaps the most widespread described a foreman asking a worker, "Joe, how come you're coming into work four days a week?" "Because I can't make a living in three," came the reply. We were told of a coal mine near Pittsburgh whose night shift was mostly younger workers. One night only eighteen of sixty workers on the shift showed up. The next day the boss called them in and dressed them down. When he threatened to fire them, they all broke into applause. Astounded, he asked why. "If you fire us, we'll all get $93 a week unemployment and won't have to work for forty-two weeks," came the reply.

Of course, the desires and life pattern of many people who grew up in the 1950s and '60s closely follow those of their parents' generation. We talked with a pipefitter in Wintersville, Ohio, a suburb of Steubensville, who was an extreme example. His father had been a pipefitter before him; at his death, he and his brothers had taken up the trade. When we asked him how he liked living in Wintersville, his only reply was, "Oh, yeah, there's plenty of work around here with the mills and all the industries in this area, and that's for me."

But in general, the differences among the different generations are visible in almost any workplace; they were described to us over and over again. Andrew Korenko at Republic Steel in Cleveland told us:

> You can see very definite differences in attitude among age groups. You can see it both in the union officials and in the regular workers. The old timers—say over fifty-five—tend to be all right. The two grievers who are fifty-five and sixty are right on their job. The old guys are full of stories about the struggle to get the union in. They'll tell you the union isn't what it used to be, that people didn't used to put up with the kind of shit they do now. The guys, say, thirty-three to fifty-five are a whole different story. The ones that hold positions in the union are still under the influence of David McDonald. They'll actually talk about cotrusteeship.

He shook his head. We asked him why he thought they were that way.

> I've wondered about that myself. These were guys that came into the mills after World War II and the Korean War. They worked themselves up to the better jobs. A lot of them came up from the South; they started off poor and ended up pretty well set up. In their terms they were successful, and they were into that whole thing.

We asked about the younger people.

> Their attitude toward the job is all right. They don't think they're going any place. A few are taking positions in the union, but most of them don't have anything to do with it. Mostly they are into absenteeism. I'm a pretty regular worker myself—I must have missed a month in the past year or so.

During the 1960s, the shift in attitudes that began with young people caused some friction between generations—the notorious "generation gap." When young people with long hair, bandanas, patched blue jeans and a fondness for pot first began appearing at work, they were frequently met with disdain and contempt by the older workers. Similarly, an older woman who had been an auto worker for many years in Detroit told us that older workers resented the absenteeism of younger workers somewhat, seeing it as improper. "They'll ask, 'How can you possibly live?' " But in the past several years, the polarization between young and old at work seems to have softened considerably. Younger workers told us over and over again that the people over thirty with whom they worked were changing their attitudes and coming around, letting their hair grow longer, doing dope with the kids, and generally loosening up in their attitudes about life. The comment of a sixty-year-old iron worker and crane operator in Portland, Oregon, with a crew-cut was not atypical:

> A lot of people complain about the kids, the long haired kids. I did too. But they're all right. There's so much bullshit in the world. Let them do something about it; they're the ones that are going to have to live with it. The radical stuff and all—the college kids even—it's all right.

There still are differences between generations, but they seem far less critical today than they did five years ago.

Even as aspirations were expanding, however, real social conditions began to deteriorate. As we have seen in Part II, the real incomes and general living conditions of most workers began to fall in the mid-1960s, and grew markedly worse as the 1970s progressed. While many older workers were protected by seniority and other forms of job security, younger workers experienced depression-level unemployment and underemployment.[7] One common result was a chronic sense of insecurity and an unwillingness to plan or sacrifice for the future. An ex-Vietnam marine, who today serves as a veterans counselor at an urban university, put it this way:

> After World War II, people knew they could buy their future. If you worked hard, you could buy thirty years. Today, nobody knows what's happening. Nobody's buying futures. People don't even plan for a few years ahead. Maybe it's because nobody knows what to expect. If even engineers can't get jobs one year, can the next, but don't know what to expect for the future, it's hard to make plans and commitments. People seem to feel insecure even when the opportunity to get ahead is there.

The resurrection of hard times, far from stimulating a return to the dedicated striving for security of the past, only increased the widespread scepticism about working hard and getting ahead as the means to a good life.

Particularly hard hit was the belief in education as an avenue of escape from low status and drudgery. During the 1960s, the jobs available to college graduates began to lose their glamour; it was widely recognized that "college jobs" could be nearly as boring, stifling, self-denying and subject to authoritarian discipline as those in industrial production. (While the student movement of the 1960s raised issues that were varied and far-reaching, much of its impetus came from students' rejection of an education whose purpose they saw as processing them to be mere cogs within the social machine.) But by the beginning of the 1970s, it had become difficult for college graduates even to get "college jobs" at all. Among young people who received B.A. degrees in 1970 and 1971 and did not go on to graduate school, there was an 8.5 percent unemployment rate; for those who majored in the humanities, the rate was 13 percent. Of those working, 42 percent were in fields not directly related to their college major.[8] By 1973, a Boston newspaperman reported:

> Anyone travelling around the city daily will encounter cab drivers with law degrees, waitresses with graduate training in social work or special education, English Ph.D. candidates who moonlight as nannies or shoe salesmen.[9]

Under such circumstances, the slogan "for a good job, get a good education" rang somewhat hollow. As a student at the University of Massachusetts at Boston said:

> When I was a kid, everyone said, "Stay in school, stay in school," so I finished high school. I worked for a while, and they told me if I wanted to do anything I had to go to college. So here I am. I know if I ever get out of here, they're going to tell me to go to graduate school. And then I declare they'll tell me I need a Ph.D. And you know what: when I get that, I still won't be able to do what I want to do. It just seems like all my yeses, they've got a no to.

The general sense of social deterioration was aggravated by the Vietnam War. Like World War II, the Vietnam War left a powerful mark on those who experienced it, whether as GIs or at home. The ex-marine explained part of why the impact of the Vietnam War was so different from World War II:

> World War II was the focus of all life at home. You should see the ads in magazines like National Geographic to get a feel for the times. There's a GI in every ad, or else farmers on tractors with flags or pictures of Hitler being beaten over the head with a corn cob. A Bell and Howell ad said, we'll make cameras for you after the war, but now we're making bomb sights. The theme was we're all making a common sacrifice. Everyone

was drafted, including lawyers, doctors—no group or stratum escaped. When they came home, they were given special treatment; in the State of Pennsylvania there was a book an inch thick with advantages for veterans—seniority, free licenses, etc. Colleges tried to recruit veterans because their full tuition was paid—nearly half of World War II vets graduated from a school, training or apprenticeship program. Veteran's organizations sprang up all over and were very powerful. Everybody got into them—everyone wanted to retain the comraderie from the war.

In Vietnam, the story was completely different. The war was unpopular at home. People were getting fat in America, but there was no common sacrifice like World War II. It was a case of business as usual. Instead of everybody getting drafted, people who could go to college often did; it was those who couldn't who went into the military.

Some factors about the war itself contributed. The officer corps deteriorated as the war expanded and inexperienced officers took over. The 1968 Tet offensive broke morale and showed that the U.S. was losing; 300 attacks starting at the same second in every part of the country showed that we weren't winning and that the South Vietnamese were totally unable and unwilling to fight. Then there was brutality to civilians. I captured two Vietcong "tax collectors." Actually they were really just solicitors; they were civilians who went around asking for contributions of food, etc. I turned them over to South Vietnamese officials. Twenty minutes later they were shot, with two U.S. officers as witnesses. I protested to my officers. They gave me a dressing down and told me to shut up. I protested to my commanding general. I was called into his office, dressed down again, and made to understand that if I ever did anything like that again I would be busted or worse. It certainly contributed to my disillusionment.

Vietnam veterans constitute a particularly disillusioned and disadvantaged group, hounded not only by memories but by high unemployment. A vet we overheard in a bar in Connecticut said:

> I was trained as a technician, but when I got out I couldn't get a job anywhere. I finally stopped telling employers I was a veteran—their immediate reaction was, oh, this guy must be a junkie.

And a black hitchhiker about twenty-two years old we picked up outside Toledo, Ohio, on his way to a construction job told us:

> I got out of the service in March. I was in 'Nam. They got all
> these programs to hire the vet—didn't do me much good. It
> took me two months to find this job.

Such experiences, combined with the traditions of resistance to
military authority that developed during the course of the war, have
helped to make veterans an unusually militant force when they
returned to jobs back home. A steelworker in Gary reported:

> Vietnam vets won't take the shit the others do—they'll yell at
> the foremen and stuff like that.

An auto worker in Detroit confirmed this:

> A lot of the younger workers come out of the army, and they've
> had it with authority. They aren't willing to take any more shit.

The experience of the war has likewise weakened the reflex
support for the state and its officials among the population as a
whole, especially young people. According to surveys by pollster
Daniel Yankelovich, the proportion of young workers who say they
consider patriotism "a very important value" dropped from 60
percent in 1969 to 40 percent in 1974. An opinion survey by Daniel
Starch in 1973 found that if Japan, Israel, Thailand, South Vietnam
or Greece were "threatened by Communist invasion and takeover,"
a majority of Americans would be opposed to sending American
troops. And willingness to serve in the military has dropped sharply.
The veterans counselor quoted earlier told us:

> The army is having trouble recruiting because the whole
> attitude toward authority has changed. Many kids would
> rather wash car windows than go in the army—they figure at
> least you're free.

Most current members of the working class, whatever their race,
sex or occupation, have shared two important historical experiences.
First, they have shared the expanding aspirations that made a steady
job and an adequate income no longer a sufficient definition of a good
life. Second, they have shared the deterioration in real incomes and
general social conditions of the past few years, which have made it
harder and harder just to get by.

It is possible, though unlikely, that in the face of hard times the
expanded aspirations that developed in the 1960s will simply fade
away as unrealistic dreams from a happier era. Whether such desires

persist or not, workers will be forced to turn to forms of collective action designed to prevent the complete destruction of their present standards of living.

But as a result of their expanded aspirations, people may well not limit the objectives of such action to economic survival and security. For as we have seen throughout this book, the deprivation and the insecurity of the majority of the population have the same root as their domination by self-denying and oppressive work—the control of social production by a special minority of owners and managers. The ultimate solution to both problems is the same—the control of production by the majority who do the work to meet their own needs. For those who have hoped for a life of pleasure and fulfilling activity, only to find themselves struggling just to get by, we believe this is the only solution to adopt.

Scott Custin/Action

IV

ACTION

"For everyone whose life is unfree and whose needs are unmet
because of minority control of productive activity, the
time has come to turn the techniques of day-to-day resistance into a
concerted struggle for direct majority control of every
aspect of social life."

It has become customary to conclude books about social problems with recommendations for actions to be taken by government officials, enlightened managers, union leaders and other "authorities." We have none to offer because we believe these "authorities" cannot solve the problems that most people face. Those who now hold power are themselves the heart of the problem. We speak instead to people like ourselves who hold no official positions of power, do not control the labor of others, and receive no special privileges from the existing organization of society.

In ordinary times, most people give little thought to the fundamental organization of society, let alone how to change it. They base their strategies for living on the assumption that the structure of society is something fixed, just a fact of life. Within that framework, they look for ways to make as good a life for themselves as they can.

But what can you do when all such ways seem blocked? When there is no way to survive except through giving up the time of your life to the domination of others? When it gets harder and harder just to get the necessities of life, and more and more of its pleasures have to be given up? When the world around you grows ugly, poisoned and dangerous? When war, large and small, becomes a chronic expectation? And when—short of some miracle magically spiriting us into an era of well-being and tranquility—there will be at best more of the same?

In the face of such conditions, life may simply seem hopeless. You can quit your job or change your life style, but what can you do when everything you try brings you back up against the same fundamental problems? It is quite natural to try to avoid even thinking about such a situation when you are in it—it seems too painful to face. And if there is nothing you can do about it, what is the point in thinking about it anyway?

But the very fact that most people share the same essential problems means that they don't have to deal with those problems alone. Indeed, if separate individuals can't solve their problems by acting alone, they have little choice but to try to create solutions through cooperation with others.

To do so requires a fundamental change in the strategies by which people try to live. Such a change inevitably involves taking risks, entering uncharted waters with no guarantee of success. But even a risky course is preferable to one that offers only sure disaster.

The core of such a new strategy must be joining together with others to eliminate those features of the existing society which make it impossible for most people to meet their needs and express their inclinations. Joint struggle to remove these barriers to a good life must become as intimate a part of people's life strategies as seeking a good education, job or home has been in the past. Only by such collective action can the fulfillment of individual goals become possible.

As we have seen throughout this book, even in normal times people use a wide range of cooperative tactics—strikes, sabotage, street actions and the like—to solve common problems and remedy immediate grievances. Under the impact of deteriorating circumstances, such tactics are being used in a more concerted way, as in the case of recent nationwide meat boycotts, truckers' blockades and strike waves. We believe that only through an expansion of the methods and goals of such action can people resist the destruction of their conditions of life. We believe, further, that such an expansion contains the possibility of completely abolishing the control of society by a minority of owners and managers.

To gain some sense of how, under pressure of social crisis, day-to-day forms of popular direct action can develop into a concerted resistance movement, and how such a movement in turn can develop into a successful challenge to a ruling minority, it is instructive to look at the revolt of the American colonies against the government and king of Britain just two centuries ago.[1]

A decade before the American Revolution, almost all the American colonists considered British rule necessary, legitimate and desirable—an unchallengable fact of life. Within the framework of colonial society, however, there were already common patterns of popular resistance to established authority which laid much of the groundwork for the revolution to come. When British naval officers exercised their power of "impressment"—capturing seamen and forcing them to serve on British ships—people from the seaport towns repeatedly poured out to prevent them. When a sailor was impressed on the British ship *St. John* in 1764, for example, a crowd in Newport, Rhode Island, protected him when he escaped to the wharf; they captured the officers who pursued him, stoned the crew and later fired on the *St. John* herself.[2] Customs laws were circumvented on a massive scale by smugglers, with wide popular support; when customs officers were considered too vigorous in enforcing the law, they were subject to direct reprisals. In Falmouth, Maine, in 1766, a customs official's home was stoned, while "persons unknown and disguised" removed imported goods that had just been impounded.[3] Action by organized crowds was likewise frequent to prevent the export of food when supplies were low, to enforce measures against epidemics, and to obstruct the enforcement of unpopular laws. Extralegal direct action was common and widespread. At first it appeared to be mainly local, aimed at immediate grievances, and in no way meant to challenge British authority as a whole—and that, at first, was indeed the case.

The British government, faced with a growing debt from its imperial wars, in 1765 passed the Stamp Act, in effect putting a sales tax on many goods and services used in America. The proposed tax was unpopular. A contemporary remembered that "even the wise and good men" were "ready to do anything or everything to obtain relief," but did not know "what, when, where, how."[4] The solution people found was to apply the existing techniques of popular resistance to the new problem. The resistance movement started in Boston, where a small group of people one morning raised an effigy of the appointed tax official for Massachusetts. Word spread, and that night a large crowd paraded with the effigy, destroyed the dock that was to become the collector's office and then burned the effigy and attacked the official's home. The next day the taxman asked to be relieved of his appointment.

Such actions spread rapidly; within four months, the stamp-tax officials had been forced to resign in all but one of the thirteen colonies.[5] Colonists likewise declared a boycott of all British products, in order to put economic pressure on Britain. "Nonimportation associations" were organized throughout the country to enforce the boycott. Finally, the intrepid simply defied the new law, conducting business, publishing newspapers and holding court without the required tax stamps. On occasion, this defiance was backed by popular force. Meetings and crowds repeatedly insisted that port officials and law courts proceed to function without the required stamps. An armed, well-organized crowd of nearly seven hundred stopped customs officials who were interfering with the commerce of vessels at Cape Fear, North Carolina.[6]

For many months, these movements had little formal organization or communication. In each locality, informal groups simply took the initiative in calling local meetings or starting actions. Many of these groups eventually took the name "Sons of Liberty." They established committees to correspond with each other, and gradually developed a communications network linking activists from Maine to Georgia. Supporters of the movement published many newspapers which helped spread the word. The whole of American society entered into political ferment as artisans, merchants and backwoods farmers published, read and debated hundreds of pamphlets on political theory and what was to be done.

In the face of such a movement, loosely organized though it was, royal authority largely disintegrated. The colonial militias sympathized with the resistance movement, and refused to suppress it when royal governors were foolhardy enough to muster them.[7] Local Sons of Liberty groups prepared to resist should the British army be turned against them. Groups in several states even formally agreed

> to march with the utmost dispatch, at their own proper costs and expense, on the first proper notice (which must be signified to them by at least six of the sons of liberty) with their whole force if required . . . to the relief of those that shall, are, or may be in danger from the stamp act.[8]

Despite its relative militance, the movement against the Stamp Act remained limited in its objectives. Except for the issue of "taxation without representation," British rule of the colonies was never questioned; even the agreement for military cooperation quoted above declared "most unshaken faith and true allegiance to his Majesty King George the Third."[9] Blame for the oppression of the colonies was invariably placed, not on the British king, Parliament or nation, but rather on their agents. When, under the pressure of the American resistance movement, the British Parliament revoked the Stamp Act less than two years after its passage, the Sons of Liberty movement felt it had accomplished its purpose and quickly dissolved.[10]

The British government, however, was still in a financial bind, and in 1767 replaced the Stamp Act with a new set of taxes on American imports. The colonists replied with a renewed boycott of all British goods, backed by a "Nonimportation Agreement." The Nonimportation Association which enforced it began as a peaceful and legal movement to demand a change in British law. Its objective was at first limited to repeal of the new taxes; the royal governor of Massachusetts reported in 1770: "In other matters which have no relation to this dispute between Kingdom and Colonies, Government retains its vigour and the administration of it is attended with no unusual difficulties."[11]

As time went on, however, the Nonimportation Associations found themselves forced to take more and more power over the actual running of American society, until they became virtual countergovernments. In New England, the Town Meeting served as a means for "uniting the whole body of the people"[12] into the movement. Elsewhere, mass meetings served the same purpose. In Charlestown, South Carolina, for example, what started as a series of meetings of artisans and others to urge participation in the boycott developed into a "General Meeting of inhabitants" at the town "liberty tree," to discuss not only enforcement of the Nonimportation Agreement, but also "other Matters for the General Good."[13] Association committees held hearings, took testimony and examined the records of those suspected of violating the agreement, judged their guilt and imposed sanctions on violators, much like courts of law. Those found guilty were subjected to social ostracism, visits by angry crowds and, at times, tar-and-feathering. Public opinion seemed to treat the Nonimportation Agreement as more legitimate than the official government; one royal governor complained that tea smuggled from Holland could "lawfully be sold" in Boston, whereas it was considered "a high crime to sell any from England."[14]

Despite substantial concessions from Britain in 1770, colonial resistance continued to mount. Tactics remained much the same—harassment of British soldiers, attacks on customs ships, circumvention of British law. The grievances that precipitated action, however, were no longer seen as isolated incidents but rather as part of a general system of oppression. Blame for that oppression was no longer placed on the local agents of the British government, but successively on the cabinet, Parliament and, finally, on the king himself. At the same time, the ultimate objectives of the movement expanded. As the royal governor of Massachusetts later recalled, "At first . . . the supreme authority [of Parliament] seemed to be admitted, the cases of taxes only excepted; but the exceptions gradually extended from one case to another, until it included all cases whatsoever."[15]

The British government dispatched additional troops and passed a series of laws designed to coerce the colonists back into line. The result, however, was only to increase their felt need for unity in resistance. Divisions within local resistance movements melted away; as one contemporary put it, measures in support of the country's liberties were more important than previous personal political loyalties.[16] Intercolonial cooperation was established by means of Committees of Correspondence among the various colonial assemblies, initiated by a group of Virginians who, Thomas Jefferson recalled, "were all sensible that the most urgent of all measures [was] that of coming to an understanding with all the other colonies, to consider the British claims as a common cause of all, and to produce a unity of action. . . ."[17] A network of county and local Committees of Correspondence made it possible to spread information and plans for action with great speed through the entire population. In many localities, residents prepared for armed defense. In

1774, the Committees of Correspondence arranged for the various colonies to send representatives to a Continental Congress, which established a Continental Association against all commerce with Britain, and, while still not declaring America independent, made plans for armed resistance to British authority. The idea was widely expressed that "it is to ourselves we ought to trust, and not to the persons who may be in power on [the other] side of the water."[18]

The mass meetings and committees of the new Association began exercising government functions even more forcefully than the old. British attempts to repress the movement led to constant skirmishes, and finally to full-scale battles at Lexington and Concord, Massachusetts. The outbreak of war generated widespread support for a total break with Britain, as did the wide distribution of Thomas Paine's revolutionary pamphlet, *Common Sense*. The second Continental Congress in 1776 finally asserted American independence—something which had been far from the minds of those who started the resistance movement a decade earlier

The American Revolution did not just create a new, independent government on the pattern of the old, however. An observer in 1763, before the resistance movement began, noted that the American colonists were "no friends to republicanism," but loyal subjects of the king and the "most ardent lovers of that noble constitution of our mother country"—despite its monarchical and aristocratic elements.[19] When the Portsmouth, New Hampshire, Sons of Liberty fearfully considered the possibility of independence in 1766, they assumed that it would imply "erecting an independent Monarchy here in America."[20] But seven years of disillusionment with the British king so shifted opinion, that by 1773, many Americans agreed that "kings have been a curse to this and every other country where they have gained a footing"; of all men, "kings . . . are the least to be trusted."[21] Instead of creating a new monarchy, the Americans, in effect, formalized the organs of their resistance movement as the new governing authority of society, thus creating a new social system based on majority rule. Town meetings and general assemblies of the population became the essential source of power and legitimacy. Committees elected by them became the local government. The insurgent assemblies and congresses to which they had sent delegates became the new governing organs of society. Thus a form of popular power from below came to replace, for a time, a system of separate authority from above.

Just as the needs of the American colonists conflicted with the interests of the British government, so today the needs of working people are in conflict with the interests of those who control their labor. But just as the colonists required a decade of social conflict to develop the aim and capacity to replace their rulers, so today people are by no means likely to take over control of their society overnight. Only in the course of a protracted struggle are they likely to discover the need and possibility of doing so.

Of course, colonial society was far different from today's. As we have seen, the American people have been divided into a small group of managers and owners who control society, and a majority who work for them. Their work has become collective, not individual. In order to take control of their social conditions, they need not so much a different political authority, but a new way of organizing their productive activity. It is the control of society by a minority class, not the control of the state by a foreign power, that needs to be eliminated today. Yet the process by which this can be accomplished may well be similar in some respects to that of the first American Revolution.

As in colonial America, so today informal patterns of popular self-organization and resistance to authority are common features of everyday life. In the course of this book we have seen such patterns in many spheres of life. They are already often effective in opposing immediate grievances, but their power to deal with more fundamental problems is still extremely limited. Their participants usually accept the status quo in general, and do not see their resistance to particular acts of those in power as part of any larger movement, let alone a challenge to the existing organization of society.

When large numbers of people are affected by the same grievances, however, such action may spread on a wider social scale. The consumer meat boycotts, truckers' blockades and strike waves that developed in response to the inflation of the early 1970s illustrate the process by which tactics often used in isolated conflicts can come to be applied by millions of people who share common problems to which they can find no other solutions.

Such large actions over particular issues may successfully resist particular grievances, but they can do little to arrest the general deterioration of living conditions most people now face. The financially pressed British rulers were determined to raise money from the colonists in one way if not in another; similarly, those who control American society today are bound to continue trying to solve their problems by taking a larger share of what workers produce. If they can't do it one way, they will try to do it another.

The key to resisting their attempts is to make the strikes, blockades, street actions and other tactics already in use the tools of a concerted social movement, in which all the various actions of working people to meet their needs are recognized as part of a common struggle. At first such a movement might well resemble the Civil Rights movement of the 1960s, with people contesting the established authorities in every sphere of life, acting on their own initiative—but with an awareness that the struggles of each are the struggles of all, and that the fundamental interests of all working people are in conflict with those of the owners and managers. Creating such a movement is the key to resisting hard times today.

In order to become the instrument of all, such a movement would need to establish meetings, popular assemblies and action committees, not only in every community like the American colonists, but in every workplace, school, military unit and other social realm as well. These in turn would need to coordinate their actions with each other. We have already seen how even small-scale resistance actions tend to create a counterpower to management and other authorities. Such assemblies, in order to achieve their objectives, would have to take over much of the actual power in the spheres in which they function.

No doubt such a movement would start with limited objectives; it would aim only to redress particular grievances, not to eliminate the source of those grievances. There can be little doubt that people will be better able to resist the deterioration of their conditions through such a movement than without it, whether or not they aim for more fundamental social changes. But what they can achieve within the framework of the present organization of society, though important, is quite limited. As long as the power of the dominant minority remains intact, society will be run for the benefit of those few, with only occasional concessions to the population whose lives they control.

Such a movement, however, might well create the conditions for a direct challenge to minority power, much as the colonial movement against taxation became a direct challenge to British and monarchical authority. In the course of such movements, people can transform their assumptions about what is possible, necessary and desirable. When ruling groups long resist the actions people take to meet their needs, it becomes apparent that not one or another official, but a whole system of minority control is at fault. The development of assemblies and other organs of popular power creates an alternative means by which society can be organized. The ability of ordinary people to direct society themselves becomes increasingly apparent. The existence of a special, separate ruling authority comes to seem increasingly undesirable and unnecessary. Under such conditions, the objective of a popular resistance movement today might widen, just as it did in the American Revolution, to aim for the creation of a new kind of society, based on the complete elimination of all kinds of minority power.

No doubt such a movement would meet serious attempts at repression from the owners, managers and their supporters; they would be unlikely to let their power slip away without a fight. Historically, American employers have used whatever means of violence were available to them to control their workers, including the police, military and private armed forces. While those who control society are themselves a small minority, they would be likely to use their control over these highly organized instruments of violence to threaten or attack those challenging their rule. Indeed, on January 26, 1975, the *New York Times* reported that all 7200 policemen in Los Angeles were being trained in ''special crowd-control techniques to enable them to cope with any protests that might occur during the current recession,'' such as ''labor strikes, student protests, and other demonstrations that might occur.''

A unified movement of the entire working class would, however, have great power to forestall and disarm such attacks. It would include the overwhelming majority of the population, defending their own interests. They would be able, through strikes and other forms of direct action, to disrupt the processes from which the dominant classes draw their strength—the activity of workers. Those whose interests opposed them would be few in number. The military and police forces are themselves drawn from the working class; their willingness to risk their lives to fight against their own interests would not be unlimited. If the popular movement were sufficiently widespread, they might well refuse to suppress it; indeed, they might even join it, much as the militia did in colonial America.

Once such repressive forces were disbanded or disarmed, people would find themselves, their assemblies and other representative organs in control of society. They would thus already be organized in a manner which allowed them to begin coordinating their activity to meet their needs. Just as the American Revolution created organs of popular democracy which made kings and aristocrats unnecessary, so there would exist instruments of social organization making a special elite of managers and capitalists superfluous. Of course, nothing but people's own determination could prevent the establishment of some new minority power. But as long as the majority were determined to keep control of society in their own hands, they would possess the means to do so.

Whether such a transformation of society will indeed occur cannot be foreseen, any more than the American Revolution could have been foretold a few years before it occurred. The future depends both on unpredictable events over which most people have little control, and on how people themselves choose to respond to those events. Only by eliminating the basic power relations of our society can people fully control their lives and meet their needs. Even if they do not succeed in doing so, however, their efforts will not be wasted: A concerted struggle for the interests of all working people is also the way to achieve the best conditions that can be won within the framework of the existing society.

For everyone whose life is unfree and whose needs are unmet because of minority control of productive activity, the time has come to turn the techniques of day-to-day resistance into a concerted struggle for direct majority control of every aspect of social life.

Throughout this book we have tried to show the essential features of our society which prevent people from directing their own activity to meeting their own needs. A successful struggle for the interests of all working people would require the elimination of those features. There is no plan which can be drawn up in advance for such a struggle. Real solutions to the problems people face depend not on any program that can be written down and put in a book, but on the real development of people's ability to get together and act cooperatively in their own interest. People can develop that ability only through a constant process of acting, evaluating the results and acting again on the basis of what they have learned.

That process has already begun in the various forms of direct resistance that are escalating today as social crisis deepens. The evaluation of those actions and the planning of future actions is a job for millions of people, in every realm of their lives. Our own evaluation of actions so far, and the analysis of society presented in this book, lead us to suggest that action—from the smallest-scale act of informal resistance to the greatest mass upheaval—be guided by the following principles:

DIRECT COOPERATION AMONG PEOPLE TO MEET THEIR OWN NEEDS

Wherever people experience a need or problem in common, it is only rational that they should get together to try to meet it. But as we have seen, many aspects of our society are organized in ways which prevent such cooperation. Instead of cooperating in their own interest, people are supposed to follow the rules and orders established by their employers and other authorities. The power of those authorities rests largely on their ability to keep the people they rule apart.

We have seen many cases, however, where instead of following those rules and orders, people get together in their own interests, even when it brings them into conflict with the established authorities. People frequently cooperate in regulating the pace of work, getting free time on the job, limiting the authority of supervisors, raising incomes, protesting higher prices, preventing the fouling of their natural and social environment—the list could go on and on. These are actions which can and should be applied by any group of people who share a common problem. It is through such action that they can lay the groundwork for a more general resistance.

Such cooperative action rests on the understanding that individuals can meet their needs through joint action with others to reach common objectives which include their own. The development of that understanding is a social process; only when many individuals share it can it be effective.

The process of getting together generally develops within the social settings in which each of us live. If you shop, use a laundromat, send children to school or go yourself, you are put into relationships with the others who relate to these same facilities. If you go to work, you find yourself together regularly with a particular group of other workers. Most people know others in the neighborhood or building in which they live. Most people have a network of relatives and friends from past associations. Many belong to organizations, clubs, churches and other voluntary associations as well.

It is within these milieux that individual thoughts and feelings, when expressed by enough people, can come to be seen as shared sentiments. They are like melting pots in which what was individual may become social. Walking through a supermarket today, you may see even total strangers communicating to each other with gestures their exasperation at the latest price increases. Eavesdropping in diners and barrooms in early 1974, you could hear violent discussions of the fuel shortage among relatives and friends at table after table. At work, discussions both about the job and the rest of life go on, even when employers try to stamp them out.

Out of the shared sentiments of such milieux, people can begin to develop their ability to act together. The ways this can happen depend entirely on the concrete situation, on how people are feeling, on the immediate problems they face and on the means they have available to act. Action may start as simply an informal agreement to follow certain common rules, such as not working beyond an agreed-to pace. Or it may take dramatic forms, like a strike or "the people out of doors." It may be preceded by a long, slow process, through which a number of individuals gradually discover or decide that they are all willing to act. Or that willingness may crystallize quite suddenly.

We had described to us a recent example of such a sudden crystallization at a nonunion print shop on the Massachusetts North Shore. Just before Christmas, everyone at work was bickering with each other, squabbling over tools, getting on each other's nerves, when suddenly the boss announced that their holidays would be cut in the next year's contract. The workers all stopped work, gathered and started talking. On the spot they decided to strike, left the plant, returned with picket signs and decided to organize themselves into a union.

Sometimes the initiative of a minority or even a single individual may trigger the cooperative action of many. A young worker at the Dodge Truck plant in Detroit described to us how he closed the entire plant one day:

> In late '72, the company was running sixty hours a week, week after week. It was an extremely uptight situation; the atmosphere was explosive. A short time before Christmas, everyone came in one Saturday with booze, got loaded and simply didn't work. The company was shrewd enough to realize that it had pushed things as far as it could, so it announced no Saturday work till after New Year. After a couple of months they started Saturdays again, though. So one night I got stoned, went over to the office of an underground newspaper and made up a leaflet saying, "What If Chrysler Called a Saturday and Nobody Came?" I went to work half an hour early the next day and taped it up all over and passed it out. Other guys I didn't even know taped it to the cars moving down the line and put it up in the bathrooms.
>
> Next Saturday, a large part of the work force didn't show up, and many of those who did hoped others wouldn't so they could go home. Chrysler tried to run the lines extremely slowly for four hours—they had to pay everyone who showed up for that much anyway—then sent everybody home. Of course it wasn't something you could repeat again.

Sometimes the trigger for cooperative action may be a particular act by those in authority. Many, perhaps most, wildcat strikes are caused by firings, rate changes and other management acts. Similarly, the East Cambridge riots were directly provoked by the arrest and death of Larry Largey. Sometimes an idea that comes from outside the immediate milieu may be the stimulus for action. The idea of a consumer boycott of meat, for example, started with housewives in one community, but most people actually heard about the idea from the news media, and then decided to try it themselves.

Through the actual experiences of action, people can build up their capacity to cooperate. Coal miners, for example, have a strong tradition of solidarity and mutual support. An old IWW organizer with wide work experience told us:

> Direct action on the job has been most traditional among underground workers. If you're a miner, it's crazy to let some office two hundred miles away, or even a manager up on the surface, tell you whether it's safe to work. So underground miners have a tradition of acting on their own. If they're not sure what to do, sometimes they'll ask a more experienced miner whether it's safe or not. You can tell good solid rock by its ringing tone when you hit it. If it gives a dull thud, you don't want to work there whether the boss says it's all right or not.

Few groups of workers in recent years have used wildcat strikes so often or effectively as miners. Not only have they struck with great frequency over safety, job assignments and other immediate issues, but in 1969 coal miners in West Virginia used a twenty-three-day, state-wide wildcat strike to force the state legislature to pass a bill compensating victims of Black Lung disease.

Cooperation has become a habitual part of the way miners deal with a wide range of problems. During the 1974 gasoline shortage, the value of that habit was strikingly illustrated. Tens of millions of Americans, in the early part of that year, found themselves passing many hours every week looking for open gas stations and waiting in gas lines. The gas lines were a perfect symbol of the powerlessness of isolated individuals—hundreds of people, each in their own cars, strung out along the road, unable to do anything but wait as the time of their lives ticked by. Although millions of people were in exactly the same position all over the country; although the newspapers and TV reported daily on capped oil wells, tankers lined up with no storage facilities available to unload, and other evidence that the entire "shortage" was artificially created to increase the price of fuel; despite the frustration that broke out occasionally in fist fights and destruction of gas station property—despite all this, people remained locked in isolation and impotence. But the reaction of miners in West Virginia, with their established patterns of coopera-

tive action, was quite different. Tired of working all day under-
ground, only to spend much of their remaining time looking for gas,
a number of them talked about what to do and decided to stay away
from work, declaring that they would strike until gasoline was made
available. They went out with mobile pickets to other mines in the
area and asked the miners to join the strike. In less than a week,
10,000 miners in West Virginia and many more in Virginia and
Kentucky had joined the strike. The governor, much against his will,
was forced to order an immediate increase in the allocation to the
mining areas, and eventually to revise his gas rationing regulations
entirely.

By taking cooperative action whenever the opportunity arises,
people can build up patterns that make future cooperation easier to
initiate and maintain. When such a way of acting becomes habitual,
people can get together, organize themselves and fight for their own
interests in whatever situation they find themselves. They can
thereby not only begin to solve their immediate problems, but can
also begin to lay the groundwork for their organized takeover of
society.

UNIFICATION OF DIFFERENT GROUPS'
STRUGGLES

Most cooperative action today remains the action of particular
limited groups. When we went on the late-night talk show in Detroit,
a young auto worker who called in put the problem perfectly. After
proposing to disband the international union, he said:

> The people I work with can get together but maybe we don't
> understand the problems of someone up the line or in another
> part of the plant. But you'd still have to get together with
> people on a larger scale in the plant and with different plants.
> How can you do that? I don't know. I've been thinking a lot
> about it. Nobody wants to get together and organize anything
> after work or anything—everyone's dog tired after twelve
> hours. I don't know. I'm either going to start to organize or
> else I'm going to quit.

As long as action remains limited to small groups, its power
remains limited as well. Only cooperation on a wide scale can
overcome this weakness..Such cooperation depends on an apprecia-
tion of the common interests that people share, even when their
immediate situations are not identical.

Action

Development toward such wide-scale cooperation can already be seen at a number of points. One of the simplest, yet most significant, is the common refusal of workers to cross each other's picket lines, even for groups of workers and industries which seem totally unrelated. Such mutual support reflects a recognition that all working people are in the same basic predicament, and that they need each other's help in dealing with it.

We saw a small but particularly dramatic example of such mutual support during the wildcat occupation of the Mack Avenue Chrysler plant in Detroit by a group of workers protesting the firing of militants (see page 74). As we hung out at a gas station across the street, we heard a middle-aged white man in the clothes of a railroad worker talking with three black strikers whom he had evidently drawn over from the plant. He told them:

> Look, we've been told to bring stuff into the plant on the railroad spur that runs along the back. You guys haven't got a single picket up there, so we don't have any excuse for not bringing the stuff in. So if you want us to help out, why don't you put a picket line up on the tracks, just like you would for trucks.

He pointed out to them where they should place the pickets, and then disappeared again into the traffic of the city.

Mutual support may develop from smaller groups reaching out to each other. For example, workers on different shifts will often come to work a little early or leave a little late in order to socialize, exchange information and coordinate activity with members of other shifts. We asked a mechanic in a truck-building factory, whose work group had helped pull a number of plant-wide actions, how to get people organized in a plant beyond those who work directly side by side. He said:

> First of all, you have to want to do it—you have to realize that it's important. Then, you just make a point of trying to get to know people in different parts of the plant—like you would anyway, but a little more deliberately. Then when a situation arises where there's some kind of action to take, you make a point of spreading the word about it to the people you know, so that those channels get built up in a kind of organized way.

At times, informal networks of friends, acquaintances and family can be made channels for communication and cooperation among people who live and work in different places. During the 1973 consumer meat boycott, whole communities were rapidly mobilized, largely by the use of such networks.

Large-scale coordination by no means develops only from smaller groups reaching out to each other; it can just as well arise through a broader movement which stimulates various groups to participate in common actions. The 1973 meat boycott illustrated this kind of organization as well: Thousands of informal and occasionally formal groups sprang up in a few weeks, as housewives all over the country latched onto the idea of the protest and made it their own.

Imitation often plays an important role in spreading large-scale actions. In the nationwide postal wildcat in 1970, for example, postal workers all over took their lead from the strikers in New York City. The New York group maintained some contact by phone with other strikers; perhaps even more important was the news of their action coming over the radio and TV. At one point in the strike, representatives from many insurgent locals met in Washington to negotiate with the government and the leaders of their own union who were opposing the strike. In the years following the strike, local militants throughout the country have maintained an informal network for exchanging information and plans in their action against both the Post Office and the leadership of the postal unions.

Another interesting example was the organization of the strike by independent truckers against government fuel policy in early 1974. These truckers were owner/operators, somewhere between ordinary workers and self-employed small businessmen. Only a minority of them belonged to either the Teamsters Union or any of a number of small independent-operator associations. Often fiercely individualistic, they are a group whose action might seem almost impossible to coordinate. Yet they were able not only to organize their strike, but to virtually drive strikebreakers from the roads throughout more than forty states. Their organization was based on two resources—the truck-stop and the short-wave radio. Strikers in each area would gather at the truck-stops, discuss their next action, and take votes to establish their policy. Many of the truckers had short-wave radios in their rigs, with which they kept in touch when patrolling for strikebreakers. (As usual, news coverage also helped strikers in different parts of the country keep informed on each other's activities.) While a motley array of individuals and groups ranging from the governor of Pennsylvania to the head of a magazine for owner/operators to Frank Fitzsimmons of the Teamsters Union rushed to Washington claiming to "represent" the truckers in negotiations with the government, the drivers stayed in the truck-stops, waiting for the government—and their "representatives"—

to make them an acceptable offer. After long negotiations the government made an offer which the "representatives" accepted. But the drivers in the truck-stops discussed the proposal, decided it wouldn't solve their problem and would only increase inflation, and voted it down all over the country. They treated those claiming to represent them as, in effect, bargaining agents for the government. Only when they got a better offer did the drivers finally vote to go back to work.

At times, mutual support can spread to seemingly unrelated groups. For example, coal miners and laundry workers in Uniontown, Pennsylvania, several years ago staged sympathy strikes in support of hospital workers who were trying to organize a union.[22] Similarly, during the 1969 strike against General Electric, 1300 workers at United Shoe Machinery in Beverly, Massachusetts, struck for nineteen days so as not to produce parts for GE.[23] In Philadelphia in 1973, we saw large numbers of workers with a wide variety of occupations joining the picket lines of striking teachers. When the city government arrested and jailed eight hundred of the teachers, the unions of Philadelphia voted to call a general strike, which was only headed off when federal intervention brought a last-minute settlement.

Such cooperation holds the potential for overcoming the separation of isolated groups. Throughout its history, the tendency toward such solidarity has been one of the most important features of working-class life. Nonetheless it remains sporadic. Only by building it into a habitual pattern of mutual support can it become a reliable means for meeting the needs of all.

PEOPLE'S CONTROL OF THEIR OWN ORGANIZATIONS

Any collective action involves some form of organization. Most organizations that exist today—unions, governments, associations of many kinds—are marked by a sharp distinction between leaders and officials on the one hand and rank-and-file members on the other. The officials may be elected, but they, not the rank and file, manage the affairs of the group.

Often such a division develops within organizations in which the ordinary participants originally held control. We have seen, for example, how many unions evolved from expressions of the direct cooperation of groups of workers to a bureaucratic apparatus through which top officials control them. Such organizations reflect not the power but the powerlessness of their members.

Throughout this book we have described actions which, in contrast, are initiated and directly controlled by those who participate in them. They have ranged from actions regulating the pace of work to wildcat strikes to boycotts to "the people out of doors." These actions contain the seeds of an alternative mode of organization, through which people can control their own cooperation.

That mode of organization may be embodied in many varying patterns. Some may be entirely informal, like the work groups we have seen engaging in resistance on the job. Others may be more formal, involving coordinating organs with elected representatives and a public visibility. Some may arise only for one occasion, like the informal group that pioneered street action in East Cambridge to protest the death of Larry Largey. Some may be sporadic, like the informal networks that often exist among militants in various parts of an industry, which only become active before and during wildcat strikes. Some may be continuous—many informal resistance groups at work, for example, go on year after year, even though individual participants may come and go.

The extent, permanence and formality of such organizations depend upon the tasks they have to perform. What they all have in common is that the ideas and plans have been discussed and agreed to by those who act. In that process, people take joint mental control of their activity and make it a tool for their own use.

Such mutual control of common activity can be a continuous process accompanying other activities, for people who are working or living side by side every day. In groups which are dispersed, or too large for such direct contact, it is more difficult to maintain a flow of information, ideas, sentiments and decisions. Often organization arises through one group's taking the initiative in action, while others simply coordinate through imitation, as in the case of the 1970 postal workers strike. More systematic organization may result when different groups send representatives to each other's discussions, or when a number of groups send members to meet to interchange ideas and coordinate plans on a larger scale.

Of course, such coordinating bodies can always become the starting point for the development of a new, centralized leadership separate from the other participants. Such a development can only be prevented if people keep their ability to discuss, decide and act for themselves, never giving it up to any separate power. This intention can be embodied in limitations on representatives. For example, the principle can be established that no representative or group of representatives holds any authority on its own; they are merely spokespeople for those they represent, and can be mandated, rotated or recalled at the will of the group. Similarly, representative organs—strike committees, councils or whatever—can be allowed to serve only as coordinating bodies, with no means of their own to impose their will on those they represent, except through the action of the groups which make them up. Even such limitations, however, are no guarantee against the development of leaders and organs with their own power, unless those they represent keep alive their capacity to think and act for themselves.

Many people argue for a different approach to organization, one with strong leaders and far more centralized power. For example, a steelworker in Gary, active in union reform, told us:

> I think we need more leaders not less of them. Like this guy Bob where I work. Everybody listens to Bob. When there's a question about what to do, people go to him. He knows the situation; he's a fighter, but he knows when to fight and when to lay low. They know they can trust him. He's a committeeman, but he's not like the rest of them. Of course, you have to have a strong rank and file to serve as a check on the leaders. I wouldn't want to be in a leadership position myself without that.

Similarly an old-time militant in Detroit, active for many years in the reform caucus of the UAW, explained to us that he believed in trying to resurrect the union because "isolated struggles will always lose eventually against employers as powerful as the auto companies."

These arguments are based on a correct perception, but they draw the wrong conclusion. People need as much knowledge, understanding and unity as they can get. But they need to get them for themselves, for everyone, not for any special group of leaders or representatives. Such distinctions between "leaders" and other people reflect not people's strength but their weakness.

Of course, people are in fact different. Some will grasp problems more quickly than others; some will be more intrepid in action; some will be good at getting people together. Everyone has their own unique contribution to make to common struggles. If leadership implies not followership but rather initiative, insight, courage and the ability to get people together, then we do indeed need more leaders, not fewer of them. Indeed, an appropriate slogan would be the statement of a group of Wobblies in Everett, Washington: Asked who their leaders were, they replied: "We don't got no leaders— we're all leaders."[24]

Social groups are composed of particular individuals with particular interests. Whatever people may say in their speeches or proclaim in their programs, they are likely, in the long run, to try to follow their own individual and group interests. When any group of officials or politicians becomes distinct from a body of people, it is likely to develop separate interests. They may claim to support the general interest, and they may indeed find it to their advantage to do so for a time. But when their interests change, they are entirely likely to follow them, even if it means "selling out" those whose support they have courted. Only by keeping control of their activity themselves can people make sure that it serves their own interests, not those of a new separate power.

EQUALITY WITHIN THE WORKING CLASS

Our society divides the working class into many groups, some with special privileges, others with special deprivations. It creates a hierarchy based on occupation, race, sex, religion, nationality, income and similar factors. Such inequality, in addition to its evident injustice, tends to divide people into competing groups, battling each other even when their long-range interests may be the same.

The very structure of a society where people have to compete for jobs, housing, education and other social resources tends to divide people into antagonistic groups. Under such conditions, many special groups have sought their own interests at the expense of others, thus further aggravating these divisions. Employers have often deliberately fostered divisions among workers as part of a strategy to "divide and rule."

There is no reason for people not to differ from each other as much as they like in taste or life style; toleration for such diversity is an important aspect of human freedom. But when inequalities among social groups result in deprivation or impede cooperation, they must be straightforwardly attacked.

As we have seen, job hierarchies with unequal pay and privileges are an important source of such divisions. They create privileged groups of workers who often side with the employer or at least "try not to rock the boat." At the same time, they create a group of workers who have little choice but to accept jobs at below-standard wages. They provide a carrot through which employers can manipulate the aspirations and behavior of those workers who hope for advancement.

Differences in income might make sense if the benefits went to those who performed the most undesirable jobs, but in reality the worst jobs are also usually the lowest paid. They also might make sense if those with the greatest needs—large families to support or

221

extra medical expenses, for example—received the highest incomes. But at present, some workers are likely to make more than others because of seniority with their employer, their sex, race or age, greater opportunities to go to school or learn skills, the economic strength of their employer and other factors that have little to do with either their sacrifices or their needs. Everyone makes the same essential sacrifice of the time of their lives when they go to work; unless they make some special additional sacrifice, or have special needs, there is no reason why all should not receive the same return for their labor.

Attacks on inequality on the job have taken various forms. Occasionally union locals have fought for and won pay equality for all of their members. For example, a woman who had worked in a factory which processed hamburgers and steaks told us that everyone from the butcher to the packer received the same wages. Similarly, it is common in Teamsters locals for the drivers, dispatchers and even the sweepers to get the same pay. In the early days of the CIO unions, many pushed for cents-per-hour rather than percentage wage increases, thus narrowing the ratios between different groups of workers with each wage increase. In the cases we have described of workers instituting job rotation, one of the main reasons for doing so has been to equalize the work, giving everyone a turn at the more and less desirable jobs. Many struggles by workers to get control over the job assignment process have been motivated by a desire to prevent it from being used as a means of favoring some individuals or groups over others.

Racial, sexual and other forms of inequality pervade our society. As long as they exist, they not only perpetuate an injustice against their victims but also greatly weaken the ability of working people to cooperate in their own interest. Struggles against such forms of inequality, therefore, are in the interest of all working people, even if they may seem to threaten temporarily the advantages of the more privileged groups. Only through such struggles can the basis for true unity of interest and action be created.

DEMOCRATIZATION OF KNOWLEDGE AND THOUGHT

Our society has centralized knowledge, planning and decision-making in the hands of a minority of managers and professionals. We have seen how employers took the skill and knowledge required to run the production process away from skilled workers and transferred it to the managerial cadre. A similar process occurred in many other spheres of life, as human intelligence came to be regarded as the function of special "experts," rather than of people in general. As a result, much of people's lives has been reduced to following instructions, obeying orders and "doing what you're told."

Most people see little reason to read or think about society, beyond perhaps what they need to know to cast a ballot every couple of years. Managerial contempt for the role of workers' intelligence is summed up in the phrase "we're not paying you to think." The feeling that they don't know or understand enough to run society is one of the prime reasons people let leaders, officials and politicians direct their activities, even when these leaders are distrusted or despised.

As long as people have no responsibility for making decisions, there is little reason for them to study or think about production or society. But as soon as they begin trying to act on their own, the need for knowledge and thought becomes evident.

In the past, the working class has had strong intellectual traditions of its own. In the early 1800s, the shoemakers of Lynn, Massachusetts, regularly hired a boy to read to them while they worked.[25] Nearly a century later, the cigarmakers of New York listened to readings from the newspapers and even from Karl Marx's *Capital*. The Wobbly halls of the West in the early years of the twentieth century maintained heavily used libraries of books ranging from the novels of Jack London to works on sociology, economics, politics and history. Many an old-timer can tell of haunting the public library in search of answers during the Great Depression of the 1930s. This tradition was made vivid for us by the recollections of an old union and radical organizer from his childhood just before World War I:

> When I was a kid in Ohio, one of my favorite spots was the land along the B&O tracks, a lone spot outside the city about ten miles.
>
> This was a recognized hobo jungle. In the afternoon the hoboes would start jumping off the trains and wandering into this place. These men came from every spot in the U.S. and these men had been in every spot of the U.S. Represented every type of life in the U.S.; some men college graduates, some from factories, some workers in transit, unemployed, the regular migrant worker that goes from harvest to harvest, also workers that were no workers at all, had no intention of working, just rebelling against conditions that existed. It was amazing how much these men knew about life, because they had lived it. They didn't need it from a book. They knew about the conditions of the western wheat fields, they knew about the

> condition of the far west fruit farms. From these men I heard the names of Herbert Spencer, Nietzsche, Plato, Aristotle, Huxley, Marx, Schopenhauer and God knows whom else. Profound philosophical discussions. Theories of how to form society. These discussions I can never forget because the profundity of them was amazing. They could only come from one who had been everywhere, done everything. Could only come from the hobo family. This was sort of my early education.

The exclusion of workers from decision-making and the emphasis on formal education as the prerequisite for decision-making responsibility have created the idea that research, study and serious thought are something for students, experts and managers. But if working people are to take control of their own activity, they need the widest knowledge and the best thought they can muster. Any basic reorganization of society will require a ferment of social and political discussion like that which preceded the American Revolution.

The development of such knowledge and thought is a social process. People need to exchange ideas and information with each other in the freest possible way, drawing on the experiences of all. In fact, people discuss their lives and their society with each other all the time, at work and in the other milieux in which they live. Where thinking is seen not just as an abstract exercise, but as something that bears on important questions of what to do, discussions can become more focused and deliberate. They may result in decisions to get together to discuss, study or write about some particular question. Through such means, people can begin to recreate an independent, working-class intellectual culture. Brain-numbing hours of labor may make this difficult. But the alternative is to be in the position of sailors who dare not mutiny because the art of navigation has been kept a secret from them.[26]

MUTUAL CONTROL OF ALL PRODUCTIVE ACTIVITY

In any society, people have to transform nature to meet their needs. In early America, as we have seen, this was done largely by individuals and families working with a relatively simple technology, producing primarily for their own personal consumption. With the development of transportation and machinery, production became ever more interdependent. Most work processes came to require the collaboration of many people, each performing different parts of the labor. Each such group produced only a narrow range of products, and was dependent on other groups for things it needed. This division of labor is actually a gigantic network of cooperation, in which millions of people produce for the needs of all.

Unfortunately, however, this cooperation did not develop under the control of all; it was controlled by those who possessed the wealth to acquire the means of production and hire others. The result has been to put the cooperative activity of millions under the control of a small minority of owners and managers. Work, far from being an expression of people's own needs and desires, has become an expression of their submission to the interests and purposes of a special ruling minority.

Returning to a society based on private production by individuals or small groups working for themselves alone would hardly be a solution to this problem. Interdependence is inevitable, unless people choose to give up the use of modern technology and return to a society where each individual or group is limited to the things they themselves can produce—thereby generating suffering and want on a colossal scale.

Nor would it be a solution to replace those who now control production with some new centralized managerial authority, such as the state. Attempts to increase the power of government over the economy are a frequent response to difficulties in the capitalist system. Such attempts may come from many directions. Liberal economist John Kenneth Galbraith, for example, has recently urged that substantial parts of the American economy be taken away from capitalist ownership and turned over to the government, while continuing to be managed by those who now run them. In times of crisis, employers themselves have turned to partial state control of the economy, as in the National Recovery Administration of the Great Depression, giving up some of their individual autonomy in order to retain their collective power. A prominent New York investment banker, for example, has recently called for a "new Reconstruction Finance Corporation" with far broader powers than that of the 1930s, which would invest public money in failing companies, spearhead development in energy and other spheres and perhaps even become the instrument of long-range federal economic planning.[27] Various left-wing political parties propose to carry out revolutions through which all production would be nationalized and controlled by the state. This type of society already exists in the various state-socialist countries, where a ruling bureaucracy, the Communist Party, governs through its control of the state, and directs the whole of a government-owned economy. All these approaches have in common an attempt to overcome the irrationalities of the present system by establishing a strong central coordination of social production—while keeping control in the hands of a minority. Instead of working for private employers, people work for the state. But the productive wealth and the productive process of society—and therefore the conditions of people's lives—are still controlled by another social group. For most people, the realities of daily life are hardly changed.

Any system in which natural resources, labor and the products of past labor are controlled by a special group of people prevents other people from getting together to define and meet their mutual needs. Only when the majority take possession in common of the means of production and organize their own labor themselves can they assure their own well-being.

Such a reorganization of society must be the goal of any movement which aims to meet the needs of working people. Likewise, it is through such a movement that this goal can be achieved. It requires the creation of organs of popular power—direct assemblies of people in various spheres of life and delegate bodies representing them—through which people can take control of their activity away from those who now possess it, to exercise it themselves. It requires that they overcome whatever forces try to prevent their emancipation. Finally, it requires that they prevent any new system of minority control from developing in the place of the old one.

Such groups of individuals would have to cooperate in common action which they discussed, planned, determined and executed themselves. Different groups would have to coordinate their activities with each other on many different levels, from those working or living side by side, to society as a whole. People would have to work mutually to meet each other's needs—the common needs of society.

The organs of coordination at first might well be those created in the struggle for majority power. No doubt groups and their interconnections would evolve over time along with changing social capacities and desires. Only constant experimentation could determine how best to combine the benefits of large-scale planning with those of individual and small-group control of the immediate environment. Even such an approach could never completely eliminate conflict between various levels and groups—precisely because it could reflect so truly people's various needs and interests, which at times must come into conflict even in a context of equality and abundance.

If the rest of social life were left unchanged, the transfer of social power in itself would mean little. Its function is to make it possible for people to overcome the barriers to a good life erected by our present system of minority rule. People would be able to make their work serve their own needs and desires as they defined them. No doubt a primary objective would be to provide for the well-being and security of all, particularly through an expansion of production in those areas where the old society most failed to meet people's needs, such as medical care and housing. Another might well be a new kind of planning, through which people would use their control of social activity to shape the entire social and natural environment to their needs and desires.

Such social reorganization would mean a complete transformation of work itself. People would no longer work as instruments of someone else's purposes, but set their purposes themselves. They would no longer work to make profits for the rich, but to meet their own needs. The authority of the employer would be gone; people would direct their own labor. The result would be a great expansion of the realm in which people could—indeed, would have to—exercise their freedom, creativity and intelligence.

Nonetheless, many jobs would at first remain unpleasant, boring, repetitive or dangerous. But those subjected to them would be in a position to eliminate unsafe and unpleasant conditions, while automating or reorganizing as much of the boring work as possible. The whole organization of work and technology as a means of controlling workers could be reversed; new engineering systems could be developed to facilitate workers' control of production. Finally, by eliminating the millions of jobs from plant guards to salesmen that produce nothing but waste or are necessary only for the old society, by including the unemployed and underemployed in useful work, and especially by a massive automating of production, people could reduce the part of their lives they spend providing the necessities to a fraction of what it is today.

Such a society would open possibilities for human development we can only dream about today. Liberated from drudgery and toil, people could use their capacity for creativity to its full extent, making possible an unprecedented blossoming of beauty and knowledge, while transforming daily life from a realm of monotony to one of free development. Freed from the constant insecurity about the future that haunts everyone today, daily life could lose much of its undercurrent of anxiety, making possible a kind of pleasure in living that most people now can experience only rarely. No longer forced to compete for the necessities of life, but rather having everything to gain from a spirit of cooperation, people would be able to reduce greatly the realm of interpersonal hostility and expand that of

227

interpersonal trust. No doubt problems and difficulties would always remain, but people would be in a position for the first time to bring the full capacities of humanity to bear in solving them.

The evolution of our society has already laid the basis for such a transformation. It has created an interdependence through which the needs of each can only be securely provided for by meeting the needs of all. Its great productive capacities have raised hopes for a life of pleasure and satisfying activity, only to dash them with the reality of want and toil. It has reduced those who own and manage the means of production to a small number, while forcing the overwhelming majority of the population to work for them. It has put in the hands of that majority the capacity to stop social production entirely, or to determine the way it proceeds. It has thereby given them the power to shape it to their will.

The time has come to use that power.

A FAREWELL: NO DRESS BEFORE THE IRON

Faced with the daily grind of a life largely sacrificed to the struggle to get by; opposed by the entire organized forces of the rich, the powerful and their supporters; buffeted by the chaos of a society controlled by others—it is no wonder that people despair that life could ever really change. And yet, ordinary people possess the greatest potential power in society. Their activity largely makes up society. All they need to do to reshape the world as they would like is to take mutual control of their own actions. The belief that they cannot do so, far from expressing what has to be, itself serves as a barrier to realizing what could be.

At the end of her haunting story, "I Stand Here Ironing," Tillie Olsen asks for her daughter:

> Help her to know—help make it so there is cause for her to know—that she is more than this dress on the ironing board, helpless before the iron. [28]

To be like that dress, a pure object of external forces, compelled to do whatever they command—a number, a thing—no human being should tolerate. We have tried throughout this book to show both the external forces that try to induce people to submit to the will and interest of others, and people's attempts to resist being reduced to passive objects. There is an old working-class saying: "It's a good life—if you don't weaken." We think "not to weaken" means not to surrender like the dress, not to accept whatever is imposed upon you, but to fight for yourself, even when the odds are against you. Through such a fight, people can try to take the time of their lives away from those who now control it and use it for themselves. Just through that struggle itself, they can take over part of the control of their activity for themselves, and give themselves a chance to make their lives more interesting, creative, friendly and pleasurable. That is why we believe it may be possible to lead a good life, even given the forces against us—if we don't weaken.

Method of Wrapping an Apple

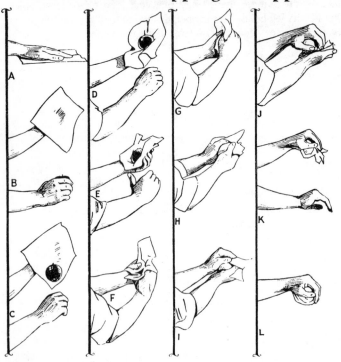

(a) Picking up the wrap.
(b) Picking up the apple.
(c) Throwing the apple into the wrap.
(d) Position of apple upon striking wrap.
(e) Wrapping process, first stage.
(f) Wrapping process, second stage.
(g) Apple held tightly in right hand, pressing apple against cup formed by left hand.

(h) Apple turned within cup formed by left hand, both wrists turning toward right.
(i) Hands turning over completely.
(j) Back of left hand upward, back of right hand downward.
(k) Apple ready for placing in box, right hand reaching for next apple.
(l) Placing wrapped apple in box.

A NOTE ON THE INTERVIEWS

In preparing this book, we talked at length with upwards of a hundred people about their lives, work, ideas and observations. All quotations, unless otherwise footnoted, come from these discussions.

We started with the idea that most people know a good deal about the social world in which they live; if they didn't, they wouldn't survive to tell about it. This doesn't mean that any individual's knowledge of his or her society is perfect; on the contrary, each of us has a view limited and distorted by our own circumscribed experience. That is why people need to learn from each other.

In our discussions, we were searching primarily for an understanding of the structure of everyday life—both the circumstances people face and what people do about them. We never considered ourselves to be studying the people we talked with, or surveying their opinions. Rather, we approached them as experts on the social worlds in which they lived and as colleagues in trying to make sense of our common situation.

In almost all cases, we told people straightforwardly that we were working on a book which dealt with what people like ourselves were thinking and doing about life and work. Most people we approached were more than willing to talk. "We want to be in the first chapter" was a frequent, smiling comment. We did not usually conduct formal interviews; mostly we had freewheeling discussions in which we asked a lot of questions, but felt free to put in our own two-cents worth as well.

We decided not to tape-record discussions, both to keep them informal and to allow discussion of sabotage and other subjects that cautious individuals would not want to put on tape. For the same reason we often changed names and identifying details in our accounts. The price of not taping discussions was to lose much of the spice and flavor of individual styles of language and storytelling, which may well be the most impressive forms of popular art in our society. We tried to write up discussions as soon after they occurred as possible. Because there were two of us, we were usually able to check each other's memories for accuracy. We do not claim that quotes are word-for-word correct, but we think we have reproduced the content of what people told us with a good degree of accuracy. Our confidence in this was bolstered when a friend who had sat in on a several-hour discussion we had with six other people read our write-up of it and commented, "If they see this, they're going to think you smuggled a tape recorder in there."

While we tried to talk with people from a wide range of occupations, backgrounds, ages, ethnic roots and locations, we have not aimed for a "random sample." Nor do we pretend that those we talked with were "typical" workers or typical anything else—we think the very idea that anyone could be typical of a whole class is as insulting as it is ridiculous. If somebody else had asked the questions we did, if we had asked different questions or if we had approached people in a different way, the answers would no doubt have been different. Readers should bear in mind the words with which an old-timer taunted us: "There's no use asking people what they think; they'll tell you one thing today—tomorrow, they'll tell you something different." The statements we quote in this book—like all such materials—are only what particular people said at particular times in the context of particular discussions.[1] We have learned much from them, nonetheless, and we think others will as well.

NOTES

INTRODUCTION

The conception of human thought and action sketched briefly here has been drawn from many sources. However, we have listed only those which were consulted specifically in the writing of this book.

George Kelly, *The Psychology of Personal Constructs* (New York: Norton, 1955), provides a useful model both for the ways individuals construct their understanding of the world and for the central role of expectation in that process. The first three chapters of the book are available in a paperback edition under the title *A Theory of Personality* (New York: Norton, 1963). Jean Piaget provides a useful developmental model for the interaction between a mental system and its environment. A good introduction to his work is Herbert Ginsburg and Sylvia Opper, *Piaget's Theory of Intellectual Development* (Englewood Cliffs, N.J.: Prentice-Hall, 1969). We also found useful Jean Piaget, *Six Psychological Studies,* trans. Anita Tenzer and David Elkind (New York: Random House, 1967). Several essays about how people learn and change in Gregory Bateson, *Steps to an Ecology of Mind* (New York: Ballantine Books, 1972), were very helpful, especially "The Logical Categories of Learning and Communication" and "Cybernetic Explanation." In thinking about the nature of human nature, we found Ernest G. Schactel, *Metamorphosis* (New York: Basic Books, 1959), particularly interesting.

We would like to stress, however, that in our view, no psychological theory can be applied directly to the explanation of social phenomena. Unfortunately, we found usable developmental social models hard to come by. Jean-Paul Sartre's later work provides an important analysis of social group formation. The first part of his *Critique of Dialectical Reason* has been translated into English with the title *Search for a Method,* trans. Hazel E. Barnes (New York: Alfred A. Knopf, 1963). The untranslated parts most relevant to the subject of this book have been carefully summarized in Wilfred Desan, *The Marxism of Jean-Paul Sartre* (Garden City, N.Y.: Doubleday, 1965). Another summary, with a greater focus on psychological issues, is R. D. Laing and D. G. Cooper, *Reason and Violence* (New York: Humanities Press, 1964). An important conception of the relation between the experience, ideas, expectations and action of social groups is presented in Georges Sorel, *Reflections on Violence* (New York: Collier Books, 1961). An attempt to view the relation of thought and action in the context of human evolution is Anton Pannekoek, *Anthropogenesis* (Amsterdam: North-Holland Publishing, 1953); although his archaeological data are somewhat dated, his ideas are still of interest. For a discussion of the background of many of these ideas in Hegel, Marx, existentialism and pragmatism, a good starting point is Richard J. Bernstein, *Praxis and Action* (Philadelphia: University of Pennsylvania Press, 1971). We have also learned a great deal from Paul Mattick, *Marx and Keynes* (Boston: Porter Sargent, 1969) and Karl Korsch, *Karl Marx* (New York: Russell & Russell, 1963). Alfred Chandler's business history, *Strategy and Structure: Chapters in the History of the American Industrial Enterprise* (Cambridge, Mass.: MIT Press, 1962), provides much food for thought about the relationship between social functions and their institutional manifestations.

1. Spendable weekly earnings of production or nonsupervisory workers with three dependents who are on private nonagricultural payrolls in constant 1967 dollars. Calculated from U.S. Department of Labor, Bureau of Labor Statistics, news release, 21 January 1976, and from the same agency's *Handbook of Labor Statistics, 1974* (Washington, D.C., 1974).
2. "Inflation: The Big Squeeze," *Newsweek,* 4 March 1974, pp. 58–62.
3. John Steinbeck, *The Grapes of Wrath* (New York: Viking Press, 1939), p. 477.
4. For a good discussion and critique of various stereotypes of the working class, see Robert Coles, "Understanding White Racists," *New York Review of Books,* 30 December 1971.
5. Thomas Paine, *Common Sense and The Crisis* (Garden City, N.Y.: Dolphin Books, 1960), p. 11.

CHAPTER 1

In this book we have only hinted at the great variety of actual work experience in different occupations and industries. We have tried instead to focus on the essential elements most employment has in common. For a massive documentation of the diversity of work experiences, stressing the lack of personal fulfillment in most contemporary work, see Studs Terkel's collection of interviews, *Working* (New York: Pantheon Books, 1974).

1. *Historical Statistics of the United States* (Washington, D.C.: U.S. Department of Commerce, 1960), which carefully compiles the most reliable available statistics from many sources, is able to give the hours of labor during the 1920s and '30s for workers in manufacturing only. During the boom years of the 1920s these hours were higher than today, but during the depression of the 1930s they were lower. The average weekly hours of production was 40.9 from 1926 to 1935 for workers in manufacturing (calculated from *Historical Statistics,* Series D 626–34, p. 92). The average weekly hours for manufacturing workers in April 1973, surprisingly enough, was 40.8 *(The American Almanac* [New York: Grosset & Dunlap, 1973], p. 228). The great decrease in hours worked preceded 1925. There has been some decline more recently in the average hours worked by all workers, but it is largely concentrated in wholesale and retail trade and results in large part from the influx of part-time workers, predominantly women, into these occupations, not from a decrease in the hours of those already employed full time.

To estimate the time spent at work and in travel to and from the job by full-time workers, we used the figure for married men presented in Michael Young and Peter Willmott, *The Symmetrical Family* (London: Routledge & Kegan Paul, 1973), table p. 348, since most married men in the United States are full-time workers, whereas a large proportion of those in other sex/marital categories are not. The figures are for men aged 18 to 64 in U.S. cities.

2. Bertolt Brecht, "Song of the Invigorating Effect of Money," *Selected Poems,* trans. H. R. Hays (New York: Grove Press, 1959), pp. 83–5.

3. *Social Indicators, 1973* (Washington, D.C.: U.S. Department of Commerce, 1973), chart 5/15, p. 164. While income statistics abound, reliable, updated information on the distribution of wealth is extremely difficult to come by.

4. The recent literature on job discontent and job enrichment is vast. A liberal, "humanitarian" approach marks *Work in America,* the Report of a Special Task Force to the Secretary of Health, Education and Welfare, prepared under the auspices of the W. E. Upjohn Institute for Employment Research (Cambridge, Mass.: MIT press, 1973). Also from the Upjohn Institute is a report on studies of job discontent, Harold L. Sheppard and Neil Q. Herrick, *Where Have All the Robots Gone?* (New York: The Free Press, 1972). *The Job Revolution,* by ex-*Fortune* editor Judson Gooding (New York: Walker, 1972), describes in inspirational tones the great gains in profits and productivity which await employers who fight employee boredom through job enrichment. The U.S. Senate Subcommittee on Employment, Manpower and Poverty of the Committee on Labor and Public

Welfare, *Hearings on Worker Alienation,* 92nd Cong., 2nd sess., 1972, includes a range of statements on this subject. So also do a series of papers presented at the Symposium on Technology and the Humanization of Work at the 139th meeting of the American Association for the Advancement of Science, Philadelphia, 27 December 1971. Georges Friedmann, *The Anatomy of Work* (New York: Free Press of Glencoe, 1962), indicates how little is really new in the so-called job revolution. A good article on efforts to involve workers in management and decision-making—one of the key elements of "job enrichment"—is Keith Dix, "Workers' Control or Control of Workers," *People's Appalachia* 3, no. 2 (Summer 1974): 16–25. It sets such efforts in historical context and offers useful suggestions for workers whose employers are proposing to institute such programs.
5. *Boston Globe,* 8 September 1974.
6. "News from Senator Edward Brooke," advance for press release, 2 June 1974, "Remarks of Senator Edward Brooke at the Dedication of the Whittier Regional Technical School."

CHAPTER 2

1. Edward G. Wakefield, *England and America* (London: R. Bentley, 1833).
2. Ibid.
3. *Historical Statistics of the United States* (Washington, D.C.: U.S. Department of Commerce, 1960), Series A 34–50, p. 9, and Series A 95–122, p. 12.
4. For a summary of available information on the early urban working class see David Montgomery, "The Working Classes of the Pre-Industrial American City, 1780–1830," *Labor History* 9, no. 1 (Winter 1968): 3–22.
5. The classic account of the early development of wage labor remains Volume 1 of John R. Commons et al., *History of Labor in the United States,* 4 vols. (New York: Macmillan, 1966). A useful model for much of this process is developed in Sam Bass Warner Jr., *The Urban Wilderness* (New York: Harper & Row, 1972). Much interesting material also appears in Norman Ware, *The Industrial Worker, 1840–1860* (Chicago: Quadrangle Books, 1964).
6. Ware, pp. xv-xvi.
7. Ibid, pp. 38–9.
8. Ibid, p. xv.
9. Ibid, p. 42.
10. Ibid, p. 28.
11. Ibid, p. x.
12. Ibid, pp. 58–9.
13. Ernest L. Bogart and Donald L. Kemmerer, *Economic History of the American People* (New York: Longmans, Green, 1942), p. 401.
14. Ibid.
15. Ware, p. 20.
16. Ibid, p. 78.

17. Ibid, p. 77.

18. Taylor quoted in Katherine Stone, "The Origins of Job Structures in the Steel Industry," *The Review of Radical Political Economics* 6, no. 2 (Summer 1974): 141–2.

19. Stone (see above note). An abridged version of this article is scheduled to appear in a forthcoming collection, *Root & Branch: The Rise of the Working Class* (New York: Fawcett, 1975). One of the authors had the opportunity to participate with Katherine Stone on much of the research for this study. For further information and references on the Homestead strike, see Jeremy Brecher, *Strike!* (San Francisco: Straight Arrow Books, 1972), pp. 53–63.

20. J. H. Bridge, *The Inside History of the Carnegie Steel Company* (New York: The Aldine Book Company, 1903), pp. 201–2, quoted in Stone, pp. 118–9.

21. John Fitch, *The Steel Workers,* vol. 3 of *The Pittsburgh Survey,* 6 vols., ed. Paul V. Kellogg (New York: Charities Publication Committee, Russell Sage Foundation, 1909–1914), p. 102, quoted in Stone, p. 119.

22. Frick to Carnegie, 31 October 1892, quoted in David Brody, *Steelworkers in America: The Nonunion Era* (New York: Harper & Row, Torchbook, 1969), p. 53.

23. For a fuller account of the Homestead Conflict, see Brecher, pp. 53–63.

24. A first-rate study of the rise of managerial structures in the context of the modern corporation is Alfred D. Chandler, Jr., *Strategy and Structure: Chapters in the History of the American Industrial Enterprise* (Cambridge, Mass.: MIT Press, 1962). According to Chandler, overproduction was the main original stimulus to business combination. See p. 30.

25. Bogart and Kemmerer, p. 550.

26. Debates on wealth, income and stock distribution are controversial and confusing. However, the figures of Robert J. Lampman, *The Share of Top Wealth-Holders in National Wealth, 1922–1956* (Princeton, N.J.: Princeton University Press, 1962), are widely accepted, even by such authorities as Herman P. Miller of the U.S. Census Bureau, who makes it his business in *Rich Man, Poor Man* (New York: Crowell, 1971) to criticize many attempts to show statistically the inequality of American society. Ferdinand Lundberg, *The Rich and the Super-Rich* (New York: Lyle Stuart, 1968), amasses vast quantities of data on these questions from all sources. Gabriel Kolko, *Wealth and Power in America* (New York: Praeger, 1962), although now somewhat out of date, puts such information in a useful perspective. Richard Parker, *The Myth of the Middle Class* (New York: Liveright, 1972) provides a more recent summary of data indicating the class divisions of American society.

27. Parker, p. 122.

28. Bogart and Kemmerer, p. 528.

29. An important discussion of the evolution of cooperation and division of labor in the early stages of capitalist society appears in Karl Marx, *Capital,* 3 vols. (Moscow: Progress Publishers, 1965), vol. 1, chs. 13 and 14.

30. Bogart and Kemmerer, p. 529.

Notes

CHAPTER 3

Material on the historical evolution of job structures is not abundant, to say the least. Most of what exists focuses on Taylorism and other aspects of "scientific management" (see Frederick Winslow Taylor, *Scientific Management, Comprising Shop Management, Principles of Scientific Management, Testimony before the Special House Committee* [New York: Harper, 1947]). A pioneer essay on the effects of "scientific management" on workers is Daniel Bell, "Work and Its Discontents," pp. 227–272 in *The End of Ideology* (New York: The Free Press, 1965). As David Montgomery (see below) has recently emphasized, the gaps between managerial ideologies and the actual practice at the point of production may be great.

Katherine Stone, "The Origins of Job Structures in the Steel Industry," *The Review of Radical Political Economics* 6, no. 2 (Summer 1974), summarizes much of the information available on other industries as well. A number of papers by David Montgomery ("The 'New Unionism' and the Transformation of Workers' Consciousness in America," mimeographed; "Immigrant Workers and Scientific Management," prepared for the Immigrants in Industry Conference of the Eleutherian Mills Historical Library and the Balch Institute, November 2, 1973; and "Trade Union Practice and the Origins of Syndicalist Theory in the United States," mimeographed) break important new ground.

Theodore Caplow, *The Sociology of Work* (New York: McGraw-Hill, 1964) summarizes a great deal of sociological research on the structure of work. Sigmund Nosaw and William H. Form, eds., *Man, Work and Society* (New York: Basic Books, 1962), contains a fairly wide sample of essays on the sociology of occupations. Stanley Aronowitz, *False Promises* (New York: McGraw-Hill, 1973) contains much interesting material on job structures, particularly in the steel industry. Volume 1, chapter 15, especially section 4, of Karl Marx, *Capital,* 3 vols. (Moscow: Progress Publishers, 1965), gives a useful analysis of the early development of the capitalist factory. For purposes of comparison, E. J. Hobsbawm, "Custom, Wages and Work-Load," in *Laboring Men* (Garden City, N.Y.: Doubleday, Anchor, 1967), pp. 405–35, is well worth reading.

This motley grab bag of sources indicates the extent to which this field is wide open for further research.

1. Norman Ware, *The Industrial Worker, 1840–1860* (Chicago: Quadrangle, 1964), p. 39.

2. Ibid, p. 40.

3. Ibid, p. 61.

4. For many additional examples of pre- and early-industrial work practices, see Herbert Gutman, "Work, Culture and Society in Industrializing America, 1815–1919," *American Historical Review* 78 (June 1973): 531–88.

5. Andrew Ure, *The Philosophy of Manufactures* (London: C. Knight, 1835)

6. Ware, p. xiv.

7. Peter Herman, "In the Heart of the Heart of the Country," in *Root & Branch: The Rise of the Working Class* (New York: Fawcett, 1975).

8. Hollis Godfrey, "Training the Supervisory Work Force," *Minutes of the First Bi-Monthly Conference of the National Association of Employment Managers, 1919,* p. 25, quoted in Stone, p. 145.

9. John Fitch, *The Steel Workers,* vol. 3 of *The Pittsburgh Survey,* 6 vols., ed. Paul V. Kellogg (New York: Charities Publication Committee, Russell Sage Foundation, 1909–1914), p. 149, quoted in Stone, p. 146.

10. Taylor, p. 40, cited in David Montgomery, *What's Happening to the American Worker?,* an interesting pamphlet distributed by *Radical America* magazine.

11. *Iron Age,* 6 July 1905, p. 24, quoted in Stone, p. 146.

12. Ware, p. 120.

13. Ibid, pp. 121–2.

14. Karl Marx, *Capital* (Moscow: Progress Publishers, 1965), p. 436.

15. Paul Douglas, *American Apprenticeship and Industrial Education* (New York: Columbia University Studies in History, Economics and Public Law, 1921), p. 116, cited in Stone, p. 165.

16. Henry Ford, *My Life and Work* (Garden City, N.Y.: Doubleday, Page, 1922), pp. 81–2.

17. J. Stephen Jeans, ed., *American Industrial Conditions and Competition* (London: The British Iron Trade Association, 1902), p. 317, quoted in Stone, p. 125.

18. Douglas, p. 116, quoted in Stone, p. 165.

19. Meyer Bloomfield, *Labor and Compensation* (New York: Industrial Extension Institute, 1917), p. 295, quoted in Stone, p. 133.

20. Taylor, p. 168, quoted in Stone, pp. 127–8.

21. Bloomfield, p. 295, quoted in Stone, p. 133.

22. "Manifesto" calling for the formation of the IWW, in *Rebel Voices,* ed. Joyce L. Kornbluh (Ann Arbor, Mich.: University of Michigan Press, 1964), p. 7. This book contains an important and entertaining wealth of material from the Industrial Workers of the World, including articles, poems, cartoons and songs.

23. *Iron Age,* 19 May 1910, p. 1190, quoted in Stone, pp. 129–30.

24. *Systems of Wage Payment* (New York: National Industrial Conference Board, 1930), p. 25.
25. Ibid, p. 118.
26. Jack Steiber, *The Steel Industry Wage Structure* (Cambridge, Mass.: Harvard University Press, 1959), p. 226, quoted in Stone, p. 157.
27. We paraphrased this poem from one author's memory of a performance of *Brecht on Brecht* in Washington, D.C. several years ago. We are extremely indebted to Martin Esslin, a leading authority on Brecht, who identified our paraphrase as part of Brecht's *Deutsche Kriegsfibel (German War Primer)*, which appears in Bertolt Brecht, *Gesammelte Werke* (Suhrkamp, 1967), vol. IV of India paper edition, p. 638. We would also like to thank Mr. Esslin for supplying us the following literal translation of the original:

> General, your tank is a strong vehicle.
> It breaks down a forest and crushes a hundred people.
> But it has one fault: it needs a driver.
> General, your bombing plane is strong.
> It flies swifter than a storm and carries more than an elephant.
> But it has one fault: it needs a mechanic.
> General, Man is a useful creature. He can fly and he can kill.
> But he has one fault:
> He can think.

CHAPTER 4

Written materials on informal worker resistance in the workplace are scarce—there are few sociologists on the job. The papers by David Montgomery (cited in the general footnote to Chapter 3) contain considerable material on the history of job resistance. We also found valuable an unpublished paper on sabotage by Steven Sapolsky, "Puttin' on the Boss—Alienation and Sabotage in Rationalized Industry" (University of Pittsburgh, July 1971). Louis Adamic, *Dynamite* (New York: Chelsea House, facsimile of 1934 ed.), contains an autobiographical chapter on "Sabotage and 'Striking on the Job.' " The wonderful descriptions of this chapter belie its own conclusions. For control of working conditions by coal miners, see Carter Goodrich, *The Miner's Freedom: A Study of the Working Life in a Changing Industry* (Boston: Marshall Jones, 1925). To see how sabotage and "soldiering" looked to management, see Stanley B. Mathewson, *Restriction of Output among Unorganized Workers* (New York: Viking Press, 1931). Alvin W. Gouldner, *Wildcat Strike* (New York: Harper & Row, 1956), gives an interesting picture of the internal dynamics of a wildcat strike in the 1950s, set in the context of a less interesting "general theory of group tensions."

For radical perspectives sympathetic to informal worker resistance, see two pamphlets by Martin Glaberman, *Punching Out*

(Detroit: Our Times Publications, 1952) and *Be His Payment High or Low* (Detroit: Facing Reality Publishing Committee, 1966), and Charles Denby, *Workers Battle Automation* (Detroit: News and Letters, 1960) and Stanley Weir, ''Rank-and-File Labor Rebellions Break Into the Open: The End of an Era,'' in *American Labor Radicalism,* edited by Staughton Lynd (New York: John Wiley & Sons, 1973).

Chapter 7 of Jeremy Brecher, *Strike!* (San Francisco: Straight Arrow Books, 1972) also has a discussion of workers' resistance on the job and its significance, with further references. Our conception of the development of groups and their resistance has drawn heavily on the ideas of Jean-Paul Sartre.

1. *New York Times,* 29 January 1974.
2. Ibid, 3 April 1973.
3. Ibid, 13 April 1973.
4. Brecher, pp. 233–4.

CHAPTER 5

The relation between workers' own struggles and trade unions is dealt with throughout Jeremy Brecher, *Strike!* (San Francisco: Straight Arrow Books, 1972). For a debate on this question, see David Montgomery, Martin Glaberman and Jeremy Brecher, ''Symposium on Jeremy Brecher's *Strike!*'' *Radical America* 7, no. 6 (Nov.-Dec. 1973): 67–112. An interesting pamphlet by Richard Hyman, *Marxism and the Sociology of Trade Unionism* (London: Pluto Press, 1971), presents a brief summary of the main trends in Marxist and academic sociological thinking about trade unionism. Unfortunately, like many studies of the subject, it has difficulty separating its thoughts about workers from its thoughts about unions.

1. Joel A. Forkosch, ''The Negotiator's Art,'' *New York Times,* 22 April 1973.
2. William Serrin, *The Company and the Union* (New York: Alfred A. Knopf, 1973), pp. 156–7.
3. A vivid analysis of the process by which union leadership becomes an agency for enforcing submission to legality and contracts is Antonio Gramsci, ''Union and Councils—II,'' *L'Ordine Nuovo,* 12 June 1920, trans., *New Left Review,* no. 51 (Sept.-Oct. 1968): 39. An unpublished paper by Steven Sapolsky on the history of the Chicago labor movement, ''Class-Conscious Belligerents—The Teamsters and the Class Struggle in

Chicago, 1901–1905'' (University of Pittsburgh, August 1973), makes a strong *prima facie* case that American employers resisted unionization much more strongly than European employers, largely because the top union leaderships in America were often unable to discipline and control their own rank and file. For a classic interpretation of the bureaucratization process in general, see Max Weber, "Bureaucracy," in *From Max Weber,* trans. and eds. H. H. Gerth and C. Wright Mills (New York: Galaxy, Oxford University Press, 1958).

4. Serrin, p. 212.

5. Summarized from Theodore Caplow, *Sociology of Work* (New York: McGraw-Hill, 1964), p. 207.

6. Brecher, p. 205.

7. Alice Lynd and Staughton Lynd, eds., *Rank and File: Personal Histories by Working-Class Organizers* (Boston: Beacon Press, 1973), pp. 107–10. This collection of interviews and autobiographical writings contains rich and fascinating material on many aspects of working-class life throughout the twentieth century, as well as considerable information on union and radical movements.

8. Emma Rothschild, *Paradise Lost* (New York: Random House, 1973), p. 133.

9. *Wall Street Journal,* 26 July 1973.

10. Ibid.

11. Ibid.

12. Quoted in Serrin, p. 170.

13. Wilfrid Sheed, "What Ever Happened to the Labor Movement?" *Atlantic* 232, no. 1 (July 1973): 44.

14. Forkosch, *New York Times,* 22 April 1973.

15. Serrin, p. 4.

16. Ibid.

CHAPTER 6

In preparing this chapter, we found useful a pamphlet by Fredy Perlman, *The Reproduction of Daily Life* (Kalamazoo, Mich.: Black and Red, 1969). An interesting attempt to summarize capitalist institutions is Louis M. Hacker, *American Capitalism: Its Promise and Accomplishment* (Princeton, N.J.: Van Nostrand, 1957). We have learned much from Karl Marx, *Capital,* 3 vols. (Moscow: Progress Publishers, 1965), that has been useful for this chapter.

1. This view conflicts with a widely held theory that, with the rise of the large modern corporation, profits are no longer key because economic power no longer resides with capitalist owners, but has been taken over by the new corporate managers, who are—or can be made—responsible to the needs of society as a whole. Such theories fail to recognize that the accumulation of profits remains as much a necessity for the new corporate

manager as it was for the private capitalist—each business still has to expand its profits and capital if it wants to stay in business. Those which do not still lose out to the competition. While oligopoly and administered prices might weaken the force of such competition within a single industry in a single country for a limited period of time, recent experience has shown that interindustry and increased international competition has repeatedly smashed through such seemingly protected corporate environments, reestablishing the imperative to accumulate. In reality, top managers usually have substantial stockholdings in the corporations they manage, and their careers are evaluated by the profitability they achieve; their own interests therefore lie in increasing profits. Even were this not the case, stockholders would still be in a position to eliminate any corporate management which pursued objectives in conflict with profitability. For a documented and extended discussion of this question, see Michael Tanzer, *The Sick Society: An Economic Examination* (Chicago: Holt, Rinehart and Winston, 1971), ch. 1.

CHAPTER 7

1. *New York Times,* 3 April 1973.
2. Ibid, 31 March 1973.
3. Ibid, 17 May 1973.
4. Ibid, 8 April 1973.
5. *Boston Globe,* 4 April 1973.
6. *New York Times,* 3 April 1973.
7. *The American Almanac* (New York: Grosset & Dunlap, 1973), p. 11.
8. Rep. Henry Reuss, "Democrat's Critique of Nixonomics," *New York Times Magazine,* 7 July 1974, p. 11.
9. More serious for him—and for millions of others—were the effects of inflation on education. During the post-Depression decades, many parents who might never have finished high school themselves were able to send their children to college. Few factors added more to people's sense that their position in the world was rising. (In a certain sense, this was an illusion. The average amount of schooling possessed by adults increased by three-and-a-half years between 1940 and 1970 [*The American Almanac,* p. 111]. An individual thus had to get several years' more schooling than his parents just to stay in the same place in relation to those his own age.) Inflation has undermined that sense of advancement. By early 1972, the chancellor of the University of Maine reported that "middle-income Americans are being priced right out of higher education . . . . Americans in the income strata of $10,000 a year are finding it increasingly difficult to send their children to college " *(Boston Globe,* 6 March 1972). The letter carrier quoted in the text indicated what this meant for his family:

> My daughter loves school. She's a great student. She took a
> chemistry test with 125 questions and got 123 right, and the
> other two were just silly little mistakes. Of course she

wants to go to college but to tell you the truth, I haven't got a dime. I work two jobs. I make around $14,000 a year and I can't save a thing. It used to be you could have a little luxury for that much money, but now it takes that much just to live. The only thing I'm hoping for is that when it comes time to send her to college the banks will have plenty of money to loan. Maybe if she can save up $1000 herself, I can borrow about $2500 a year, take out a new loan each time I pay an old one back. But you only make so much money; I'm not sure how I can pay the loans back. I'll tell you, if I hit that $50,000 lottery, I'd send her to one of those private colleges.

10. "Inflation: The Big Squeeze," *Newsweek,* 4 March 1974, p. 61.

11. *New York Times,* 11 November 1973.

12. Ibid, 20 June 1974.

13. *New York Times,* 1 February 1975.

14. *New York Times,* 16 February 1975 and 8 February 1975.

15. The explanation of business cycles is controversial, to say the least. John Maynard Keynes's classic explanation appears in his *General Theory of Employment, Interest and Money* (New York: Harcourt, Brace, 1936). Unlike many of his followers, Keynes did not believe that this problem could, in the long run, be solved within the framework of private capitalism, and therefore advocated a "comprehensive socialization of investment."

Marx presents elements of an alternative explanation of these phenomena, based on a totally different general theory, in *Capital,* 3 vols. (Moscow: Progress Publishers, 1965). vol. 3, part 3. An important attempt to apply Marx's model to "post-Keynesian" capitalism is Paul Mattick, *Marx and Keynes* (Boston: Porter Sargent, 1969). An interesting view of the problems of the American economy in the late 1960s and early '70s is Michael Tanzer, *The Sick Society: An Economic Examination* (Chicago: Holt, Rinehart and Winston, 1971).

16. John Steinbeck, *The Grapes of Wrath* (New York: Viking Press, 1939), p. 477.

17. *Wall Street Journal,* 15 July 1974.

18. Much attempt has been made to blame the current economic crisis on the exhaustion of mineral and fossil energy reserves. Numerous studies show that reserves are sufficient for scores and often hundreds of years, but our economic system currently finds it unprofitable to extract them. Our "shortages" result from our social organization, not from an unbountiful earth.

19. "Slowdown: The Amber Lights Begin to Flash," *Citibank Monthly Economic Letter,* August 1973, p. 3.

20. Wilfrid Sheed, "What Ever Happened to the Labor Movement?" *Atlantic* 232, no. 1 (July 1973): 66.

21. *New York Times,* 7 November 1971.

22. Gabriel Kolko, *Wealth and Power in America* (New York: Praeger, 1962), p. 78.

23. *New York Times,* 1 July 1974.
24. Ibid.
25. Ibid, 23 March 1973.
26. Ibid, 1 July 1974.
27. Ibid, 1 May 1970. For an account of the strike, see Jeremy Brecher, *Strike!* (San Francisco: Straight Arrow Books, 1972), pp. 274–6.
28. *New York Times,* 14–17 July 1974.
29. Ibid, 1 July 1974.
30. Charles Walker, "Relief and Revolution," *Forum* 88 (Aug.-Sept. 1932):156. For further information and references on the action of the unemployed and impoverished during the Great Depression, see Brecher, pp. 144–50.

CHAPTER 8

1. *New York Times,* 17 December 1972.
2. Sam Bass Warner Jr., *The Urban Wilderness* (New York: Harper & Row, 1972), p. 148. The first two parts of this book provide a magnificent synopsis of the development of the entire United States urban environment. We have drawn on it extensively in this chapter. For an even broader historical view, see Louis Mumford, *The City in History* (New York: Harcourt, Brace & World, 1961).
3. Barry Commoner, *The Closing Circle* (New York: Alfred A. Knopf, 1971), p. 138. This book provides an excellent guide to ecological issues and the recent destruction of the natural environment.
4. Ibid, p. 175.
5. *New York Times,* 30 June 1974.
6. Commoner, p. 215.
7. Warner, p. 107.
8. Ibid, pp. 83–4.
9. Ibid, pp. 107–9.
10. For a further discussion of urban growth patterns, stressing the central role of waterfront, high ground and other valuable geographical features in the pattern of urban growth, see Michael Young and Peter Willmott, *The Symmetrical Family* (London: Routledge & Kegan Paul, 1973), ch. 2.
11. Joseph P. Fried, *Housing Crisis, U.S.A.* (New York: Praeger, 1971), p. 49. The effects of technology and transportation on plant size have not been all toward centralization. The same old-timer told us: "The auto companies have tended away from giant complexes like River Rouge, which build the entire car. Instead they are building smaller, more specialized plants in semirural parts of the industrial belt. They are also smaller in manpower because productivity has increased so much. The result is to break up great concentrations of workers, but to give groups of 8000 workers at, for example, stamping plants, power to close down huge parts of the industry." This results in part from advanced technology, in part from the ability to move parts from plant to plant more cheaply. High

technology factories, like the Route 128 electronic and engineering complex outside Boston, tend to be of moderate size.

12. Seymour Wolfbein, *Work in American Society* (Glenville, Ill.: Scott, Foresman, 1971), p. 70.

13. *New York Times,* 4 June 1974.

14. *Social Indicators, 1973* (Washington, D.C.: U.S. Department of Commerce, 1973), table 8/13, p. 258.

15. Robert C. Joiner, "Trends in Homeownership and Rental Costs," *Monthly Labor Review* 93, no. 7 (July 1970): 30.

16. Ibid, p. 29.

17. *New York Times,* 27 May 1974.

18. Ibid, 11 June 1973.

19. Quoted in Fried, p. 41.

20. Ibid.

21. *New York Times,* 21 April 1974.

22. Ibid, 24 February 1974.

23. Ibid, 25 April 1974. It is significant that the difference in distance for central city dwellers (five miles) and suburbanites (six miles) is small. The movement of jobs to the urban rim means that for most people living in the city is not living substantially closer to the job.

24. Commoner, p. 169.

25. Dorothy Nelkin, "Massport vs. Community," *Society* 11, no. 4 (May-June 1974): 31. Our account of the East Boston conflict has been drawn largely from this study. See also her *Jetport: The Boston Airport Controversy* (New Brunswick, N.J.: Transaction Books, 1974).

26. In our account of the East Cambridge riots we have drawn on our own participation and interviews, news accounts and a taped radio broadcast on the subject, "A Hero for the Projects," from WBCN, Boston, generously supplied us by Andrew Kopkind.

27. *Boston Real Paper,* 1 November 1972.

28. *Boston Globe,* 26 October 1972.

29. *Boston Phoenix,* 31 October 1972.

30. *Boston Globe,* 29 November 1972.

31. William Simon, John H. Gagnon and Stephen A. Buff, "Son of Joe: Continuity and Change among White Working-Class Adolescents," manuscript prepared to appear in *The Journal of Youth and Adolescence* 1, no. 1 (Winter 1972): 3.

PART III: INTRODUCTION

A massive and useful bibliography on the American working class and its historical roots can be found in Marc Fried, *The World of the Urban Working Class* (Cambridge, Mass.: Harvard University Press, 1973). Fried's demarcation of the working class is similar to our own. An introductory discussion of the issues raised by applying concepts of class to modern society is T. B. Bottomore, *Classes in Modern Society* (New York: Random House, Vintage Books, 1968). An interesting and subtle approach to the nature of social class can be found in Karl Marx, *18th Brumaire of Napoleon Bonaparte* (New York: International Publishers, 1963). The social function of different conceptions of class is brought out in Stanislaw Ossowski, *Class Structure in the Social Consciousness* (New York: The Free Press, 1963); this book can help increase one's awareness of the social issues and ideological presuppositions implicit in most discussions of class.

We have chosen to focus on broad social classes as the most important groups in our present society, and to define these classes in a particular way, because we found it the most useful way to think about three problems:

1. The overall process by which social wealth and power are produced and distributed.

2. The various opportunities people experience in daily life at work, at home and in between, as a result of their position in that process.

3. The process by which the differences in social position and life possibilities of different individuals can be overcome.

Other purposes could no doubt justify other definitions of class.

Social classes are notoriously hard to define. There is rarely a clear line separating one from another, and many individuals do not fall neatly into just one class. That does not make thinking about class position pointless; many kinds of classification suffer from the same problem, yet are still useful. For a discussion of this question as it applies to classification in a variety of scientific fields and the increasing recognition of "polythetic" forms of classification, in which no single uniform property is required to define a group, see Robert R. Sokal, "Classification: Purposes, Principles, Progress, Prospects," *Science* 185 (27 September 1974): 1115–23.

Several other difficulties in studying class require mention. Class categories are not static; class structures evolve. For this reason, they always include groups which are in transition from one category to another, and therefore have some of the characteristics of each.

An illustration of this is the problem of determining whether class is an individual or a family attribute, that is, whether the occupations of family members other than the head are to be taken into account in establishing class. This is the result of a particular historical situation, in which women are becoming increasingly independent from fathers and husbands, but still remain subordinate to them in many respects.

A further difficulty is that many of the categories used in government and sociological studies—white- and blue-collar, professional, technical, kindred, etc.—cut across class lines. In one category you may find some of the highest-paid and most prestigious jobs in society alongside some of the lowest-paid and most menial. One result, pointed out by sociologist Christopher Jencks, is that income inequality is far greater within than between government occupational categories (Christopher Jencks et al., *Inequality* [New York: Basic Books, 1972], p. 226). Whatever the purpose of this category selection, it gives the impression of a far greater equality among different segments of the population than actually exists, making it extremely hard to differentiate statistically among different social groups.

1. For a useful presentation of occupational data, see Seymour Wolfbein, *Work in American Society* (Glenville, Ill.: Scott, Foresman, 1971).

2. Herman P. Miller, *Rich Man, Poor Man* (New York: Crowell, 1971), p. 212.

3. The strata that lie between capitalist and working classes are a good example of how historical development itself redefines the categories with which society must be understood. At an earlier stage of capitalist society, the miscellaneous social functions performed by intermediate groups could only be classified by the undescriptive phrase ''middle class.'' With the development of a group of professional bureaucratized managers distinct from capitalists, and with the proletarianization of many formerly ''middle-class'' functions, it becomes possible to place most of the ''intermediate strata'' in the loose functional category of managers of the production and distribution of social wealth. Since the occupational structure of government and other nonprofit institutions has developed along the same general pattern as the private economy, employees in the ''public sector'' can be reasonably divided between the same managerial and working classes as those in the ''private sector.''

4. *The American Almanac* (New York: Grosset & Dunlap, 1973), p. 324.

5. Ferdinand Lundberg, *The Rich and the Super-Rich* (New York: Lyle Stuart, 1968), p. 13.

6. Many members of this class use the term ''middle class'' to mean very much what we have used ''working class'' to mean. Which word people use has limited significance for revealing what the word actually means to them. As Richard Parker wrote in *The Myth of the Middle Class* (New York: Liveright, 1972): ''The American middle class is synonymous with the word majority. To Americans, to be middle class is to stand literally in the middle, to be average, to be the typical man in the street, the Good Joe.''

The interchangeability of the two terms was indicated by a policeman in a working-class suburb of Washington, D.C., who referred to "the middle-class folks, the working people," in an interview with Joseph Howell *(Hard Living on Clay Street* [Garden City, N.Y.: Doubleday, Anchor Books, 1973], p. 274). For an excellent discussion of this subject, see Bennett M. Berger, *Working-Class Suburb: A Study of Auto Workers in Suburbia* (Berkeley: University of California Press, 1971), ch. 6. Berger quotes the revealing statement of a suburban auto worker: "Around here, the working class *is* the middle class" (p. 84). Berger concludes: "To be 'middle class,' then, probably means to them, not what sociologists mean by middle class, but rather *middle of the working class*" (p. 86).

7. The 75 percent of the population lowest in income receives less than one-half of the country's income; the other 25 percent receives the other half (see *The American Almanac*, table 529, p. 324). The figures are calculated by adding the two highest tenths and half the 8th tenth. The share going to the top quarter of the population is in reality probably even higher, since income is certainly concentrated in the upper half of the 8th tenth.

Evidence indicates that the income gap between managerial and working classes is increasing. A study published by the Department of Labor found that between 1958 and 1970, the share of wage and salary income received by the highest-paid one-fifth of male workers increased from 38.2 percent to 40.6 percent, while the lowest one-fifth declined from 5.1 percent to 4.6 percent (Peter Henle, "Exploring the Distribution of Earned Income," pp. 16–27 in *Monthly Labor Review* 95, no. 12 [December 1972], and *New York Times*, 22 December 1972). S. M. Miller and Martha Bush, examining whites in the age group born between 1926 and 1935, report that the mean family income of blue-collar workers fell from 82.7 percent of professionals and managers in 1960 to 69.8 percent in 1970 ("Can Workers Transform Society?" in Sar A. Levitan, ed., *Blue-Collar Workers* [New York: McGraw-Hill, 1971], pp. 230–52).

8. "Current Labor Statistics," *Monthly Labor Review* 97, no. 3 (March 1974): 95.

9. Howell, p. 338.

10. *New York Times*, 2 July 1974. See also James N. Morgan et al., *Five Thousand American Families—Patterns of Economic Progress* (Ann Arbor: Institute for Social Research, University of Michigan, 1974) and Michael C. Barth et al., *Toward an Effective Income Support System: Problems, Prospects and Choices* (Madison: Institute for Research on Poverty, University of Wisconsin, 1974).

CHAPTER 9

Considerable quantities of material from numerous sources on various aspects of the lives of industrial workers in America are put together in a somewhat dubious frame of reference in Arthur B.

Notes

Shostak, *Blue-Collar Life* (New York: Random House, 1969). Sar Levitan, ed., *Blue-Collar Workers* (New York: McGraw-Hill, 1971), reveals all too well the current level of academic studies of this topic. However, we recommend from it Lee Rainwater's essay, "Making the Good Life," for a picture of the mainstream suburban working class in the late 1960s.

1. Samuel Lane Loomis, *Modern Cities and Their Religious Problems* (New York: The Barker and Taylor Co., 1887), quoted in Herbert Gutman, "Work, Culture and Society in Industrializing America, 1815–1919," *American Historical Review* 78, no. 3 (June 1973): 557.

2. Ernest L. Bogart and Donald L. Kemmerer, *Economic History of the American People* (New York: Longmans, Green, 1942), p. 741.

3. Seymour Wolfbein, *Employment and Unemployment* (Chicago: Science Research Associates, 1967), p. 190.

4. *World Almanac 1974* (New York: Newspaper Enterprise Association, 1973), p. 97.

5. Richard A. Cloward and Frances Fox Piven, *Regulating the Poor: The Functions of Public Welfare* (New York: Vintage Books, 1972), p. 201. This book contains a useful description of the most recent phase of the migration from the land to the city. We also recommend it to anyone interested in welfare, poverty and the low-paid labor market.

6. Shostak, p. 7.

7. Ibid, p. 6.

8. The development of such a class culture is the central theme of E. P. Thompson's magnificent *The Making of the English Working Class* (New York: Random House, 1966). See also *The Uses of Literacy* by Richard Hoggart (Boston: Beacon Press, 1961). For an interesting analysis of the extent to which American workers had a distinctive class culture in 1934, see Charles R. Walker, *An American City: A Rank-and-File History* (New York: Farrar & Rinehart, 1937), pp. 239ff.

9. For a synopsis of research on class, race and ethnicity in urban neighborhoods, see Sam Bass Warner Jr., *The Urban Wilderness* (New York: Harper & Row, 1972), ch. 6. Two other books by Warner, *The Private City: Philadelphia in Three Periods of Its Growth* (Philadelphia: University of Pennsylvania Press, 1968) and *Streetcar Suburbs: The Process of Growth in Boston, 1870–1900* (New York: Atheneum, 1969), bring out more fully the central role of class in urban life.

10. Quoted in Bogart and Kemmerer, p. 434.

11. Norman Ware, *The Industrial Worker, 1840–1860* (Chicago: Quadrangle Books, 1964), p. 23.

12. Ibid, pp. 68–9.

13. Ibid, p. 7.

14. Katherine Stone, "The Origins of Job Structures in the Steel Industry," *The Review of Radical Political Economics* 6, no. 2 (Summer 1974), provides much insight into the development of such occupational ladders.

See also the other papers presented at the Conference on Labor Market Stratification, Harvard University, March 16–17, 1973. Within economics, there is now considerable literature on "dual labor markets." See, for example, Peter B. Doeringer and Michael J. Piore, *Internal Labor Markets and Manpower Analysis* (Lexington, Mass.: Lexington Books, 1971).

15. For a fine portrait of contemporary mainstream and lower working-class life patterns, see Joseph T. Howell, *Hard Living on Clay Street* (Garden City, N.Y.: Doubleday, Anchor Books, 1973).

16. Ware, pp. 16–17.

17. Ibid, p. 13. It is hardly surprising that the same report estimated that the average length of life for the Irish in Boston was not over fourteen years (Ware, p. 14). Conditions of equal horror could be described in the South Bronx today, where dead bodies are gnawed by rats while they wait in the corridors of hospitals for medical personnel to discover that they have died.

18. For an insight into working class attitudes toward education in the 1920s, see Robert S. Lynd and Helen Merrell Lynd, *Middletown: A Study in Contemporary American Culture* (New York: Harcourt, Brace, 1929), Part 3.

19. Stanley Aronowitz, *False Promises* (New York: McGraw-Hill, 1973), gives much useful information on the central role of ethnicity in dividing the working class, particularly within the unions.

20. For more information see Jeremy Brecher, *Strike!* (San Francisco: Straight Arrow Books, 1972). For the development of a commitment to workers' control of production, see David Montgomery, "The 'New Unionism' and the Transformation of Workers' Consciousness in America, 1909–1922," mimeographed.

21. Brecher, p. 248.

22. One of the more statistically accurate presentations of the view that the importance of the industrial work force is declining can be found in Daniel Bell, *The Coming of Post-Industrial Society* (New York: Basic Books, 1973).

CHAPTER 10

The basic book on American white-collar workers remains C. Wright Mills, *White Collar* (London: Oxford University Press, 1951). We have also drawn on two unpublished studies, Frederick D. Weil, "The Economic Class Position of Clerical Workers" (1973) and Frank Ackerman, "Employment of White-Collar Labor, 1910–1960" (1970).

1. Seymour Wolfbein, *Employment and Unemployment* (Chicago: Science Research Associates, 1967), p. 194.

2. Ibid, p. 195.

3. Ibid, p. 184.

4. Daniel Bell, *The Coming of Post-Industrial Society* (New York: Basic Books, 1973), p. 133.

A great deal has been made of the fact that, according to government statistics, more workers are now employed in "service-producing" than in "goods-producing" sectors of the economy. Two important points need to be borne in mind in evaluating this statistic, however. First, the "decline" of the "goods-producing" sector is largely a result of the dramatic decline in agricultural workers. Second, more than three-fourths of the so-called service-producing jobs are actually in transportation, public utilities, trade, finance, insurance, real estate and government—hardly what we normally think of as "service."

The decline of "goods-producing" relative to "service-producing" employment is often explained as a shift in demand to services as basic needs are met by rising income levels. However, relative productivity and wage rates are an important part of the story. The relative decline in blue-collar employment is largely a result of labor-saving technology introduced in response to the relatively high wages of the predominantly male workers in that sector. If female "service-producing" workers achieved wage parity with male blue-collar workers tomorrow, it would unquestionably lead to a relative decrease in "service-producing" employment as some jobs became unprofitable to perform and others became cheaper to perform by machine.

Those who celebrate the increasing proportion of the labor force engaged in "service" as opposed to "goods" production should note that the expanding retail trade and service sectors of the economy are among the lowest paid and most backward. The number of workers in these two sectors has roughly tripled since World War I (Wolfbein, p. 184). The average hourly income in retail trade in 1967 was $2.01 before deductions. The average spendable income after taxes was $75 a week in retail and wholesale trade; $64 a week in building services, laundries and dry cleaners and $50 a week in hotels and motels (Richard Parker, *The Myth of the Middle Class* [New York: Liveright, 1972], pp. 148–9). A substantial proportion of workers in some of these categories work part time, which may bring down the weekly averages, but also indicates the marginal nature of many jobs in this allegedly humanizing "services" sector of the economy.

5. Robert S. Lynd and Helen Merrell Lynd, *Middletown: A Study in Contemporary American Culture* (New York: Harcourt, Brace, 1929), p. 22.

6. Weil, p. 17. The relatively low pay of clerical workers is not just a symptom of the concentration of women in clerical work. In 1971, the income of *male* clerical workers fell almost halfway between operatives and craftsmen and foremen (Weil, chart, p. 20). In 1939, male clerical workers earned 8 percent more than craftsmen and foremen; in 1971, 11 percent less (ibid). Male clerical workers in 1970 made less than 90 percent of the average income for all full-time workers (ibid, p. 55).

7. Weil, p. 34.

8. *New York Times,* 14 October 1973.

9. Ibid, 15 October 1974.

10. *Work in America,* the Report of a Special Task Force to the Secretary of Health, Education and Welfare, prepared under the auspices of the W. E. Upjohn Institute for Employment Research (Cambridge, Mass.: MIT Press, 1973), p. 40.

11. Weil, p. 21.

12. Some "experts" on occupational statistics somewhat peculiarly interpret this transition from blue- to white-collar work as an expression of upward mobility.

13. Bell, p. 145.

14. Mills, p. 254.

15. Weil, p. 41.

16. Stanley Aronowitz, *False Promises* (New York: McGraw-Hill, 1973), p. 301.

17. Jeremy Brecher, *Strike!* (San Francisco: Straight Arrow Books, 1972), pp. 283–4.

CHAPTER 11

Much of the economic history of black workers is summarized in Harold M. Baron, "The Demand for Black Labor: Historical Notes on the Political Economy of Racism," *Radical America* 5, no. 2 (Mar.-Apr. 1971):1–46. A collection of documents on black resistance is Joanne Grant, *Black Protest: History, Documents and Analysis* (New York: Fawcett, 1968). A number of interesting papers appear in Julius Jacobson, ed., *The Negro and the American Labor Movement* (Garden City, N.Y.: Anchor Books, 1968). Other books we found of interest included the classic W. E. B. DuBois, *Black Reconstruction in America* (Cleveland: Meridian Books, 1964) and his *Dusk of Dawn* (New York: Schocken Books, 1968); C. Vann Woodward, *The Strange Career of Jim Crow* (New York: Oxford University Press, 1966) and *Origins of the New South* (Baton Rouge: Louisiana State University Press, 1972); and Robert L. Allen, *Black Awakening in Capitalist America* (Garden City, N.Y.: Anchor Books, 1970).

1. Quoted in Ernest L. Bogart and Donald L. Kemmerer, *Economic History of the American People* (New York: Longmans, Green, 1942), pp. 489–90.

2. Jacobson, p. 36.

3. Harold M. Baron, "The Demand for Black Labor," p. 14.

4. Ibid, p. 13.

5. Charles Johnson, *The Shadow of the Plantation* (Chicago: University of Chicago Press, 1934), p. 210, quoted in Baron, "The Demand for Black Labor," p. 25.

6. Baron, "The Demand for Black Labor," p. 16.

7. Ibid, pp. 20–1.

8. Ibid, p. 20.

9. Ibid, p. 26.

10. Richard A. Cloward and Frances Fox Piven, *Regulating the Poor: The Functions of Public Welfare* (New York: Vintage Books, 1972), p. 202.

11. Harold M. Baron and Bennett Hymer, "The Negro Worker in the Chicago Labor Market," in Jacobson, p. 262.

12. Ibid.

13. Ibid, p. 280.

14. *Boston Globe*, 6 January 1974.

15. Herbert G. Gutman, *"The Negro and the United Mine Workers of America,"* in Jacobson, p. 49.

16. Ibid, pp. 119–20. This article contains many other interesting historical examples of cooperation between black and white workers.

17. Alice Lynd and Staughton Lynd, eds., *Rank and File: Personal Histories by Working-Class Organizers* (Boston: Beacon Press, 1973), pp. 163–4.

18. For a thorough review of survey data on racism, strongly indicating that it is not primarily a phenomenon of the white working class, see Richard F. Hamilton, "Class and Race in the United States," in *The Revival of American Socialism,* ed. George Fischer, (New York: Oxford University Press, 1971).

19. William Serrin, *The Company and the Union* (New York: Alfred A. Knopf, 1973), p. 235, reports that this plant "employed a crew of men to go into toilets to paint over racial slurs written on the walls."

20. For an account of a similar attitude among railroad workers in the early 1960s, see Alice Lynd and Staughton Lynd, p. 240.

21. For a good discussion of this phenomenon in one neighborhood, see Joseph Howell, *Hard Living on Clay Street* (Garden City, N.Y.: Doubleday, Anchor Books, 1973), pp. 350–1.

CHAPTER 12

A useful though somewhat dated introduction to the history of women's labor, originally published in 1959, is Robert W. Smuts, *Women and Work in America,* 2nd ed. (New York: Schocken, 1971). A more general account of women's changing social roles is William H. Chafe, *The American Woman* (New York: Oxford University Press, 1972). Eleanor Flexner, *Century of Struggle* (New York: Atheneum, 1972), presents a history of the women's rights movement in the United States. A good analysis of factors affecting women's participation in the labor force is Valerie Kincade Oppenheimer, *The Female Labor Force in the United States,* Population Monograph Series #5 (Berkeley: University of California Press, 1970). On wage differentials and job segregation, we benefited from reading Mary Stevenson, "Women's Wages and Job Segregation," *Politics and Society* 4, no. 1 (Fall 1973): 83–96; an unpublished draft of her 1973 Ph.D. thesis; and Mary E. Corcoran, "Sex-Biased Wage Differentials" (MIT, February 1974). A useful guide for action for women who face job discrimination is Katherine Stone, *Handbook for OCAW Women* (Denver: Oil, Chemical and Atomic Workers International Union, 1973). *The Handbook on Women Workers,* issued every few years by the Women's Bureau of the U.S. Department of Labor, contains a first-rate collection of facts and statistics on women and work. Michael Young and Peter Willmott, *The Symmetrical Family* (London: Routledge & Kegan Paul, 1973), contains much interesting material on many of these questions for England.

1. Smuts, pp. 7–8.
2. Ibid, p. 5.
3. Ibid, pp. 23–4.
4. Ibid, p. 23.
5. Herman Miller, *Rich Man, Poor Man* (New York: Crowell, 1971), p. 224.
6. Ibid.
7. Caroline Bird, *Born Female* (New York: Pocket Books, 1969), p. 33.
8. *Handbook on Women Workers,* p. 58.
9. Ibid, pp. 7–8.
10. Ibid, p. 57.
11. *Why Women Work* (Washington, D.C.: U.S. Department of Labor, Women's Bureau, 1971), p. 1.
12. Flexner, p. 53.
13. Smuts, p. 91.
14. Edward Gross, cited in Stevenson, p. 6.
15. This "earnings gap" can hardly be attributed to differences in amounts of education. A study by Valerie Oppenheimer found that 42 percent of all women workers are in occupations which have higher than average educational levels but lower than average median earnings (Valerie K. Oppenheimer, "The Sex-Labeling of Jobs," *Industrial Relations* 7, no. 3 [May 1968]: 224–8). Throughout most of the twentieth century, women in the labor force have had substantially more education than men, and the gap has still not quite been closed. A rapidly rising college graduation rate for men, however, has recently contributed to the relative decline of women in professional occupations. In 1940, women were 45 percent of professional

and technical workers; in 1968, only 39 percent (*Handbook on Women Workers*, p. 94).

16. *Handbook on Women Workers*, p. 94.

17. Esther Peterson, "Working Women," in *The Woman in America*, ed. Robert Jay Lifton (Boston: Beacon Press, 1964), p. 163–4.

18. *Handbook on Women Workers*, p. 15.

19. Stevenson, "Women's Wages," pp. 83–96.

20. *Handbook of Women Workers*, p. 94.

21. Ibid, p. 92.

22. Stevenson, unpublished study, computed from *Current Population Reports*, Consumer Income Series no. 69 (April 1970): 60.

23. *Handbook on Women Workers*, p. 92.

24. Calculated from *Handbook on Women Workers*, p. 92.

25. Ibid.

26. *Women Employed Investigation of Kraft Foods* (Chicago: Women Employed, May 1973), pp. 4–5.

27. *Handbook on Women Workers*, p. 111.

28. Ibid, pp. 109–13.

29. Stevenson, "Women's Wages," pp. 83–96.

30. Ivar Berg, *Education and Jobs: The Great Training Robbery* (New York: Praeger, 1970), pp. 105–6. Among books on "manpower," this one is striking for its mordant humor and tendency to penetrate myths and stereotypes, giving some sense of how things really work.

31. *Background Facts on Women Workers* (Washington, D.C.: U.S. Department of Labor, Women's Bureau, n.d.), p. 1.

32. *Handbook on Women Workers*, p. 84.

33. *Supervisor's Manual for State Employees*, developed by the Bureau of Personnel and Standardization, Commonwealth of Massachusetts, pp. 167–72.

34. The proportion of women in heavy industry has gradually increased over the past twenty-five years (*Handbook on Women Workers*, p. 113), and we found that women were coming into many previously all-male plants and jobs, often in response to government pressure on employers.

CHAPTER 13

The central role of shared experience and a cultural recognition of that shared experience in the process of class formation is eloquently emphasized in E. P. Thompson, *The Making of the English Working Class* (New York: Random House, Vintage Books, 1966). For a view complementary to our own, though with differences of emphasis, see Stanley Aronowitz, *False Promises* (New York: McGraw-Hill, 1973). In our thinking about the life experiences of various generations, we have drawn on the masses of data analyzed by Joseph Eyer, "Living Conditions in the U.S.," in *Root &*

Branch: The Rise of the Working Class (New York: Fawcett, 1975), and in a wide-ranging series of unpublished studies by Joseph Eyer and Ingrid Waldron.

1. Christopher Jencks et al., *Inequality* (New York: Basic Books, 1972), p. 211.
2. Eli Ginzberg, "The Long View," in *Blue-Collar Workers,* ed. Sar A. Levitan (New York: McGraw-Hill, 1971), p. 29.
3. Bennett M. Berger, *Working-Class Suburb: A Study of Auto Workers in Suburbia* (Berkeley: University of California Press, 1971). This short book contains much interesting information and insight about the American working class in the 1950s.
4. Harvey Swados, *A Radical at Large* (London: Rupert Hart-Davis, 1968), p. 64. Swados's comment is particularly significant in that it comes in the midst of an essay devoted to debunking the "Myth of the Happy Worker." Swados perceptively concluded this passage, "but only for that long."
5. Levitan, p. 206.
6. This shift shows up sharply in a series of surveys taken by Daniel Yankelovich, Inc., during the 1960s and 1970s. See Daniel Yankelovich, *Changing Youth Values in the '70s* (New York: John D. Rockefeller III Fund, 1974).
7. Certain trends in the growth patterns of the American population have aggravated the problems faced by young people starting work today. As with the economic trends, these population trends favored the generation which started work during the 1950s and early 1960s, and created disadvantages for those who entered during the later 1960s and the 1970s.

During the depression decade of the 1930s, most people had many fewer children than either before or since. The small generation born during the 1930s entered the work force during the 1940s and '50s. This age group's chances of finding secure, well-paid jobs were improved because its members were relatively few. Consequently, this generation has experienced one of the lowest unemployment rates and one of the steadiest improvements in income of any in American history.

After World War II, however, there was a dramatic change in the number of children families wanted and had. Throughout the nineteenth and early twentieth centuries, the average number of births per married woman had declined until it reached about 2.5. But among women born in the 1930s, the number rose to about 3.5. The result was the much discussed "baby boom"—a tremendous increase in the number of people born in the two decades following World War II.

In the course of time, these people began to reach job-seeking age. According to *Youth: Transition to Adulthood,* the Report of the Panel on Youth of the President's Science Advisory Committee (Washington, D.C.: Executive Office of the President, 1973), from which the statistics used in this note are drawn, the number of people 14–24 increased from 26.7 million in 1960 to 40.5 million in 1970—an increase of more than 50 percent in one decade. The following table shows the effects of this change on the size of generations:

Year	Population 14–24 years old
1940	26.3 million
1950	24.2 million
1960	26.7 million
1970	40.5 million

By the late 1960s and early 1970s, the increasing number of young people was clearly contributing to a relative deterioration of their economic position. Between 1967 and 1971 the median weekly earnings of men 16 to 24 fell about 12 percent compared to those 25 and over.

However, the greatest impact of the "baby boom generation" on the workplace has yet to be felt. As the report cited above pointed out in 1973:

> The crest of the wave has only now begun to reach the full-time, education-completed labor market and will be inundating it in the years to come. Until now, much of this wave has been deflected and delayed by an increase in the number of youths staying on within the educational system and an increase in the duration of their stay there. For example, while the population of 16- to 19-year-olds increased between 1957 and 1970 by 6 million, the "not enrolled in school" labor force component of this age group increased by only 0.6 million. Similarly, in the 20–24 age group, which increased by 6.5 million between 1960 and 1970, the "not enrolled" labor force increased by only 2 million in the same period.

Thus, these two age groups together increased by 12.5 million, all but 2.6 million of whom remained in school. It is the remaining 9.9 million increase which is now flooding into the labor market, contributing to the elevated unemployment rates of the late 1970s.

8. *New York Times,* 8 January 1973.
9. *Boston Globe,* 30 May 1973.

PART IV

Materials we consulted bearing on the creation of a society based neither on private nor state control of the production process include Anton Pannekoek, "Workers Councils," in *Root & Branch: The Rise of the Working Class* (New York: Fawcett, 1975); Paul Mattick, "Workers' Control," in *The New Left,* ed. Priscilla Long (Boston: Porter Sargent, 1969); Peter Kropotkin, *The Conquest of Bread* (New York: New York University Press, 1972); Paul Goodman and

Percival Goodman, *Communitas* (New York: Vintage Books, 1960); Murray Bookchin, *Post-Scarcity Anarchism* (Berkeley: Ramparts Press, 1971); Jeremy Brecher, "A Post-Affluence Critique," a review of *Post-Scarcity Anarchism,* and Murray Bookchin's reply, "Listen, Marxist: A Reply," in *Root & Branch,* no. 4, pp. 7–31. Staughton Lynd and Gar Alperovitz, *Strategy and Program* (Boston: Beacon Press, 1972); Gerry Hunnius, G. David Garson and John Case, eds., *Workers' Control* (New York: Random House, 1973); André Gorz, *Strategy for Labor* (Boston: Beacon Press, 1967); "Notes on the Economic Theory of Decentralized Socialism," Seminar Report from the Exploratory Project for Economic Alternatives, Cambridge Institute, March 1973.

For a brief review of past working-class efforts to take control of production in Russia, Italy and Spain, with further references, see Jeremy Brecher, *Strike!* (San Francisco: Straight Arrow Books, 1972), ch. 9. For analysis of the May-June 1968 upheaval in France, see R. Gregoire and F. Perlman, *Student/Worker Action Committees* (Kalamazoo, Mich.: Black and Red, n.d.); Daniel Cohn-Bendit and Gabriel Cohn-Bendit, *Obsolete Communism: The Left-Wing Alternative* (New York: McGraw-Hill, 1969); *Caw!* (the magazine of Students for a Democratic Society), no. 3 (Fall 1968); and "Mass Strike in France," in *Root & Branch.* For documents of recent working-class activity in Italy, providing considerable insight into the character of one concerted working-class movement today, see *Radical America* 5, no. 5 (Sept.-Oct. 1971): 3–38 and 7, no. 2 (Mar.-Apr. 1973): 1–121.

1. In our account of the development of the American Revolutionary movement, we have drawn primarily on Pauline Maier's *From Resistance to Revolution* (New York: Random House, Vintage Books, 1974). Like her, we have abstracted from the very real and significant differences in attitude and social position among the American colonists. Our purpose has not been to deal with the social context and results of the Revolution, but simply to point out certain developmental characteristics it shares with many other revolutions. We have also consulted Lawrence Henry Gipson, *The Coming of the Revolution* (New York: Harper Torchbooks, 1962); Staughton Lynd, *Intellectual Origins of American Radicalism* (New York: Vintage Books, 1969); Gordon S. Wood, *The Creation of the American Republic* (Chapel Hill: University of North Carolina Press, 1969); and Samuel Eliot Morison, *The Oxford History of the American People* (New York: New American Library–Mentor, 1972), vol. 1.

Notes

2. Maier, p. 6.
3. Ibid, p. 7.
4. Ibid, p. 52.
5. Ibid, pp. 54–5.
6. Ibid, p. 84.
7. Ibid, p. 92.
8. Ibid, p. 94.
9. Ibid, p. 104.
10. Ibid, p. 111.
11. Ibid, p. 134.
12. Ibid, p. 118.
13. Ibid.
14. Ibid, p. 137.
15. Gipson, p. 201.
16. Maier, p. 222.
17. Gipson, p. 209.
18. Maier, p. 243.
19. Ibid, p. 288.
20. Ibid.
21. Ibid, p. 291.
22. David Montgomery, *What's Happening to the American Worker?* (pamphlet distributed by *Radical America*), p. 8.
23. Ibid, p. 20.
24. Joyce L. Kornbluh, ed., *Rebel Voices* (Ann Arbor: University of Michigan Press, 1964), p. 204.
25. Norman Ware, *The Industrial Worker, 1840–1860* (Chicago: Quadrangle Books, 1964).
26. We have borrowed this phrase from Daniel Cohn-Bendit.
27. Felix G. Rohatyn, "A New R.F.C. is Proposed for Business," *New York Times*, Business Section, 1 December 1974. (Mr. Rohatyn is a partner in Lazard Frères and Co.)
28. Tillie Olsen, "I Stand Here Ironing," *Tell Me a Riddle* (New York: J.J. Lippincott, 1961), p. 89.

A NOTE ON THE INTERVIEWS

1. For a provocative and important discussion concerning the multiple conceptions people often hold of social reality, and the dependence of conceptions expressed upon social context, see Robert R. Jay, "Conception and Actuality," in *Javanese Villagers: Social Relations in Rural Modjokuto* (Cambridge, Mass.: MIT Press, 1969), ch. 2. We also benefited from an unpublished paper on "Anthropologist's Accounts of Informant's Accounts" by Nancy B. Jay.

BIBLIOGRAPHY

BOOKS

Ademic, Louis. *Dynamite*. New York: Chelsea House, facsimile of 1934 ed.

Allen, Robert L. *Black Awakening in Capitalist America*. Garden City, N.Y.: Anchor Books, 1970.

American Almanac, The. New York: Grosset & Dunlap, 1973.

Aronowitz, Stanley. *False Promises*. New York: McGraw-Hill, 1973.

Barth, Michael C., et al. *Toward an Effective Income Support System: Problems, Prospects and Choices*. Madison: Institute for Research on Poverty, University of Wisconsin, 1974.

Bateson, Gregory. *Steps to an Ecology of Mind*. New York: Ballantine Books, 1972.

Bell, Daniel. *The Coming of Post-Industrial Society*. New York: Basic Books, 1973.

Bell, Daniel. *The End of Ideology*. New York: The Free Press, 1962.

Berg, Ivar. *The Great Training Robbery*. New York: Praeger, 1970.

Berger, Bennett M. *Working-Class Suburb: A Study of Auto Workers in Suburbia*. Berkeley: University of California Press, 1971.

Bernstein, Richard J. *Praxis and Action*. Philadelphia: University of Pennsylvania Press, 1971.

Bird, Caroline. *Born Female*. New York: Pocket Books, 1969.

Bloomfield, Meyer. *Labor and Compensation*. New York: Industrial Extension Institute, 1917.

Bogart, Ernest L. and Kemmerer, Donald L. *Economic History of the American People*. New York: Longmans, Green, 1942.

Bookchin, Murray. *Post-Scarcity Anarchism*. Berkeley: Ramparts Press, 1971.

Bottomore, T. B. *Classes in Modern Society*. New York: Random House, Vintage Books, 1968.

Brecher, Jeremy. *Strike!* San Francisco: Straight Arrow Books, 1972.

Brecht, Bertolt. *Selected Poems*. Translated by H. R. Hays. New York: Grove Press, 1959.

Bridge, J. H. *The Inside History of the Carnegie Steel Company*. New York: The Aldine Book Company, 1903.

Bibliography

Brody, David. *Steelworkers in America: The Nonunion Era.* New York: Harper & Row, Torchbook, 1969.

Caplow, Theodore. *The Sociology of Work.* New York: McGraw-Hill, 1964.

Chafe, William H. *The American Woman.* New York: Oxford University Press, 1972.

Chandler, Alfred D., Jr. *Strategy and Structure: Chapters in the History of Industrial Enterprise.* Cambridge, Mass.: MIT Press, 1962.

Cloward, Richard A. and Piven, Frances Fox. *Regulating the Poor: The Functions of Public Welfare.* New York: Vintage Books, 1972.

Cohn-Bendit, Daniel and Cohn-Bendit, Gabriel. *Obsolete Communism: The Left-Wing Alternative.* New York: McGraw-Hill, 1969.

Commoner, Barry. *The Closing Circle.* New York: Alfred A. Knopf, 1971.

Commons, John R., et al. Vol. 1, *History of Labor in the United States,* 4 vols. New York: Macmillan, 1966.

Desan, Wilfred. *The Marxism of Jean-Paul Sartre.* Garden City, N.Y.: Doubleday, 1965.

Doeringer, Peter B. and Piore, Michael J. *Internal Labor Markets and Manpower Analysis.* Lexington, Mass.: Lexington Books, 1971.

Douglas, Paul. *American Apprenticeship and Industrial Education.* New York: Columbia University Studies in History, Economics and Public Law, 1921.

DuBois, W. E. B. *Black Reconstruction in America.* Cleveland: Meridian Books, 1964.

DuBois, W. E. B. *Dusk of Dawn.* New York: Schocken Books, 1968.

Fischer, George, ed. *The Revival of American Socialism.* New York: Oxford University Press, 1971.

Fitch, John. *The Steel Workers.* Vol. 3 of *The Pittsburgh Survey,* 6 vols. Edited by Paul V. Kellogg. New York: Charities Publication Committee, Russell Sage Foundation, 1909–1914.

Flexner, Eleanor. *Century of Struggle.* New York: Atheneum, 1972.

Ford, Henry. *My Life and Work.* Garden City, N.Y.: Doubleday, Page, 1922.

Fried, Joseph P. *Housing Crisis U.S.A.* New York: Praeger, 1971.

Fried, Marc. *The World of the Urban Working Class.* Cambridge, Mass.: Harvard University Press, 1973.

Friedmann, Georges. *The Anatomy of Work.* New York: Free Press of Glencoe, 1962.

Ginsburg, Herbert and Opper, Sylvia. *Piaget's Theory of Intellectual Development.* Englewood Cliffs, N.J.: Prentice-Hall, 1969.

Gipson, Lawrence Henry. *The Coming of the Revolution.* New York: Harper Torchbooks, 1962.

Gooding, Judson. *The Job Revolution.* New York: Walker, 1972.

Goodman, Paul and Goodman, Percival. *Communitas.* New York: Vintage Books, 1960.

Goodrich, Carter. *The Miner's Freedom: A Study of the Working Life in a Changing Industry.* Boston: Marshall Jones, 1925.

Gorz, André. *Strategy for Labor*. Boston: Beacon Press, 1967.

Gouldner, Alvin W. *Wildcat Strike*. New York: Harper & Row, 1956.

Grant, Joanne. *Black Protest: History, Documents and Analysis*. New York: Fawcett, 1968.

Hacker, Louis M. *American Capitalism: Its Promise and Accomplishment*. Princeton, N.J.: Van Nostrand, 1957.

Hobsbawm, E. J. *Laboring Men*. Garden City, N.Y.: Doubleday, Anchor Books, 1967.

Hoggart, Richard. *The Uses of Literacy*. Boston: Beacon Press, 1961.

Howell, Joseph. *Hard Living on Clay Street*. Garden City, N.Y.: Doubleday, Anchor Books, 1973.

Hunnius, Gerry; Garson, G. David, and Case, John, eds. *Workers' Control*. New York: Random House, 1973.

Jacobson, Julius, ed. *The Negro and the American Labor Movement*. Garden City, N.Y.: Anchor Books, 1968.

Jay, Robert R. *Javanese Villagers: Social Relations in Rural Modjokuto*. Cambridge, Mass.: MIT Press, 1969.

Jeans, J. Stephen, ed. *American Industrial Conditions and Competition*. London: The British Iron Trade Association, 1902.

Jencks, Christopher, et al. *Inequality*. New York: Basic Books, 1972.

Johnson, Charles. *The Shadow of the Plantation*. Chicago: University of Chicago Press, 1934.

Kelly, George. *The Psychology of Personal Constructs*. New York: Norton, 1955.

Kelly, George. *A Theory of Personality*. New York: Norton, 1963.

Keynes, John Maynard. *General Theory of Employment, Interest and Money*. New York: Harcourt, Brace, 1936.

Kolko, Gabriel. *Wealth and Power in America*. New York: Praeger, 1962.

Kornbluh, Joyce L., ed. *Rebel Voices*. Ann Arbor: University of Michigan Press, 1964.

Korsch, Karl. *Karl Marx*. New York: Russell & Russell, 1963.

Kropotkin, Peter. *The Conquest of Bread*. New York: New York University Press, 1972.

Laing, R. D. and Cooper, D. G. *Reason and Violence*. New York: Humanities Press, 1964.

Lampman, Robert J. *The Share of Top Wealth-Holders in National Wealth, 1922–1956*. Princeton, N.J.: Princeton University Press, 1962.

Levitan, Sar A., ed. *Blue-Collar Workers*. New York: McGraw-Hill, 1971.

Lifton, Robert Jay, ed. *The Woman in America*. Boston: Beacon Press, 1964.

Long, Priscilla, ed. *The New Left*. Boston: Porter Sargent, 1969.

Loomis, Samuel Lane. *Modern Cities and Their Religious Problems*. New York: The Barker and Taylor Co., 1887.

Lundberg, Ferdinand. *The Rich and the Super-Rich*. New York: Lyle Stuart, 1968.

Lynd, Alice and Lynd, Staughton, eds. *Rank and File: Personal Histories by Working-Class Organizers*. Boston: Beacon Press, 1973.

Bibliography

Lynd, Robert S. and Lynd, Helen Merrell. *Middletown: A Study in Contemporary American Culture.* New York: Harcourt, Brace, 1929.

Lynd, Staughton, ed. *American Labor Radicalism.* New York: John Wiley & Sons, 1973.

Lynd, Staughton. *Intellectual Origins of American Radicalism.* New York: Vintage Books, 1969.

Lynd, Staughton and Alperovitz, Gar. *Strategy and Program.* Boston: Beacon Press, 1972.

Maier, Pauline. *From Resistance to Revolution.* New York: Random House, Vintage Books, 1974.

Marx, Karl. *Capital,* 3 vols. Moscow: Progress Publishers, 1965.

Marx, Karl. *18th Brumaire of Napoleon Bonaparte.* New York: International Publishers, 1963.

Mathewson, Stanley B. *Restriction of Output among Unorganized Workers.* New York: Viking Press, 1931.

Mattick, Paul. *Marx and Keynes.* Boston: Porter Sargent, 1969.

Miller, Herman P. *Rich Man, Poor Man.* New York: Crowell, 1971.

Mills, C. Wright. *White Collar.* London: Oxford University Press, 1951.

Morgan, James N., et al. *Five Thousand American Families—Patterns of Economic Progress.* Ann Arbor: Institute for Social Research, University of Michigan, 1974.

Morison, Samuel Eliot. *The Oxford History of the American People.* New York: New American Library–Mentor, 1972.

Mumford, Louis. *The City in History.* New York: Harcourt, Brace & World, 1961.

National Industrial Conference Board. *Systems of Wage Payment.* New York: National Industrial Conference Board, 1930.

Nelkin, Dorothy. *Jetport: The Boston Airport Controversy.* New Brunswick, N.J.: Transaction Books, 1974.

Nosaw, Sigmund and Form, William H., eds. *Man, Work and Society.* New York: Basic Books, 1962.

Olsen, Tillie. *Tell Me a Riddle.* New York: J. J. Lippincott, 1961.

Oppenheimer, Valerie Kincade. *The Female Labor Force in the United States,* Population Monograph Series #5. Berkeley: University of California Press, 1970.

Ossowski, Stanislaw. *Class Structure in the Social Consciousness.* New York: The Free Press, 1963.

Paine, Thomas. *Common Sense and The Crisis.* Garden City, N.Y.: Dolphin Books, 1960.

Pannekoek, Anton. *Anthropogenesis.* Amsterdam: North-Holland Publishing, 1953.

Parker, Richard. *The Myth of the Middle Class.* New York: Liveright, 1972.

Piaget, Jean. *Six Psychological Studies.* Translated by Anita Tenzer and David Elkind. New York: Random House, 1967.

Root & Branch, ed. *Root & Branch: The Rise of the Working Class.* New York: Fawcett, 1975.

Rothschild, Emma. *Paradise Lost.* New York: Random House, 1973.

Sartre, Jean-Paul. *Search for a Method*. Translated by Hazel E. Barnes. New York: Alfred A. Knopf, 1963.

Schactel, Ernest G. *Metamorphosis*. New York: Basic Books, 1959.

Serrin, William. *The Company and the Union*. New York: Alfred A. Knopf, 1973.

Sheppard, Harold L. and Herrick, Neil Q. *Where Have All the Robots Gone?* New York: The Free Press, 1972.

Shostak, Arthur B. *Blue-Collar Life*. New York: Random House, 1969.

Smuts, Robert W. *Women and Work in America,* 2nd ed. New York: Shocken, 1971.

Sorel, Georges. *Reflections on Violence*. New York: Collier Books, 1961.

Special Task Force to the Secretary of Health, Education and Welfare, prepared under the auspices of the Upjohn Institute for Employment Research. *Work in America*. Cambridge, Mass.: MIT Press, 1973.

Steiber, Jack. *The Steel Industry Wage Structure*. Cambridge, Mass.: Harvard University Press, 1959.

Steinbeck, John. *The Grapes of Wrath*. New York: Viking Press, 1939.

Swados, Harvey. *A Radical at Large*. London: Rupert Hart-Davis, 1968.

Tanzer, Michael. *The Sick Society: An Economic Examination*. Chicago: Holt, Rinehart and Winston, 1971.

Taylor, Frederick Winslow. *Scientific Management, Comprising Shop Management, Principles of Scientific Management, Testimony before the Special House Committee*. New York: Harper, 1947.

Terkel, Studs. *Working*. New York: Pantheon Books, 1974.

Thompson, E. P. *The Making of the English Working Class*. New York: Random House, Vintage Books, 1966.

Ure, Andrew. *The Philosophy of Manufactures*. London: C. Knight, 1835

Wakefield, Edward G. *England and America*. London: R. Bentley, 1833.

Walker, Charles R. *An American City: A Rank-and-File History*. New York: Farrar & Rinehart, 1937.

Ware, Norman. *The Industrial Worker, 1840–1860*. Chicago: Quadrangle Books, 1964.

Warner, Sam Bass, Jr. *The Private City: Philadelphia in Three Periods of Its Growth*. Philadelphia: University of Pennsylvania Press, 1968.

Warner, Sam Bass, Jr. *Streetcar Suburbs: The Process of Growth in Boston, 1870–1900*. New York: Atheneum, 1969.

Warner, Sam Bass, Jr. *The Urban Wilderness*. New York: Harper & Row, 1972.

Weber, Max. *From Max Weber*. Translated and edited by H. H. Gerth and C. Wright Mills. New York: Galaxy, Oxford University Press, 1958.

Wolfbein, Seymour. *Employment and Unemployment*. Chicago: Science Research Associates, 1967.

Wolfbein, Seymour. *Work in American Society*. Glenville, Ill.: Scott, Foresman, 1971.

Wood, Gordon S. *The Creation of the American Republic*. Chapel Hill: University of North Carolina Press, 1969.

Bibliography

Woodward, C. Vann. *Origins of the New South*. Baton Rouge: Louisiana State University Press, 1972.

Woodward, C. Vann. *The Strange Career of Jim Crow*. New York: Oxford University Press, 1966.

World Almanac 1974. New York: Newspaper Enterprise Association, 1973.

Young, Michael and Willmott, Peter. *The Symmetrical Family*. London: Routledge & Kegan Paul, 1973.

PERIODICALS

Baron, Harold M. "The Demand for Black Labor: Historical Notes on the Political Economy of Racism." *Radical America* 5, no. 2, March–April 1971.

CAW! The Magazine of Students for a Democratic Society, no. 3, Fall 1968.

Coles, Robert. "Understanding White Racists." *New York Review of Books*, 30 December 1971.

"Current Labor Statistics," *Monthly Labor Review* 97, no. 3, March 1974.

Dix, Keith. "Workers' Control or Control of Workers." *People's Appalachia* 3, no. 2, Summer 1974.

Gramsci, Antonio. "Union and Councils—II." *L'Ordine Nuovo*, 12 June 1920. Translated in *New Left Review*, no. 51, September-October 1968.

Gutman, Herbert. "Work, Culture and Society in Industrializing America, 1815–1919." *American Historical Review* 78, June 1973.

"Inflation: The Big Squeeze." *Newsweek*, 4 March 1974.

Iron Age: 6 July 1905, 19 May 1910.

Joiner, Robert C. "Trends in Homeownership and Rental Costs." *Monthly Labor Review* 93, no. 7, July 1970.

Montgomery, David. "The Working Classes of the Pre-Industrial American City, 1780–1830." *Labor History* 9, no. 1, Winter 1968.

Montgomery, David; Glaberman, Martin, and Brecher, Jeremy. "Symposium on Jeremy Brecher's *Strike!*" *Radical America* 7, no. 6, November-December 1973.

Nelkin, Dorothy. "Massport vs. Community." *Society* 11, no. 4, May-June 1974.

Oppenheimer, Valerie K. "The Sex-Labeling of Jobs," *Industrial Relations* 7, no. 3, May 1968.

Radical America 5, no. 5, September-October 1971.

Radical America 7, no. 2, March-April 1973.

Reuss, Rep. Henry. "Democrat's Critique of Nixonomics." *New York Times Magazine*, 7 July 1974.

Sheed, Wilfrid. "What Ever Happened to the Labor Movement?" *Atlantic* 232, no. 1, July 1973.

Simon, William; Gagnon, John H., and Buff, Stephen A. "Son of Joe: Continuity and Change among White Working-Class Adolescents." Manuscript prepared to appear in *Journal of Youth and Adolescence* 1, no. 1, Winter 1972.

"Slowdown: The Amber Lights Begin to Flash." *Citibank Monthly Economic Letter*, August 1973.

Sokal, Robert R. "Classification: Purpose, Principles, Progress, Prospects." *Science* 185, 27 September 1974.

Stevenson, Mary. "Women's Wages and Job Segregation." *Politics and Society* 4, no. 1, Fall 1973.

Stone, Katherine. "The Origins of Job Structures in the Steel Industry." *Review of Radical Political Economics* 6, no. 2, Summer 1974.

Walker, Charles. "Relief and Revolution." *Forum* 88, August-September 1932.

NEWSPAPERS

Boston Globe: 6 March 1972, 26 October 1972, 31 October 1972, 1 November 1972, 29 November 1972, 4 April 1973, 30 May 1973, 6 January 1974, 8 September 1974.

Boston Phoenix: 31 October 1972.

Boston Real Paper: 1 November 1972.

New York Times: 1 May 1970, 7 November 1971, 17 December 1972, 22 December 1972, 8 January 1973, 23 March 1973, 31 March 1973, 3 April 1973, 8 April 1973, 13 April 1973, 22 April 1973, 17 May 1973, 11 June 1973, 14 October 1973, 15 October 1973, 11 November 1973, 24 February 1974, 21 April 1974, 25 April 1974, 27 May 1974, 4 June 1974, 20 June 1974, 30 June 1974, 1 July 1974, 2 July 1974, 9 July 1974, 14 July 1974, 15 July 1974, 16 July 1974, 17 July 1974.

Wall Street Journal: 26 July 1973, 15 July 1974, 4 September 1974, 1 December 1974, 1 February 1975, 8 February 1975.

GOVERNMENT PUBLICATIONS

Background Facts on Women Workers. Washington, D.C.: U.S. Department of Labor, Women's Bureau, n.d.

Current Population Reports. Consumer Income Series, no. 69. Washington, D.C.: U.S. Bureau of Census, April 1970.

Handbook on Women Workers, The. Issued every few years by the U.S. Department of Labor, Women's Bureau.

Hearings on Worker Alienation. U.S. Senate Subcommittee on Employment, Manpower and Poverty of the Committee on Labor and Public Welfare, 92nd Cong., 2nd sess., 1972.

Historical Statistics of the United States. Washington, D.C.: U.S. Department of Commerce, 1960.

Panel on Youth of the President's Science Advisory Committee. *Youth: Transition to Adulthood.* Washington, D.C.: Executive Office of the President, 1973.

Bibliography

Social Indicators 1973. Washington, D.C.: U.S. Department of Commerce, 1973.
Why Women Work. Washington, D.C.: U.S. Department of Labor, Women's Bureau, 1971.

PAMPHLETS

Denby, Charles. *Workers Battle Automation*. Detroit: News and Letters, 1960.

Glaberman, Martin. *Be His Payment High or Low*. Detroit: Facing Reality Publishing Committee, 1966.

Glaberman, Martin. *Punching Out*. Detroit: Our Times Publications, 1952.

Gregoire, R. and Perlman, F. *Student/Worker Action Committees*. Kalamazoo, Mich.: Black and Red, n.d.

Hyman, Richard. *Marxism and the Sociology of Trade Unionism*. London: Pluto Press, 1971.

Montgomery, David. *What's Happening to the American Worker?* Distributed by *Radical America* magazine.

Perlman, Fredy. *The Reproduction of Daily Life*. Kalamazoo, Mich.: Black and Red, 1969.

Stone, Katherine. *Handbook for OCAW Women*. Denver: Oil, Chemical and Atomic Workers International Union, 1973.

Yankelovich, Daniel. *Changing Youth Values in the '70s*. New York: John D. Rockefeller III Fund, 1974.

UNPUBLISHED PAPERS

Ackerman, Frank. "Employment of White-Collar Labor, 1910–1960." 1970.

Conference on Labor Market Stratification, Harvard University, 16–17 March 1973. Various papers.

Corcoran, Mary E. "Sex-Biased Wage Differentials." MIT, February 1974.

Exploratory Project for Economic Alternatives. "Notes on the Economic Theory of Decentralized Socialism." Cambridge Institute, March 1973.

Jay, Nancy B. "Anthropologist's Accounts of Informant's Accounts."

Montgomery, David. "Immigrant Workers and Scientific Management." Prepared for the Immigrants in Industry Conference of the Eleutherian Mills Historical Library and the Balch Institute, 2 November 1973.

Montgomery, David. "The 'New Unionism' and the Transformation of Workers' Consciousness in America." Mimeographed.

Montgomery, David. "Trade Union Practice and the Origins of Syndicalist Theory in the United States." Mimeographed.

Sapolsky, Stephen. "Class-Conscious Belligerents—The Teamsters and the Class Struggle in Chicago, 1901–1905." University of Pittsburgh, August 1973.

Sapolsky, Stephen. "Puttin' on the Boss—Alienation and Sabotage in Rationalized Industry." University of Pittsburgh, July 1971.

Stevenson, Mary. Unpublished draft of 1973 Ph.D. thesis.

Symposium on Technology and the Humanization of work at the 139th meeting of the American Association for the Advancement of Science, 27 December 1971. Various papers.

MISCELLANEOUS PUBLICATIONS

Godfrey, Hollis. "Training the Supervisory Work Force." *Minutes of the First Bi-Monthly Conference of the National Association of Employment Managers, 1919.*

"News from Senator Edward Brooke," advance for press release, 2 June 1974. "Remarks of Senator Edward Brooke at the Dedication of the Whittier Technical School."

Supervisor's Manual for State Employees. Developed by the Bureau of Personnel and Standardization, Commonwealth of Massachusetts.

INDEX

absenteeism, worker, 193, 194
action committees, 208–9, 218–21.
    See also collective action;
    Committees of Correspondence;
    JET-STOP; nonimportation
    committees
action techniques. *See* anti-eviction
    riots; boycotts; blockades;
    collective action; resistance on
    the job; riots; strikes; wildcat
    strikes
AFL-CIO, 86–87, 136, 157–58, 222.
    See also unions
agribusiness, 133
agriculture: decrease of farm workers,
    115, 154, 159, 167–69, 252;
    profit syndrome in, 117–18, 133;
    self-sufficiency of, 23–25, 106;
    wage labor in, 36, 39
alienation, worker. *See* nonwork;
    unions, bureaucratization; work
Amalgamated Association of Iron,
    Steel and Tin Workers, 31–32
American Federation of Labor (AFL).
    See AFL-CIO; unions
American Revolution, 9, 142, 203–8
anti-eviction riots, 128, 144, 189
artisans, 23–26, 28, 39, 106, 153
assembly line, 48, 49
automotive industry: built-in
    obsolescence, 115; conditions
    in, 18–20, 42, 48–49, 74–75,
    89, 192; five-year contract of,
    93; job equalization in, 51; job
    rotation in, 67–68; militance in,
    70, 164–65; plant location,
    245–46; racism in, 172, 174;
    resistance in, 63, 67–68,

192–94, 213; strikes in, 49,
    74–75, 82, 89, 216;
    unemployment benefits in, 114;
    and unionism, 82, 89, 92–93,
    96–97, 98, 215; and veterans,
    198. *See also* United Auto
    Workers
automation, 28–29, 48. *See also*
    technology
Awl, quoted, 26

baby-boom, post-war, 137, 177,
    257–58
"baby-carriage blockade," 140
Barakumin, 170
black Americans, 135, 167–75
blockades. *See* Logan Airport
    controversy; truckers' blockade;
    worker strategies
blue-collar workers, 149–59, 248;
    contrasted with white-collar,
    161–65; housing of, 136;
    solidarity of, 60; supervised by
    technicians, 44. *See also* work;
    working class
Blumfield, Meyer, quoted, 51–52
boycotts, 4, 107, 111, 151. *See also*
    meat boycott; nonimportation
    associations
Braidwood, Illinois, strike of 1877,
    171
Brecht, Bertolt, 13, 57
bureaucrats. *See* government;
    management; socialism, state;
    unions

Index

Jeremy Brecher has worked as a research assistant, a congressional speech writer, and an editor. He attended Reed College in Portland, Oregon, and has been a student and an Associate Fellow at the Institute for Policy Studies in Washington, D.C. He holds a Ph.D. from The Union Graduate School. His previous book, *Strike!,* was listed as one of the "Noteworthy Titles" of 1972 by *The New York Times Book Review.* He has recently helped edit the collection *Root & Branch: The Rise of the Working Class Movements.* He is twenty-nine years old and lives and writes in West Cornwall, Conn. Next year he has been invited to teach at Ezra Stiles College, Yale University.

Tim Costello has been a truck driver for the past eight years. He has also worked a number of factory and construction jobs. He has intermittently attended Goddard College in Vermont, Franconia College in New Hampshire, and the New School in New York. Aged thirty, he lives in Rockport, Massachusetts with his wife, Helen, and their daughter, Gillian.

About Jeremy Brecher's first book, Strike!:

"Clearly the best single-volume summary yet published of American general strikes."
WASHINGTON POST

"Scholarly, genuinely stirring"
NEW YORK TIMES BOOK REVIEW

"A magnificent book. I hope it will take its place as the standard history of American labor."
STAUGHTON LYND

"The best book I have seen on American labor as a social movement. An important contribution to sociology as well as history."
WILLIAM KORNHAUSER, PROFESSOR OF SOCIOLOGY, UNIVERSITY OF CALIFORNIA AT BERKELEY

"A really impressive piece of work."
DAVID MONTGOMERY, CHAIRMAN, DEPARTMENT OF HISTORY, UNIVERSITY OF PITTSBURGH

Dear Institute for Policy Studies:

Please send me _____ paperback copies of **Common Sense for Hard Times** by Jeremy Brecher and Tim Costello. Enclosed is a check for $_____. (Please include $3.95 per copy, plus $.55 per order for postage and handling. Write for prices on larger quantities.)

Name _____

Street & Number _____

City & State_____ Zip_____

Send to: Common Sense
             Institute for Policy Studies
             1901 Q St., N.W.
             Washington, D.C. 20009

16